Defence of Regional Economic Development

DEFENCE OF REGIONAL ECONOMIC DEVELOPMENT

Manoj Kumar Singh

PRASHANT PUBLISHING HOUSE
DELHI- 110094

PRASHANT PUBLISHING HOUSE
C-34, 28 Foota Road, Gali no-3,
West Karawal Nagar, Delhi-110094
Mob:- 9810396373, 8826258746

Email: prashantpublishinghouse@gmail.com
web- www.pphbooks.co.in

DEFENCE OF REGIONAL ECONOMIC DEVELOPMENT

Reserved
First Published 2019
ISBN- 978-93-88526-06-7

PRINTED IN INDIA
Published by Mr. R. K. Jha M/s Prashant Publishing House and Published at H.S. Offset House Prees, Delhi.

Preface

Trends in global defence industry have impinged India in many ways. India's defence industry has witnessed significant changes since the end of the Cold War. In the 1990s, changes in both institutional and policy spheres became more prominent. The most far reaching change that has occurred in recent years in India's defence-industrial sector is related to its opening up to the market. Long protected as a closed sector, India's defence industry has now opened up for private participation. As if this was not enough, it is also showing enough willingness to become an exporter and dares to venture into the competitive global arms market.

At the same time, it is also showing willingness to diversify its range of products, which not only include modern weapons systems but also technologies for wide and popular civilian uses. The Indian defence-industrial sector targets the national, and even global, civilian market to sell its products, especially in the fields of civilian space, medical, and electronics. Thus conversion through diversification has been witnessed in many areas of defence production in India.

Defence markets and defence industries are changing. They have been adjusting to disarmament, to 'revolutions' in both military and financial affairs and to further technical change affecting defence industries. New forms of industrial organisation have emerged as defence companies have developed their prime contracting and systems integration capabilities and have changed from national to international (global) companies. The major defence companies have both military and civil businesses, whilst some are specialist defence companies (eg. embracing air, land and sea systems).

This book makes an interesting reading for historians, defence and policy analysts, researchers and general readers alike.

—*Editor*

Contents

1

New Criticism in Defence Economics Development

There is a developing field in the economics of conflict: an area traditionally the preserve of political scientists. Here, one contribution by economists is to focus on the costs of conflict. Wars are costly. However, there is a lack of empirical work on the costs and benefits of conflict (Sandler and Hartley, 2003). For example, a cost-benefit framework for considering a possible conflict with Iraq.

Problems of Estimating Costs

For the participants, estimates of military costs involve the following:

- The *additional costs* of the conflict
- The need to include the costs of replacing equipment
- The need to value the human capital losses (ie. based on the discounted value of future earnings)
- Recognition that estimates will differ from out-turns
- Possible long-term costs such as the need for peacekeeping forces and a greater threat from terrorism
- Possible financial contributions from nations not participating in the conflict.

There are costs for the civilian economy. These include impacts on oil prices; on airline and tourist markets; on share prices and the state of general confidence in various economies;

possible recession effects; and on public spending plans (e.g. greater spending on defence at the expense of social welfare programmes). In undertaking such analysis, the counterfactual cannot be ignored, namely, what would have happened without any conflict? For example, would the airlines have experienced a recession in their markets? Nor can the costs incurred by and imposed upon Iraq be ignored: these involve physical and human capital losses.

Estimating Profits

A cost-benefit approach to conflict requires estimation of both costs and benefits. For the participants, what are the likely benefits from a war with Iraq and how highly are such benefits valued ? Here, one possible approach is to use costs to indicate the *minimum valuation* which must be placed on the benefits. For example, the Gulf War cost the UK some £2.5 billion with contributions to the UK from other nations of over £2 billion (1991 prices). Today's costs to the UK of a Gulf-type war with Iraq would be over £3 billion.

Scope and Definitions

Consider how economists might analyse the events of September 11th 2001. These attacks on the USA involved macro- and micro-economic impacts, the economics of military alliances and the challenge of modelling terrorist behaviour. Throughout, there is also the need to recognise the counterfactual: what would have happened in the absence of September 11th?

The end of the Cold War has led to the growth of non-conventional conflict in such forms as revolutions, civil wars, guerilla warfare and terrorism. These result in new threats to national security. Terrorism is defined as "... the premeditated use of, or the threat to use, extra-normal violence or brutality to gain a political objective through intimidation or fear". Terrorism is not new. There are examples from World War II and the German occupation of Europe.

More recently, there is the example of Northern Ireland which demonstrated the costs of terrorism in the form of deaths and injuries to military and civilian personnel, adverse effects on trade and exchange and the loss of foreign investment and tourists. Peace resulting from the Good Friday Agreement provided a range of economic and other benefits, with peace representing a public good. The features of recent terrorism involve individuals or groups attacking civilian targets: these are asymmetric attacks (not the traditional armies versus armies). The attacks are also transnational and some are state-supported.

Macroeconomic Impacts

The immediate cost to the US economy from the September 11th attacks were lives lost, property destroyed or damaged and lost output. Initial estimates of lost output were $100 billion, with a present value of economic damage to the USA estimated at $2 trillion. Lloyds of London reported losses of almost £2 billion on the World Trade Centre and the Pentagon buildings. Other macroeconomic impacts included:

- A loss of confidence affecting firms and their investment plans and households shifting from consumer spending to savings.
- The role of government reflected in counter-cyclical policies. Monetary policy favoured lower interest rates and fiscal policy resulted in increased government spending (e.g. increased US defence spending). Microeconomic impacts on US markets

There were direct impacts on four markets:

The property and building industry. There was an increased demand for replacement office accommodation in New York and Washington possibly leading to higher rents. There was also an increased demand for demolition and rebuilding work, all of which affected the construction industry.

The insurance market. There were losses to insurers, higher premiums following the attacks, a restructuring of the insurance industry to meet greater and new risks and insurers offering lower premia for increased security measures in buildings.

The defence market. New security threats have emerged (e.g. terrorism; weapons of mass destruction in 'rogue states'). New threats require new structures and equipment for the Armed Forces (e.g. forces with a worldwide capability; rapidly-deployable forces and equipment). Armed Forces have also acquired new roles in deterring terrorism and in emergency response to terrorist attacks (e.g. responding to chemical-biological attacks on civilians). The result is pressure to raise defence budgets to meet the new threats.

The airline market. This market and the associated travel market was directly affected by the September 11th attacks. There was a reduced demand for air travel resulting in job losses, capacity reductions (e.g. aircraft stored or scrapped) and exits from the airline industry (e.g Sabena and Swissair in Europe). Airlines incurred substantial losses.

For example, the major US airlines reported losses of £2.4 billion in the first quarter of 2002: but how large would the losses have been in the absence of September 11th? The US government responded by providing cash assistance to US airlines (are such losses a case for subsidy?). Interestingly, the low-cost European airlines were reporting increased business and major orders for new aircraft! There was also an increased demand for substitutes such as rail travel, telecommunications (fax; e-mail), private corporate jets and low-cost airlines. Increased airport security has meant higher costs for passengers (including waiting time). Nor have aircraft manufacturers been immune (e.g. Boeing; Airbus). Cancellations of orders for new aircraft have meant job losses, including supply chain impacts, and lower prices for new airliners.

The Economics of Military Alliances

Following September 11th, a US-led coalition conducted military operations in Afghanistan. This raises the general question of whether a nation benefits from being a member of a military alliance (e.g. NATO). There is a considerable defence economics literature on military alliances (Hartley and Sandler, 2001). This literature models alliances as 'clubs' providing a public good in the form of collective defence-security (e.g. US strategic nuclear umbrella which is non-rival and non-excludable for members of the alliance). One prediction of this model is free riding whereby the more defence a nation's allies provide, the less the nation will spend on defence. As a result, there is exploitation with small nations exploiting the willingness of large nations to provide alliance defence.

Are there economic models explaining terrorist behaviour? Whilst there is a complex literature in this area, the topic can be approached by considering the economics of crime and punishment (ie. illegal activities). Consider the example of theft. Criminals considering theft will evaluate its likely benefits and costs. The benefits of theft include the value of the goods which are stolen (in present value terms) as well as the possibility that some criminals might be risk-seekers and enjoy the 'thrills of robbery. Benefits have to be compared with costs to assess whether the robbery is 'worthwhile.' The costs of crime include the 'set-up' costs which might be for an individual or group (e.g. planning; search; observation; bribery of insiders). Then there are the costs of implementation (the robbery and escape) and the probability of capture and a penalty (fine or imprisonment).

The possible policy solutions to crime include changes in the distribution of income and wealth in society, private insurance, private security systems, more police and social penalties providing greater deterrents such as longer imprisonment for criminals. Economic models of terrorist behaviour use the standard consumer choice models with individuals and groups facing an allocation and choice problem. Terrorists aim to maximise their individual or group utility. But they are subject to limited resources (income, wealth, labour, time) which have to be allocated between various terrorist and non-terrorist activities. Further allocation decisions are needed between alternative terrorist attack options, such as skyjackings, kidnappings, bombings, assassinations and the use of chemical, biological and nuclear weapons. These economic models of terrorism offer various predictions:

Substitution effects. If a government increases the price of one form of attack, terrorists will seek lower-cost alternatives. For example, increased airport security might mean more bombings of other civilian targets (e.g. city centres).

Income effects. Governments can try to reduce terrorist activity by denying access to funds (budget constraints).

Increase the costs of terrorism. Deterrence is one option (tit for tat policies). Or, costs might be imposed on nations supporting terrorist groups (e.g. Afghanistan).

Free riding. Nations have incentives to free ride on any nation (e.g. USA) which actively pursues international terrorist groups.

DEFENCE INDUSTRY AND THE ECONOMIC CHARACTER OF THE PLA

The transformation of China's defence establishment into a system capable of independently sustaining modern armed forces was one of the major goals of the military modernization program. In the late 1970s and 1980s, defence spending remained relatively constant despite the shift in resources in favour of overall economic development. Reforms focused on reorganizing the defence research-and-development and industrial base, more closely integrating civilian and military science and industry, and selectively utilizing foreign technology. China sold arms for hard currency to provide additional funds for defence industries. The PLA continued to play its role in economic development by participating in selective construction projects, providing dual-use training, and producing most of its food needs.

Military Expenditures

In the 1980s Chinese statistics indicated that defence spending represented a decreasing percentage of government expenditures, falling from 16 percent in 1980 to 8.3 percent of the state budget in 1987. However, United States Department of Defence studies suggested that the published budget figures understated defence spending by about one-half. With the growth of the Chinese economy under the modernization program, defence spending also represented a smaller percentage of the gross domestic product (GDP) than previously. United States Central Intelligence Agency analysts estimated that defence expenditures in 1978 absorbed 8 to 10 percent of GDP; in 1986 United States Department of Defence analysts estimated that China's military expenses fell within the range of 6 to 8 percent of GDP. Comparison of indices of defence procurement spending and industrial production from 1971 to 1983 revealed that the former increased by 15 percent, whereas the latter rose by 170 percent. These studies indicated that Chinese leaders have indeed subordinated military modernization to economic development. United States Department of Defence officials in 1986 estimated Chinese defence spending by resources and force categories for the 1967 to 1983 period. Roughly 50 percent of defence expenditures were for weapons, equipment, and new facilities; 35 percent for operating costs; and 15 percent for research, development, and testing and evaluation.

By service, these costs broke down to 25 percent for the ground forces; 15 percent for the Navy; 15 percent for strategic air defenses; 5 percent for ballistic missile forces; 5 percent for tactical air forces; and about 35 percent for command, logistics, personnel, intelligence, medical care, administration, research, development, testing and evaluation, and other support. Beginning in the late 1970s, China devoted more resources to its Strategic Missile Force, indicating an effort to increase its strategic security while modernizing the economy, and to national command and support activities, reflecting an emphasis on modernization of the defence structure.

MILITARY R&D AND NDSTIC

The National Defence Science, Technology, and Industry Commission was the coordinating body for military research and development and industrial production. The NDSTIC reported to the party Central Military Commission's National

Defence Industries Committee and the State Council's Leading Group for Science and Technology. The NDSTIC supervised weapons research and development, coordinated military production of defence industries, and controlled funding for weapons procurement. The establishment of the NDSTIC was a reform measure designed to break down the barriers between civilian and military research and development and industry. Military science and industry previously had been secretive, segregated, and privileged sectors, having material, financial, and personnel resources superior to those available to the civilian sector. The creation of the NDSTIC was one measure by which Chinese leaders hoped to facilitate the transfer of technology between the military and civilian sectors. The NDSTIC, in particular through its trading arm, China Xinshidai Corporation, coordinated procurement of foreign technology for military purposes.

Defence Industry

Beginning in 1978, Chinese leaders set out to transform the defence industries, which had a huge excess capacity and were criticized for having a "golden rice bowl" (rich but always begging for more). To utilize this excess capacity better and to break down the barriers between military and civilian industry, the machine-building ministries were reorganized, and civilians were appointed to manage them.

The civilianized, renamed ministries and their responsibilities consisted of the Ministry of Nuclear Industry—nuclear weapons; Ministry of Aeronautics—aircraft; Ministry of Electronics Industry—electronics; Ministry of Ordnance Industry— munitions and armaments; Ministry of Astronautics—ballistic missiles and space systems; and China State Shipbuilding Corporation—naval construction. In 1986 the Ministry of Machine Building, which produced civilian heavy machinery and industrial equipment, and the Ministry of Ordnance Industry were consolidated into the new State Machine-Building Industry Commission as a way to strengthen the unified management of the national machine-building and weapons enterprises. In 1987 little information was available about this new commission or its relationship to the NDSTIC or to the State Economic Commission, whose Defence Bureau coordinated the civilian production of the defence industry. Further changes in defence industry structure occurred in 1986 and 1987, when inland defence enterprises were either relocated closer to transportation links or cities, closed down, or transferred to local civilian control and production.

Weapons Production

In 1987 China adopted a new contractual system for weapons research, development, and production. It was not clear from available information how this contract system would affect the role of the NDSTIC as the coordinating body for defence science and industry. Previously, the NDSTIC controlled procurement funding, reviewed proposals for weapons requirements funneled through the General Staff Department's Equipment Subdepartment, and coordinated with defence industries to produce the needed equipment.

Under the new system, the state divided defence research and development funds into three categories: military equipment research, basic and applied sciences research, and unidentified technological services. The first type of appropriation went to military arms and services, which signed contracts with research institutes or enterprises to develop and manufacture the required weapons.

The contract system involved the PLA, which had been removed to a large extent from such activities, in the development and manufacture of the weapons it would use. The second category of funds was devoted to basic research and applied science to help modernize the defence industry. The third category went to technological services necessary for research programs. This reform was another measure designed to integrate military and civilian industry by placing the military production of defence industries within the framework of the planned-commodity economy. The new system further sought to provide the military with better equipment at a minimum cost, to force the defence industry to upgrade weapons designs and improve production, to improve the management of weapons research and development through state application of economic levers, to promote cooperation between research institutes and factories, and to increase the decision-making powers of the enterprises.

Procurement of weapons and equipment represented 45 percent of the defence budget during the 1967 to 1983 period. This figure included 25 percent for aircraft, 15 percent for ground forces weapons, and about 10 percent each for naval and missile systems. China's military-industrial complex, the third largest in the world, produced a wide variety of weapons, including light arms and ammunition, armor, artillery, combat aircraft, fast-attack craft, frigates, destroyers, conventional and nuclear submarines, electronic equipment, tactical missiles, and ballistic missiles.

With the notable exception of China's indigenously produced nuclear submarines, nuclear missiles, and satellites, most Chinese weaponry was based on Soviet designs of the 1950s and 1960s. Much of this equipment was obsolete or obsolescent, and beginning in the late 1970s China made great efforts to upgrade the equipment by changing indigenous design or by incorporating Western technology. The greatest weaknesses were in conventional arms, precision-guided munitions, electronic warfare, and command, control, communications, and intelligence. China attempted to address these weaknesses by focusing military research on electronics—essential to progress in the previously mentioned areas—and by selectively importing key systems or technologies.

TRENDS OF INDIA'S DEFENCE INDUSTRY

Trends in global defence industry have impinged India in many ways. India's defence industry has witnessed significant changes since the end of the Cold War. In the 1990s, changes in both institutional and policy spheres became more prominent. The most far reaching change that has occurred in recent years in India's defence-industrial sector is related to its opening up to the market. Long protected as a closed sector, India's defence industry has now opened up for private participation. As if this was not enough, it is also showing enough willingness to become an exporter and dares to venture into the competitive global arms market. How far it will succeed in its objectives is examined elsewhere, but changes are certainly a product of and response to the contemporary changes in the global industrial defence scenario. At the same time, it is also showing willingness to diversify its range of products, which not only include modern weapons systems but also technologies for wide and popular civilian uses. The Indian defence-industrial sector targets the national, and even global, civilian market to sell its products, especially in the fields of civilian space, medical, and electronics. Thus conversion through diversification has been witnessed in many areas of defence production in India.

India's defence industry has come a long way from being at the lowest end of the production spectrum, catering to the maintenance and repair and overhaul of imported weapons, to a stage where it can boast of designing and developing a range of state-of-the-art weapons systems. Half a decade of defence-industrial experience in India shows that while it started from scratch, it has been able not only to learn and absorb various stages of production intricacies but also produce complex systems that are primarily an indigenous activities. Another important factor is that the Indian defence industry has produced various weapons systems under licenses acquired from various foreign sources.

Although the first Prime Minister of India, Jawaharlal Nehru, believed in 'self sufficiency' in arms production, which became a policy mantra for subsequent years, it had to be supplemented by what is roughly called 'self-reliance in defence'. Self-reliance does not preclude accessing external sources for technology and systems, or external help in any stage of the production cycle. It is the degree of dependency on external sources that is tested in the case of India's quest for self-reliance.

India opted to choose an incremental path, in which it was necessary to continue to meet urgent requirements through imports while striving hard on achieving indigenous capabilities in defence production. Both policies continued till the late 1980s and many of the components of both still continue till today. The 1990s witnessed a series of far-reaching initiatives in the field of national security, of which defence industry was a critical component.

The creation of six Special Task Forces to reform major aspects of national defence coordination and management, under the Chairmanship of the then Defence Minister in 1994 may effectively be considered as the first major step after a long time to initiate and implement much-desired reforms in the defence-industrial sector. This was followed by a series of intensive interactions between various organs of the armed forces, government departments and institutions like the Confederation of Indian Industries (CII). The 'Army-Industry Partnership', a partnership between CII and the Indian Army to get acquainted with each other's needs and to facilitate channels of communication between the armed forces and the private industry, was a result of this process and, in turn, led to other cooperative initiatives. Events like India's nuclear tests in mid-1998 and the Kargil conflict in mid-1999 provided grounds for an intense debate on various aspects of India's national security. Also, as a by-product of the current disinvestment programme, which is primarily aimed toward lessening or wiping out government control and responsibilities in state-owned public enterprises in India, the debate on a reform of the defence industry got a major boost as demands for a privatisation of and private participation in this hitherto closed sector grew more in tune with the changing times.

In January 2001, the Government of India initiated a series of major initiatives that, among others, included Foreign Direct Investment (FDI) up to about 26 percent and full private participation in certain sectors in the defence industry. This policy indeed marks a critical departure from the past. Followed by this, the Group of Ministers (GoM) Report on 'Reforming the National Security System' was made public in early 2001. This laid stress on reforms in all-encompassing aspects of national security; of which changes sought in higher defence management emphasised the need to create specific institutions like the Defence Acquisitions Board to adapt and facilitate changing needs of the defence industry.

While these far-reaching institutional and policy-oriented changes have been underway for quite some time especially since the early 1990s, the demand for private participation has assumed significance in recent years. In such a scenario, analyses of India's defence-industrial sector and policies have become critically important to understand the complex web of linkages that determine national policies in the defence-industrial sector.

This, in turn, needs a closer look into the past performance of the defence industry, lessons learnt and a peep into the likely future course.

The Major Defence Industries

The world's major defence industries over the period since the end of the Cold War in 1990. Employment has fallen at the world level and especially in the industrialized nations (e.g Europe; former Soviet Union). Nonetheless, total world employment in arms industries was 8.7 million in 1997 with 55% of this employment in industrialized countries and 45% in developing nations. China, the USA and Russia accounted for some 70% of world arms industry employment.

Countries have differed in the magnitude of the decline in their defence industry employment. Europe and Russia experienced major employment reductions over the period 1990 to 1997. Within Europe, employment reductions were especially severe in central and eastern Europe (e.g in 1990, Hungary with an index of 600 and Bulgaria with an index of 400).

In contrast, compared with the world average, employment reductions were below average in the USA, the UK, France and China. Even so, output reductions in nations such as the United States have been substantial. For example, the annual output of military aircraft for US Armed Forces declined from 3,085 units in 1970 to 664 units in 1990 and 150 units in 1998.

RISING DEFENCE EXPENDITURE IN INDIA

The Government of India has been investing heavily into its Defence industry due to strained relations with its neighboring countries and growth in international terrorism. The Defence budget for the year 2005 was $17.80 billion, a growth of 7.6 percent from the budget allocation of 2000. Typically 5.0 percent to 10.0 percent of the Defence budget is allocated for modernization and weapon induction. The larger share is allocated for payment, allowances, and for maintenance of aging military equipment. The Government of India expects its Defence expenditure to exceed $20.00 billion by 2008.

Private Investments on the Rise in the Indian Defence Industry

The Defence industry in the past has been dominated by the government-run public sector undertakings (PSU). This scenario has changed significantly with the Ministry of Defence providing license to private companies to manufacture select aerospace and Defence products.

In 2001, the country opened for up to 100 percent Indian private sector investments in the Defence industry and allowed foreign direct investment (FDI) of up to 26.0 percent in select areas of the Defence industry. Some of the key non-PSU industry participants supplying Defence equipment and services include Mahindra & Mahindra, Tata Group, Kirloskar Brothers, Larsen & Toubro, Ashok Leyland, Jindal, Max Aerospace & Aviation, and Ramoss India.

Increasing Public-Private Collaborations

The Defence industry is gradually liberalizing and the public sector is facilitating greater private sector participation in the area of Defence goods production. There are about 5,100 companies supplying around 20.0 percent to 25.0 percent of components and subassemblies to state-owned contractors and the market size is expected to be around $6.20 billion in 2005. Of India's current Defence procurement of capital items, more than 30 percent is imported, however, this is expected to change with the creation of more public-private partnerships.

The Indian Space Research Organization (ISRO) has a strong partnership with the Indian industrial sector for space programs execution. Over 500 small, medium, and large-scale enterprises work with ISRO, supplying hardware, undertaking fabrication jobs, and establishing fabrication and test facilities. The Indian industrial sector provides all raw materials and high-tech electronic items required by ISRO and has also contributed toward developing systems for launch vehicle spacecraft, remote sensing, and ground equipment. Around 231 technologies developed by ISRO were transferred to the Indian industrial sector for commercial use. ISRO also undertakes technical consultancy projects for industries.

INDIA'S OFFSET POLICY TO ENCOURAGE DOMESTIC PRODUCTION

India's offset policy for Defence goods has been designed to leverage the country's position as a large buyer and exporter. India's offset policy for the Defence industry states that any purchase from a foreign supplier in excess of $70.0 million will require a reinvestment of 30.0 percent of the total purchase amount in terms of components and services from India. The offset policy applies to imports by Defence PSU's, ordinance factories, and private participants of the industry.

The offset policy is also expected to act as a driver to create market-entry opportunities for mid-rung companies, which are looking at investing in research and development and manufacturing of Defence goods. The proposed offset policy is conducive for the private companies to have a larger presence.

Growth Opportunities in the Indian Defence Industry

The domestic capability of the Indian Defence industry is largely concentrated around the production of the PSUs and ordinance factories. This trend is expected to change with the recent selective liberalization of the Defence industry and a sound offset policy, which are expected to create greater private sector participation and facilitate bigger FDI inflows into the Indian Defence industry.

The Government of India has shown keenness in allowing international collaboration for the production of weapon systems, which are purely used for non-lethal purposes. The production of the following weapon systems are expected to be promoted in the future:

- Technologies/equipment for counter terrorism
- Surveillance, communication equipment, and sensors for border management
- Cyber security-synergies in the field of information technology
- Devices to neutralize improvised explosive devices (IEDs).

Suppliers and manufacturers of the above-mentioned weapon systems are expected to be some of the chief beneficiaries of the increased indigenization of the production process in the Indian Defence industry. Key areas of growth identified within the industry are expected to arise from the up gradation of the production capacity expansion, technology transfer, and modernization of Defence infrastructure.

ECONOMIC EFFECTS OF DEFENCE INDUSTRIAL BASES

Generally, economic theory has no distinctive role for military spending; it is just another form of government spending. Briefly (and superficially), for neoclassical theory, security may be necessary for trade, but there is a trade-off between 'guns and butter.' For Keynesians, security – as government spending – can have a positive demand effect. For Marxists, the story is mixed (Dunne, 1990). The Underconsumptionists, however, do have a clear and positive role for military spending, though it is not backed up empirically.

There are a number of channels through which the DIB can affect the economy. It can support jobs, but can also divert resources from other uses. It can create negative externalities through its influence on other areas of the economy and can crowd out investment from the civil sector. A positive impact may be that it spins off technology to the civil sector, but while this may have been the case a few decades ago, increasingly there is what is termed 'spin in,' with civil technology being increasingly used in weapons systems. A positive impact could be achieved through the creation of demand, but this might create bottlenecks in the economy and impact negatively on the civil economy. Military spending has sociopolitical effects, such as militaristic nationalism, or helping control labour, which may impact on the economy. It can, however, lead to the creation of a coherent set of vested interests, the 'military industrial complex,' which acts in its own interests and invents threats to bargain for increased resources. Whether the overall impact is positive or negative is clearly an empirical question.

A number of forms of empirical analysis have been undertaken. These include institutional and historical studies, econometric analyses and model simulations. Overall, the results suggest: a negative effect of military spending on economic growth for advanced economies, at the expense of investment rather than consumption; and that reductions in military spending can improve economic performance, particularly when the savings are reallocated.

To this can be added the fact that the threats facing countries are different than during the Cold War period and are likely to require non-traditional responses. In the post-Cold War period, the focus was on pariah states, terrorism, crime and peacekeeping. The activities of the armed forces – as well as what they do, where they do it and how – are likely to be very different. They are likely to require different equipment and force structures. Strategic mobility and global information and communications systems are likely to be increasingly important and there is considerable dependence on the US for these. With changes in technology, it is becoming impossible for countries to maintain the capability to independently produce a comprehensive range of weapons. The UK defence industry has moved from strategic justification to economic justification for its existence. It is, however, a declining employer and is heavily subsidised. It is also now stuck with programmes and industries that are a legacy of the Cold War. The economics of maintaining this capability have meant a push for arms exports, but there is excess capacity in the market, with weapon systems selling at near marginal cost and the extensive use of offsets and other measures.

Clearly, the South African defence industry has undergone considerable restructuring in the last few years in response to internal and external changes. This has manifested in the breaking off of state arms production to form Denel, although until recently, the government had adopted a 'hands off' approach. The massive reductions in procurement have led to downsizing, increased concentration and a push for exports. The changing international scene, both on the supply and demand sides, has also influenced the industry and continues to do so. The declining demand for exports has exacerbated local cuts in procurement and the changing nature of international arms producers has made maintenance of a national DIB impossible. This has heightened the spread of the major players into other countries to expand their network of component and sub-product suppliers and their search for markets. The changes in procurement relations in major arms-producing companies has been reflected in South Africa to some degree, with marketing and lobbying becoming an increasingly important tool of the public and private industries. There is still a strong set of interests around arms production that has influenced and is influencing government policy and these interests have been strengthened by the involvement of a number of major international players.

The defence industry remains a relatively important part of the South African economy and still has a substantial state-owned component. This suggests that there is still some restructuring to be undertaken. The form it will take is dependent on the outcomes of two major policy initiatives: the privatisation of Denel; and the recent R30 billion procurement package (now costing more than R40 billion), with associated offsets to provide advanced weapon systems to the SANDF. The outcome of these initiatives will determine the size, structure and performance of the industry in the future, with associated implications for the economy. As research suggests, there are substantial economic costs to maintaining a DIB. This is an important issue for the future of the South African economy and industry.

THE PRIVATISATION OF DENEL

The performance of Denel in the first five years of its life was not impressive and did not augur well for its future. From the mid-1990s, however, it appears to have forged a more coherent and mutually beneficial working relationship with the government. Since 1998, moves to restructure and privatise Denel have become closely bound with the arms procurement deal and associated industrial participation programme (Defence Industrial Participation – DIP). In addition, there have been efforts to find a large international defence company to take a strategic equity partnership in Denel.

The visit of British Prime Minister Tony Blair to South Africa in 1998 saw the signing of a memorandum of understanding between BAE Systems and Denel. Denel was then internally restructured in 1999, shifting from a looser network of companies and divisions to a more autonomous set of business groupings. The current business units are Denel Aerospace, Denel Ordnance, and a commercial and IT division. There is also a small training grouping, the Kentron Training College, which provides bridging programmes for aspirant military engineers.

This at least partly reflected the policy developments outlined in the 1999 National Conventional Arms Control Committee discussion document "Policy on the South African Defence Related Industry," which sets out proposals for industry restructuring. This included breaking up Denel by selling off less than 100% in clusters, breaking off the attractive bits first to maximise revenue, and a proposal to encourage rationalisation of both the private and public industry.

In October 2000, Cabinet approved BAE Systems as the preferred strategic equity partner for the Denel Aerospace and

Ordnance Groups. Within Denel Aerospace, Snecma/Turbomeca was approved as the strategic equity partner at the divisional level for the business unit Airmotive. Similarly, within Denel Ordnance, the UK pyrotechnic manufacturer Pains Wessex Defence was confirmed as strategic equity partner for the Swartklip division. At the macro level, it was hoped that the finalisation of a strategic equity partnership with BAE Systems could be achieved by March 2001, but the negotiations have proved lengthier than initially expected.

There have also been pressures within Denel to return to concentrating on the Group's perceived traditional strengths – although this is not without its contradictions – and to downsize in areas such as small arms. The Commercial and IT group is to shift away from Denel Aerospace and Denel Ordnance, and ultimately will be hived off as a completely separate entity. The recent establishment of Arivia. Kom, as a joint venture between the IT divisions of Eskom, Datavia in Transnet and Ariel Technologies in Denel, is also a step in this direction.

These partnerships at macro and meso levels are not necessarily discrete or self-standing. Turbomeca, for instance, will provide engines for a new light helicopter, the Augusta A109, and the Hawk advanced trainers on order from BAE Systems. As part of the Snecma group, Turbomeca has an extensive set of manufacturing and aircraft maintenance operations internationally.

This is clearly a continuing process, but reflects the policy of breaking up Denel using strategic partners, with privatisation planned later when the issues of black empowerment have been considered. There are a number of concerns that arise from recent changes and future plans. Firstly, the issue of regulation could be problematic. The links between Denel and Armscor may compromise the role of regulation, and some consideration has to be given to the control of state and private entities that have major strategic partners. There is some concern that rentseeking behaviour among the state, industry and foreign players may impact upon the success of privatisation measures. Indeed, the role and influence of international companies is of concern as it may be difficult to control and may lead to the creation of a strengthened 'military industrial complex.' This could produce further pressure to increase military spending and loosen export controls. Finally, the shared/overlapping interests of companies such as BAE Systems, Snecma/Turbomeca and Westland Augusta in South Africa – which, in terms of the current defence offset programme in South Africa, are not uncommon – may raise concerns that companies can collude in their own interest.

THE SANDF PROCUREMENT PACKAGE

The decision to procure weapons systems for the SANDF from foreign suppliers made clear an already implicit government view that the maintenance of a general capability in military production was not feasible. As we have seen, developments in international markets suggest that the future might entail a small industry operating in niche markets, possibly in collaboration with a major international player. This recognition of the new reality, where even second-level producers are unable to sustain a comprehensive arms industry, led to the decision to procure externally. Once this decision was made, a considerable amount of effort was put into attempts to wring as much from the potential suppliers as possible, both in the form of defence-related industrial participation, and in order to maintain the competitive parts of the industry and of non-defence products. A major justification for the packages was the economic benefits through these offset deals.

The proposals included: direct contracts with South African defence firms; investment in Denel; and diverse non-defence investments ranging from automotive components, manufacturing, telecommunications, stainless steel and specialty steel plants, gold jewellery, plastics and high-quality textiles. Credits were given for technology transfers and for economic empowerment. Under guidelines that took effect from September 1996, all government and parastatal contracts with an import content exceeding US $10 million must include an industrial participation component. The value of the offsets was to comprise a minimum 30% of a bid's imported component for civilian contracts. For defence contracts, the offsets should comprise 50% of a bid's imported components.

The industrial participation portion of the bid was assessed according to 'credits' awarded for each type of benefit. To illustrate, the number of credits for job creation should equal the estimated value of salaries and wages. New investments, research and development, and links with previously disadvantaged persons (either as shareholders or contractors) earned double credits. Bidders must fulfil their obligations within seven years, and must provide a performance guarantee equal to 5% of the offset component. Once the contract is awarded, the supplier must file bi-annual progress reports.

Ministry of Finance and the Department of Trade and Industry personnel – who assisted in the final stages of negotiation once the structure of the deal was essentially in place – are convinced that they achieved a particularly good deal. The anticipated export percentages of the projects well exceed the stipulated 50% level, and returns on investment on the overall cost of the procurement package are estimated to be approximately 94.5%. Furthermore, throughout the duration of the deal, exports are expected to be in the region of 280% of the original purchase price. Many of the projects under the DIP scheme are still to be finalised, and others are in the exploratory and negotiation phases.

The defence offsets, especially the DIP components, have certainly provided a substantial lifeline to the South African defence industry, while at same time undercutting any remaining aspirations for South Africa to maintain its own DIB. While the industry response in general has been favourable, there are some dissenting voices, especially from the aviation sector. The impact of the deal has been more on defence and related industries, as more progress has been made on the DIP side of the offsets than with the non-defence industrial participation scheme. Batchelor and Dunne (2000) raised concerns about the capability of the local industry to benefit from the deals. They suggested that while the aerospace sector seemed best placed to benefit and to prove themselves attractive to foreign companies, the electronics sector might have a harder time, and the maritime sector was likely to struggle. This would seem to have been borne out by recent developments.

The impact has been to provide orders to domestic companies and opportunities for companies to develop niches in the international market through links with the foreign companies. Private companies and Denel have been drawn into international circuits of defence production, both in terms of indirect and direct DIP. For instance, Denel has been contracted to build the tail section of the RAF's fleet of Hawk fighter trainers. It is also building landing gear fuselage sections for the Gripen jet fighter, and rudders and ailerons for other BAE Systems aeroplanes. These are not overly high-tech manufacturing operations and may reflect some watering down of the technological path/expertise of Denel. Other DIP contracts are of a nature that is obliging contractors to rethink their niche business, e.g. Tellumat/Eloptro and their form.

There is increasing participation of European defence groupings and investors in the South African industry, at prime contractor and sub-contractor levels. This participation is part of ongoing restructuring and expansion of international defence groups such as EADS and Thales. Local divisions can influence government-to-government dealings to the benefit of the parent company and local subsidiary.

There have been some concerns raised over the value of the offset deal to the South African economy. The limited but growing international literature on defence offsets and their economic effects does not instill confidence. The impact of offsets is often found to be problematic in terms of job creation, the strengthening of backward and forward linkages, and technology enhancement. Nor do offsets constitute a 'third way' for the economic development of least developed countries. A recent study of Saudi Arabia's defence offset programmes reveals that instead of a proclaimed 75 000 local jobs, the various programmes had generated approximately 2 000 jobs. Few countries appear to have been successful in using defence offsets to sufficiently utilise, embed and extend technology transfers. Those domestic defence industries that are expected to benefit from offset deals are often characterised by a 'technologically sophisticated conservatism' (BAEC 1998: 33; Batchelor and Dunne 2000), which does not lend itself to the densification of intellectual and social capital. What is required is a 'high degree of local technological absorptive capacity' to be achieved through a state-sponsored 'civil-military, science and technology strategy'. In addition, new modes of structuring technology-intensive production appropriate for the 'new economy' are needed.

While still in their formative stages, the policies have come under public criticism on a number of fronts. The prices of the systems have been condemned as being inflated by the offset arrangements, while reports have identified beneficiary companies that are linked to the head of the weapons procurement committee. Hidden costs have been highlighted, including unanticipated capital expenditure to activate imported equipment and the research and development expenditure required to benefit from technology transfers. Furthermore, as is acknowledged by Denel staff, there will be a variety of possibilities arising from defence offsets for technology transfer and other opportunities that the economy is not in a position to exploit. The government claimed that the impact on the budget would be 'relatively attenuated and is entirely manageable.' In addition, it claims that the 'net effect on the total procurement on the South African economy is broadly neutral'. By contrast, the Institute for Democracy in South Africa (IDASA) Budgetary Group, anticipates that the R30-43 billion procurement package, despite being spread out over several years, will increase defence's share of the budget and somewhat reduce the percentage allocated to infrastructure and public works programmes. This will, in turn, undercut the provision of more funds for poverty relief and affect the more peripheral provinces such as the Eastern Cape. Moreover, Batchelor and Dunne (1999) suggest that the arms acquisition programme could lead to more imports and place pressure on South Africa's balance of payments.

As regards regional development, there are promises of important contributions, but these are not tied into a clear policy framework. The initiative is project-driven, but there is little in the way of public awareness of the investment possibilities on offer. There is no doubt that the procurement programme will impact on the economy, but its spatial effects are more difficult to estimate. The initial estimate of 65 000 jobs and earnings of R110 billion for the original R31 billion investment have been downscaled, and even these figures have been questioned. The DIP may have a positive effect on the defence industry, but it is at a cost to the economy and there is a clear opportunity cost for the use of these resources.

These concerns raise important questions as to the value of this particular deal, but also the use of offset deals in arms procurement generally. The move to justify procurement of weapons systems by economic rather than security benefits is problematic and obscuring the true price of weapons systems by offsets creates problems. It provides scope for corruption and policy confusion, as well as compromising debates over alternative paths to security and development. The impact of companies – used to operating in the world of arms trading with its commissions, bribes and murky deals – in a new democracy is unlikely to be a positive one. The restructuring of the South African defence industry still has some way to go and there are many lessons to be learned, both for future policy and for other countries facing similar policy choices.

The analysis in this paper suggests that there have been significant shifts in the nature, scope and workings of the South African defence industry in recent years, and that these have to be understood within the context of: changes in the international arms market; restructuring of the international defence industry; and the discourses accompanying these processes. The changes cannot be understood in terms of globalization, but rather are a complicated process of internationalisation, where companies remain wedded to their home countries but increasingly have international joint ventures and other links. With the concentration and growth of major defence companies, brokered and networked production has become pervasive.

Another discernible trend is that new generation defence conglomerates are becoming more like non-defence companies and are increasingly influenced by financial capital. In both developed and developing countries, the 'military industrial complex' is reconstituting itself in more informal and less visible forms.

As part of this process, the larger companies have found new ways to influence governments. This has clear implications for any country with a defence industry, as it implies that a comprehensive DIB is impossible to maintain. For relatively small economies, the only possible future lies in becoming a niche producer. A standard argument is that defence industries are vital to national economies; however, a growing body of research suggests that military spending has essentially adverse macroeconomic effects. Increasingly too, defence companies are more reliant upon exports and use economic arguments to justify them. Nevertheless, arms exports are subsidised heavily by the government and the economic benefits are not clear.

There has been a marked restructuring of the South African defence industry, with downsizing coming to an end due to the termination of military spending cuts and the offsets from the procurement package. The industry still maintains a state producer that, prior to privatisation, is restructuring with foreign strategic partners. Compared with similar countries, it could be argued that there is still potential for further reductions in military spending, although the defence actions of the concerned vested interests seem to have stopped reductions. This reflects similar developments in other countries of a renewed but less visible 'military industrial complex,' which is enhanced by the involvement of powerful international arms companies. Future government policymaking will need to recognise this important feature of the political terrain. Given the evidence of the economic costs of defence industries, a large opportunity cost is likely to be attached to any strengthening of their importance in the economy. It would seem better that the government aim to retain intelligent customer status – allotting a recognisable subsidy where needed – rather than develop policies that require a potentially costly resource, where subsidies and costs may be hidden from view through the brokering of procurement deals with offsets. At present, these proposals are based upon concerns and warnings emanating from recent developments. It is important that research is conducted for the life of the projects to inform future policymaking and to provide important lessons to other countries considering similar policies.

ECONOMIC COST OF THE MILITARY INDUSTRIAL COMPLEX

These must be the words of some liberal Democratic Senator running for President in 2008. But no, these are the words of Republican President Dwight D. Eisenhower, the Supreme Allied Commander during World War II, five decades ago. The United States, the only superpower remaining on earth, currently spends more on military than the next 45 highest spending countries in the world combined. The U.S. accounts for 48% of the world's total military spending. Where did the peace dividend from winning the Cold War go?

The United States spends on its military 5.8 times more than China, 10.2 times more than Russia, and 98.6 times more than Iran. The Cold War has been over for 20 years, but we are spending like World War III is on the near term horizon. There is no country on earth that can challenge the U.S. militarily. So, why are we spending like we are preparing for a major conflict? The impression on the rest of the world is that we have aggressive intentions. The administration is posturing like Iran is a threat to our security. Iran spends $7.2 billion annually on their military. We could make a parking lot out of their cities in any conflict. Does anyone really believe that they would create a nuclear weapon and use it on Israel? Their country would be obliterated.

Defence spending had peaked at just under $500 billion in 1988. The fall of communist Russia did result in a decline to the $350 billion range from 1995 through 2000, and an economic boom ensued. Since 9/11 we have doubled our spending on defence. This seems like an overly extreme reaction to 19 terrorists attacking our country. Bin Laden and his terrorist network numbered less than 10,000. The initial response of invading Afghanistan, defeating the Taliban, and cornering bin Laden in the mountains was supported by the entire world. The success of this response was sufficient to deter any other country from allowing terrorist organizations to operate freely within their borders.

The natural response of the United States should have been to increase spending on border protection, upgrading the CIA, and increasing our ability to gather intelligence. Instead, we spent billions on weapons, aircraft, tanks, and missiles. The neo-cons, led by Cheney, Rumsfeld, and Wolfowitz, saw the 9/11 attack as their opportunity to change the world. They've gotten their wish. Of course, we took our eye off of bin Laden and Afghanistan. The Taliban has experienced a resurgence, recently freeing 800 fighters from a prison. Bin Laden continues to issue videotapes exhorting his followers to continue the fight.

Dwight D. Eisenhower's farewell speech in January 1961 is a brilliantly perceptive analysis of the future of our country. *Throughout America's adventure in free government, our basic purposes have been to keep the peace; to foster progress in human achievement, and to enhance liberty, dignity and integrity among people and among nations. To strive for less would be unworthy of a free and religious people. Any failure traceable to arrogance or our lack of comprehension or readiness to sacrifice would inflict upon us grievous hurt both at home and abroad.*

This last sentence describes what George Bush has managed to do in the last 5 years. The arrogance of believing that we could invade a country on the other side of the world and expect to be treated as liberators is beyond comprehension. Our reputation abroad has been grievously damaged. The voluntary sacrifices we've made in the U.S. were to receive tax cuts and multiple tax rebates, paid for by our grandchildren. President Bush has sacrificed by not playing golf for the last 5 years.

How noble. Not exactly the Greatest Generation, quite yet. Did President Eisenhower envision that the U.S. would have troops stationed in 70% of the world's countries? According to the Defence Department's latest "Personnel Strengths" report, the United States now has troops stationed in 147 countries and 10 territories. This is the greatest number of countries that the United States has ever had troops in. Why are we policing the world? What is the point of having 57,000 troops in Germany and 33,000 troops in Japan? Germany and Japan each spend $40 billion per year on their military. Can't they defend themselves at this point? We defeated them 60 years ago. It is time to leave. This is a prelude to decades of occupation in Iraq. Don't believe the blather about withdrawal. The military has no intention of withdrawing.

It is a shame that after 9/11, George Bush didn't read President Eisenhower's farewell speech. I wonder if he has ever read the speech. Instead he chose to follow the "wisdom" of Dick Cheney, Donald Rumsfeld, and Paul Wolfowitz. President Eisenhower's words describe the crisis that occurred on September 11, 2001. President Eisenhower, as a former commanding general of Allied forces in World War II, knew exactly what the implications of having a permanent armaments industry were to the United States. He was also worried about the implications. These words were spoken 5 decades ago, but are just as true today.

The top five U.S. defence contractors generated almost $129 billion in revenues and $8 billion in profits in 2006, double the revenue and profits in 2000 when George Bush became President. The War on Terror has been a windfall for the defence industry and their shareholders. These companies have intertwined themselves into the fabric of our government and defence department. They contribute tremendous amounts of money to Congressional candidates and have thousands of lobbyists pushing for more defence contracts. Many politicians end up working for defence contractors (i.e. Dick Cheney) after they leave public service. This leads to conflicts of interest negatively impacting the American public.

It appears that the biggest winners of the War on Terror are the CEOs of the defence contractors. I wonder if they realized how rich they would become as they watched the Twin Towers crumble to the ground. They have virtually tripled their annual income, while the average American scratched out a 20% increase over 6 years. They have managed to generate the tremendous profits and personal wealth while only employing 10% more employees. Boeing and Raytheon were actually able to reduce their workforce. How productive. These contractors will do everything in their power to retain and increase these fabulous profits.

President Eisenhower clearly understood the moral implications of a huge armaments industry and the costs to a free society. *This conjunction of an immense military establishment and a large arms industry is new in the American experience. The total influence — economic, political, even spiritual — is felt in every city, every State house, every office of the Federal government. We recognize the imperative need for this development. Yet we must not fail to comprehend its grave implications. Our toil, resources and livelihood are all involved; so is the very structure of our society.*

We have some of the brightest engineers in the country developing weapons to kill human beings more efficiently. There is an opportunity cost that is being paid. These engineers could be concentrating their brilliance on developing alternative energy solutions which could free us from our drug dependence on the Middle East. Which effort would benefit our country more, weapons development or energy independence? President Eisenhower's final words are the most chilling. *In the councils of government, we must guard against the acquisition of unwarranted influence, whether sought or unsought, by the military industrial complex. The potential for the disastrous rise of misplaced power exists and will persist.* We did not heed his wisdom. Laurence Vance, author of *What's Wrong with the U.S. Global Empire? contends* that our foreign policy *is not right, it's unnatural, it's very expensive, it's against the principles of the Founding Fathers, it fosters undesirable activity, it increases hatred of Americans, it perverts the purpose of the military, it increases the size and scope of the government, it makes countries dependent on the presence of the U.S. military, and finally, because the United States is not the world's policeman.*

War and non-stop conflict benefit the military industrial complex. It is in their best interest for them to support candidates that favour an aggressive foreign policy. This could lead to Defence companies using their influence to provoke conflict throughout the world. If as a country we continue to allow our politicians and their military industrial complex corporate sponsors to spend $700+ billion per year on weapons, to the detriment of higher education, alternative energy projects, and national infrastructure needs, we will be paying an extremely high price.

We are in a classic guns or butter scenario. The Bush Administration has decided to choose guns while borrowing from our grandchildren and the Chinese to pay for the butter. This can work for awhile, but as deficits accumulate, the dollar plummets, and inflation rears its ugly head, our great country will decline as other empires who overstepped their bounds declined.

GLOBALIZATION ON MILITARY EXPENDITURE AND ARMS TRANSFERS

Although the term 'globalization' did not appear until recently, the notion of globalization has existed for a long time. The concept is being used for a wide variety of phenomena and trends and the descriptions of current trends in globalization and the conclusions as regards its impact differ accordingly. There exists not one discourse of globalization but several. In a recent survey of the debate and the literature, five major discourses on globalization are identified, basically falling into the areas of economics, sociology, political science, culture and ecology. All these aspects of globalization, together with the globalization of technology, have an impact of the trends and patterns in military expenditure and arms transfers, directly or indirectly by their impact on the causes of military expenditure, arms production and arms transfers.

The process of globalization has gone through several phases during which the various aspects have assumed different importance. During the cold war period, the political aspects were predominant. The impact of this phase of globalization on trends and pattern of military expenditures and arms transfers was significant and is well documented. During the subsequent, current, phase of globalization, the politico-military dynamic of the cold war has been overtaken by a mainly financial phase. It began in the second half of the 1980s, with the enormous expansion of trading in foreign currency after the breakdown in the 1970s of the international Bretton Woods currency system, and has resulted in the abolishing of state controls of capital markets and opening up of new financial world markets, in privatizations of public enterprises and services, in a break-up of national champion monopolies, and in a general encouragement of global competition. Simultaneously with the globalization of financial and economic activities, the end of the cold war has meant a deglobalization of political action.

These factors, around the existence of which there is fairly broad consensus, have an impact on military expenditure and arms transfers in several ways, perhaps primarily through its effect on the arms industry. While the military sector has been the sector most resistant to privatization, commercialization and reduced political control, all these trends are currently affecting the production, procurement and international transfers of arms. The arms industry is increasingly being privatized and commercialized. The European arms industry is going through a process of internationalization, until now relatively limited and primarily through cross-border joint ventures, but more recently also through cross-border mergers of arms producing companies. European companies are also acquiring armsproducing companies in other continents, recent examples include Australia, South Africa and South Korea, while transatlantic military-industrial links are still rare in spite of the lively debate on both sides of the Atlantic about their potential. The increasing privatization, commercialization, competition and internationalization of arms production, have resulted in an increased pressure from the arms industry to export their excess supply of weapons, and thus to increased commercialization also of the arms trade, in which marketing and generous sales terms play an increasing role. At the same time, increased internationalization means reduced possibilities for national governments to implement national arms export regulations, since companies can choose to export their products from a business unit in another country with more liberal export regulations. For this reason, national export laws are becoming increasingly irrelevant. This points to the need for common or international export rules.

However, globalization may render also international control more difficult. The globalization of technology in general, and in the context of a gradual closing of the gap between military and civil technology, will make it increasingly difficult to control the international transfer of militarily relevant technologies in the future. The challenge is to achieve international limitations in the transfer of military technology without resorting to controls which will inhibit international transfers of all types of advanced technology, that is, also civil technologies which would benefit economic growth in the recipient countries.

A relatively new development is the impact of globalization on armed conflict and the financing of these. The fragmentation and decentralization of the state has produced a new type of wars and with it increasingly financing of wars outside traditional government defence budgets. As described by Mary Kaldor, these new wars take place in the context of extreme globalization, under which territorially-based production has more or less collapsed and production continues only of a few valuable commodities (diamonds, emeralds, drugs), which provide a source of income for whoever can provide 'protection'. These wars are fought by various types of fighting units, public and private, state and non-state, including regular armed forces or remnants thereof, paramilitary groups, self-defence units, foreign mercenaries, and regular foreign troops, usually under international auspices. During these conditions governments, like privatized military groups, need alternative sources of funding for their military activities, many of which involve criminal activities. These fall into the following categories: 1) 'Asset transfer', i.e. the redistribution of existing assets to benefit the fighting units (such as loot, robbery, hostage-taking, and deriving profits from control over market prices); 2) 'war taxes' or 'protection' money from the production of primary commodities and various forms of illegal trading; and 3) external assistance, in particular for imports, such as (a) remittances from abroad to individual families, b) direct assistance from the Diaspora living abroad; (c) assistance from foreign governments; and 4) humanitarian assistance diverted by governments and warring factions for their own use.

For countries involved in such new wars, data on government military expenditure are irrelevant for measuring military expenditure. What is more important is that the set of social relationships which are formed by these systems for financing wars constitute strongly resisting factors for the ending of war.

Privatization of security is an increasing trend also in countries which are not involved in regular armed conflict but where there is a demand for more security services than the government can offer. There is an emerging group of private security companies whose main task is the provision of security in many Third World countries, especially in Africa. The demand for private security services has emerged from a combination of factors, including from western governments seeking to reduce defence budgets, African governments in search of security, international mining corporations and rebel movements. They provide a variety of services, ranging from guarding installations, protecting convoys, supporting humanitarian assistance operations to performing reconnaissance and intelligence services, providing logistical and transport support, military training, strategic planning, and engaging in combat. These companies have developed to fill the need for security in the current context of conflict in Africa, in weak states with limited government legitimacy and with limited economic resources, and in which the international community is increasingly reluctant to intervene.

INDIA'S UNENDING DEFENCE EXPENDITURE

Despite criticism from various circles that India is not investing more to tackle development issues as millions remain mired in poverty; the Indian government's ambitious modernisation plan for its military is in full swing. In February this year, Indian military procurement units descended on the DefExpo 2010 trade fair in New Delhi. Inaugurating the Indian Defence Exhibition, Defence Minister A.K. Antony said that India's defence expenditure, which is 2.5 percent of its gross domestic product (GDP), is going to increase.

He pointed out, "our defence industry is open up to 100 percent for Indian private sector, while foreign direct investment is allowed up to 26 percent." Antony further indicated that our government is committed to rapid modernisation of armed forces. Over the next 12 years, India is set to spend a whopping US$200 billion on defence acquisitions to replace its outdated inventory. In this regard, on February 15, 2010, a report of the Indian strategic defence magazine (India Strategic's DefExpo) revealed that 70 per cent of the inventory of the Indian armed forces is 20-plus years old, and needs to be replaced with the modern technology.

It explained that nearly half of this funding ($100b) will go to the Indian Air Force (IAF), which would need to replace more than half of its combat jet fleet as well as the entire transport aircraft and helicopter fleet. The army needs new guns, tanks, rocket launchers, multi-terrain vehicles, while the navy needs ships, aircraft carriers and new range of nuclear submarines.

In three from 1994 to 1997 India's defence budget was increased from 20 percent to 24.4 percent. For the financial year 2001-2002 defence has been allocated Rs 620,000.00 million. This amount shows an increase of Rs 75,000 million as compared to previous year's revised estimates of Rs 544,610 million. In 2009, India increased its defence budget by a whopping 28.2 percent or Rs 130,000.00 million. Some experts estimate that military spending will increase further, totalling as much as 200 billion dollars over the period to 2022.

India's military has planned a massive upgrade of its mainly 1990s-era weapons systems which is mostly from the former Russia. The plans include the purchase of 126 new combat aircraft to replace an ageing fleet of MiG-21s..The US has emerged as a potential military supplier to India since the two countries signed a deal of civil energy technology in 2008, which lifted sanctions on New Delhi in order to import nuclear technology. India is likely to become a major customer for the US military-industrial complex over the next few years. During the recent visit of the US Secretary of State Robert Gates to New Delhi, American Defence officials, however, have said that US weapons sales to India would not be a focus of the trip. Regardless of such denials, the key reason for the Gates' visit can be found in the fact that India is planning to raise its military budget by 50% to almost $40 billion, making military expenditure 3% of the annual GDP. In contrast to India's planned defence expenditures, Pakistan's entire 2009-10 budget amounts to little over $30 billion.

India, the largest arms buyer among emerging nations, accounted for 7.5 per cent of all international arms sales between 2000 and 2007. It has spent billions of dollars in the past few years on purchases of planes, radars and ships from Britain, France, Germany and Russia and Israel.

In recent years, India has bought reconnaissance aircraft from US aerospace major Boeing worth 2.1 billion-dollars, medium range missiles for 1.4 billion dollars from Israeli Aerospace Industries, and signed an upgrade service contract with the Russian Aircraft Corporation to upgrade its MiG 29 squadrons for 965 million dollars. Several deals are planned for the near future including one of the largest arms contracts of recent times—a 11-billion-dollar project to acquire 126 multi-role combat aircraft.

It is mentionable that after 9/11, both India and Israel which had openly jumped on Bush's anti-terrorism enterprise are acting upon a secret diplomacy, targeting Pakistan China, Iran and Syria. In this context, Indo-Israeli secret diplomacy could be assessed from the interview of Israel's ambassador to India, Mark Sofer published in the Indian weekly Outlook on February 18, 2008.

Regarding India's defence arrangements with Tel Aviv, Sofer had surprisingly disclosed "We do have a defence relationship with India, which is no secret" and "with all due respect, the secret part will remain a secret." As regards joint exercises, Sofer replied, "Certain issues need to remain under wraps for whatever reason."

Notably, India's 'The Tribune' wrote on September 10, 2003, "India and Israel took giant leaps forward in bolstering the existing strategic ties", and Tel Aviv has "agreed to share its expertise with India in various fields such as anti-fidayeen operations, surveillance satellites, intelligence sharing and space exploration." With the support of Israel, New Delhi has been acquiring an element of strategic depth by setting up logistical bases in the Indian Ocean for its navy. In fact, India wants to become a mini-superpower of the region and hence it uses the pretext of deterrence against Pakistan and China. In this context, New Delhi with the support of US and Israel has presumed peace-loving Pakistan and China as their arch enemies, but it does not admit officially.

In May, 1998, when India detonated five nuclear tests, Islamabad was compelled to follow the suit through its own atomic experiments. But Pakistan which so far relied upon the minimum nuclear deterrence has again been forced by India's unending spending on arms purchases to counterbalance the former. In this regard, Pakistan has signed a number of agreements with China. Nevertheless, currently, more than half of India's budget is allocated for military, paramilitary, various security forces and debt servicing. That leaves less than half for everything else including infrastructure development projects, education, healthcare, poverty alleviation, and various human services. New Delhi' s latest arms buildup will leave even less for what India needs most to lift hundreds of millions of its citizens from abject poverty, hunger illiteracy and disease. Indian civil society organisations, while complaining of excessive defence spending indicated that the government spends 2.35 per cent of GDP on defence, but only 1.72 per cent on the social sector. The defence budget for 2009-2010 is 29 billion dollars, up 34 percent over the previous one. Indian defence analyst Ravinder Pal Singh, while calling New Delhi's unending defence spending at the cost of poverty-alleviation—with security requirements competing with socioeconomic concerns for money calls it guns-versus-butter question.

Even some of Indian officials are surprised in relation to Indian defence expenditure which has no bounds. For example, an official of the country's finance ministry remarked, "There is a dilemma...poverty needs to be eradicated to prevent men from taking to the guns...but more funds for security means less money for poverty alleviation." Meanwhile, a report of United Nations pointed out that India ranks 134th of 182 countries on the United Nations Development Programme's Human Development Index. It estimated that 50 per cent of the world's undernourished population lives in India. Nearly 31 per cent of the billion-plus Indians earn less than a dollar a day.

Secretary General of the Control Arms Foundation of India Binalakshmi Nepram said, "When people are dying of poverty and bad sanitation, what protection will arms provide them?" On the one hand, international community has been making strenuous efforts for world peace in wake of global financial crisis and war against terrorism, on the other, India has initiated deadly nuclear arms in South Asia where people are already facing multiple problems of grave nature. Majority of South Asian people are living below the poverty level, lacking basic facilities like fresh food and clean water. While yielding to acute poverty, every day, some persons commit suicide in India, Pakistan, Sri Lanka etc.

Setting aside regional problems, and resolution of Indo-Pak issues-especially thorny dispute of Kashmir, Indian rulers state that they don't have any aggressive designs. But it becomes a big joke of the 21st century, reminding a maxim, "armed to the teeth, but no enemy", if we take cognisance of India's unending defence expenditure.

Sajjad Shaukat writes on international affairs and is author of the book: US vs Islamic Militants, Invisible Balance of Power: Dangerous Shift in International Relations.

2

Information in Economics Development

Development economics is increasingly becoming an empirical discipline today. Where theory reigned during the 1980s and early 1990s, in the last ten years or so the primary research concerns have become increasingly driven by empirical and policy issues. In this essay we wish to reflect on the balance between theory and the rest in the discipline, thinking aloud about the question whether the pendulum has shifted away a bit too far, and whether there is need for some reorientation of the dominant research agenda or methodology.

We will revisit classic 'theory versus empirics' debates involving some of the great 20th century economists, and distil from this a notion of alternative stages in the maturation of any given field of economics. Following this, we will attempt to place the evolution of methodology in development economics within this general scheme, in order to gain some perspective of where the field currently stands, and the role of theory at the current frontiers of research.

Given the nature of this symposium, we will attempt to be brief and succinct, rather than embark on an expansive and scholarly essay. Accordingly we will eschew accuracy and detail for the sake of breadth and brevity. Indeed, we see this as an opportunity to air and thus clarify my own subjective views, and invite feedback from others.

TRADITIONAL 'THEORY VERSUS EMPIRICS' DEBATES

Regarding the appropriate balance between theory and empirics, the great economic thinkers of the first half of the 20th century had strikingly diverse views. In his preface to his monumental *History of Economic Analysis,* a thousand page historical account on the evolution of economic theory, Joseph Schumpeter expressed the judgment that the study of economic history and economic statistics should precede theory.

At the other extreme John Maynard Keynes maintained a profoundly distrustful attitude towards statistics. Towards the beginning of his well-known review of Jan Tinbergen's monograph on statistical testing of business cycle theories , Keynes writes:

"Prof. Tinbergen is obviously anxious not to claim too much. If only he is allowed to carry on, he is quite ready and happy at the end of it to go a long way towards admitting, with an engaging modesty, that the results probably have no value. The worst of him is that he is much more interested in getting on with the job than in spending time in deciding whether the job was worth getting on with. He so clearly prefers the mazes of arithmetic to the mazes of logic, that we must ask him to forgive the criticisms of one whose tastes in statistical theory have been, beginning many years ago, the other way around."

He then goes on to list various possible sources of bias, which in the vocabulary of modern econometrics would translate into problems of omitted variables, errors in variables, multicollinearity, simultaneity, incorrect functional form, time lags, trend corrections, parameter instability, and problems in extrapolation. Gathering these together, he expresses his skepticism concerning the usefulness of regression analysis in the process of inference concerning the validity of theories:

"Thirty years ago we used to be occupied in examining the slippery problem of passing from statistical description to inductive generalization in the case of simple correlation; and today in the era of multiple correlation we do not find that in this respect practice is much improved."

The review ends thus: "we hope that we have not done injustice to a brave pioneer effort....we have a feeling that Prof. Tinbergen may agree with some of my comment, but that his reaction will be to engage another ten computers and drown his sorrows in arithmetic. It is a strange reflection that this book looks likely, as far as 1939 is concerned, to be the principal activity and *raison d'etre* of the League of Nations."

Fortunately Tinbergen did not give up, and neither did the fledgling field of econometrics, despite the rapid demise of the League of Nations. Tinbergen's patient and detailed reply to Keynes reads like the rejoinder that any modern econometrician would probably have written. Specifically, that many influences could be excluded from the estimated regression and collected as a residual, suitable assumptions regarding which would validate the inference, assumptions that can themselves be tested from the data; that multicollinearity is a only problem of degree not of kind; that nonlinear functional forms can be approximated by polynomials, and so on. The rejoinder hardly affected Keynes' skepticism, whose subsequent reply ended by labeling econometrics as 'statistical alchemy' rather than a science.

Yet it is undeniable that econometric analysis has progressed impressively since the time of the Keynes-Tinbergen debate, particularly with respect to combating the very problems that they discussed. The scientific status of econometrics is far less in doubt today, an issue argued persuasively by David Hendry in his inaugural lecture at the London School of Economics in 1980 : "Forty years after Keynes wrote his review should still be compulsory reading for all who seek to apply statistical methods to economic observations. ....To Keynes' list of problems, we would add stochastic mis-specification, incorrect exogeneity assumptions ..., inadequate sample sizes, aggregation, lack of structural identification and an inability to refer back uniquely from observed empirical results to any given initial theory.

That the subject is exceedingly complicated does not entail that it is hopeless. Considerable progress has been made on the technical aspects, such as studying the consequences of the various problems just listed, designing means of detecting these, developing methods that mitigate some of their ill effects or handle several complications at once, and analyzing the properties of estimators when the sample size is small...Much of this technical work is essential background to understanding and correctly interpreting empirical findings and, although some work may have turned out to be otiose in retrospect, the ever increasing level of technique is not a symptom of alchemy."

We doubt that many economists today would disagree with this assessment. The contemporary relevance of the Keynes-Tinbergen debate to development economics is confined to those first generation empirical and field studies that are essentially descriptive accounts, yet aspire to have relevance for inferring the validity of some (frequently implicit) theory of the development process, predicting the future, or recommending suitable policies. Many such studies aim to avoid the latter explicitly, in the standard anthropological approach of 'description for description's sake' —— yet often make implicit inferences and policy judgments from their descriptions. Description is one thing, but inference is quite another — what Keynes referred to as the ' slippery problem of passing from statistical description to inductive generalization'. This is exactly the purpose of modern econometrics, i.e., explicitly specify the hypothesis to be tested, derive their observable implications, use these in inference, and test as far as possible assumptions required for the validity of the inference. Such studies are now common at the frontier of contemporary empirical research in development economics.

A decade later a similar debate arose between Tjalling Koopmans, and Rutledge Vining, following Koopmans' critical review of an empirical analysis of business cycles by Burns and Mitchell. Koopmans' critique provides an eloquent statement of the shortcomings of 'measurement without theory', drawing analogies from the relationship between the empirical Keplerian stage and theoretical Newtonian stage in celestial mechanics. He provides three main arguments.

"My *first argument*, then, is that even for the purpose of systematic and large scale observation of such a many-sided phenomenon, theoretical preconceptions about its nature cannot be dispensed with....(their) analysis employs the following seven series...There is no systematic discussion of the reasons for selecting these particular variables as most worthy of study....The lack of guidance from theoretical considerations is perceivable also in the choice of the measures computed from the variables selected...The rejection of the help that economic theorizing might give leaves a void. For now there is a need for some organizing principle to determine on what aspects of the observed variables attention should be concentrated..."

"The movements of economic variables are studied as if they were the eruptions of a mysterious volcano whose boiling cauldron can never be penetrated. There is no explicit discussion at all of the problem of prediction, its possibilities and limitations, with or without structural change, although surely the history of the volcano is important primarily as a key to its future activities. There is no discussion whatever as to what bearing the methods used, and the provisional results reached, may have on questions on economic policy. This, then, is my *second argument* against the empiricist position: without resort to theory, in the sense indicated, conclusions relevant to the guidance of economic policies cannot be drawn."

"...the extraction of more information from the data requires that, in addition to the hypotheses subject to test, certain basic economic hypotheses are formulated as distributional assumptions, which often are not themselves subject to statistical testing from the same data. Of course, the validity of information so obtained is logically conditional on the validity of the statistically unverifiable aspects of these basic hypotheses. The greater wealth, definiteness, rigor, and relevance to specific questions of such conditional information, as compared with any information extractable without hypotheses of the kind indicated, provides the *third argument* against the purely empirical approach." Vining's response is rich and detailed, which among various other points refers back to a classification of different stages of research that originated with Trygve Haavelmo:

"Haavelmo gives a rough fourfold classification of the main problems encountered in quantitative research: first, the construction of tentative theoretical models; second, the testing of theories; third, the problem of estimation; and fourth, the problem of prediction. It may be noticed that the first problem (possible the second, depending upon one's interpretation) is the only one of the four that is not a problem of strictly modern statistical theory. He goes on to say that the "explanation of phenomena" consists of digging down to more fundamental relations are those that have a great degree of invariance or autonomy with respect to the ordinary or reasonably expected changes in economic structure, and a theory is a construction of a system of autonomous relations."

Vining then goes on to discuss the shortcomings of the prevailing theoretical paradigm and therefore argue that business cycle research was still in the first stage: "Is the Walrasian conception not in fact a prétty skinny fellow of untested capacity upon which to load the burden of a general theory accounting for events in space and time which take place within the spatial boundary of an economic system? When we think of the enormous body of factual knowledge digested and systematized in the other fields of variation and the meagerness of our own results from efforts to systematize, are we quite ready to leave Haavelmo's first problem and launch into the last three problems in estimation theory?....Burns and Mitchell presumably are still on Problem 1. Koopmans has vaulted over, some would say hastily if the research is in the field of economics, to Problems 3 and 4. This is not to deny the very great interest that economic research has in the results of Koopmans' group on Problems 3 and 4. But it is to express belief that, so long as a field of knowledge continues tc develop, workers will be puttering around, and not in vain, within the unexplored expanses of Problem 1 — the searching for regularities and interrelations of regularities and the feeling around for interesting theoretical models. Not all this work will find formal mathematics of immediate use, and much of it will be such an explorative character as to render almost meaningless the notion of a planned maximization of information from given data."

Vining's rejoinder is an important reminder of the value of exploratory data analysis as a preliminary stage of research on any given economic phenomenon, which precedes and aids the formulation of concrete theories of that phenomenon. The large masses of data on planetary motion collected by Tycho Brahe were no doubt a useful step for Kepler in his effort to organize the observed phenomena into a number of empirical laws, which in turn were a precondition for the Newtonian stage. In most areas of economics where the relevant theory is far from obvious, the value of similar exploratory data analysis in helping the evolution of such theories cannot be understressed.

Accordingly we would modify Haavelmo's classification to add a pre-theory stage prior to his stage 1, and for purposes of brevity merge the second and third stages of testing and estimation. The modified classification would then constitute the following:

Stage 1: empirical description of the relevant phenomenon, consisting of exploratory data analysis aimed at helping identify empirical regularities that need to be explained by a suitable theory, and in addition the nature of assumptions that such a theory can make without gross violation to the empirical patterns.

Stage 2: the formulation of a relevant theory, including derivation of potentially observable (hence falsifiable) implications.

Stage 3: The testing and estimation of theories, a stage which may lead back to modification or replacement of the previous theories, in an iterative back and forth with Stage 2.

Stage 4: use of the least unsuccessful theory from the standpoint of empirical verification for purposes of prediction and policy evaluation. From the standpoint of this classification, we can interpret Koopmans' critique of empirical work as pertaining to Stages 3 and 4, while Vining's rejoinder can be interpreted as a defense of Burns and Mitchell's work as pertaining to the pre-theory Stage 1.

We shall review the ebb and flow of the role of theory and empirical research in the field of development economics over the past century in the light of this particular classification.

The Role of Assumption in expansion Economics

Barring important isolated contributions in the earlier part of the century such as the work of Allyn Young, development economics emerged as a distinct field in the 1940s and 1950s. The principal protagonists in the early decades combined both Stage 1 empiricists such as Kuznets and Myrdal, and Stage 2 theorists such as Rosenstein-Rodan, Hirschman, Leibenstein, Lewis, Nurkse, Scitovsky and Sen.

The field remained quite aloof and isolated from mainstream neoclassical economics, as the principal ideas of that literature —— coordination failures, poverty traps, take-off into self-sustained growth, critical minimum effort, pecuniary externalities, balanced and unbalanced growth, dualism, surplus labour, institutional failures — were not quite consistent with the Walrasian paradigm. Instead they were based on implicit assumptions of pervasive externalities, missing markets, economies of scale, imperfect competition, and imperfect information, for which satisfactory theories comparable in logical completeness, detail and elegance to the Walrasian theory were then lacking. The key policy concern was the suitable design of strategies of development planning led and regulated by the state.

Later in the 1960s and 70s the theories followed in a similar tradition, addressing issues such as cost-benefit analysis, migration and optimal growth, in the work of Lefeber, Little, Mirrlees, Chakravarty, Sen, Dasgupta, Marglin, Harris, Todaro and many others. During this stage theoretical research predominated, or gained more visibility, with limited interchange between theoretical and empirical researchers. The field was definitely at somewhere between Stages 1 and 2. Stage 3 involving detailed testing and estimation of the theoretical models had not yet begun.

The next phase involved a shift to a different set of phenomena and theoretical framework, which brought development economics closer to the mainstream. Key to this were theoretical developments in mainstream economics the 1970s, which began to incorporate departures from the Walrasian paradigm systematically, especially with respect to theories of imperfect competition and of asymmetric information. On the one hand these led to rigorous theories of some of the ideas that the early pioneers had discussed in less formal terms, such as coordination failures, endogenous growth theory, incomplete markets and efficiency wages. The literature on asymmetric information and contract theory began to be applied to agrarian institutions in developing countries, motivated by the empirical patterns documented for the latter by Bardhan and Rudra in the 1970s. The 1980s saw a large range of theoretical contributions of this kind, a broadening of issues including dynamic implications of contractual imperfections, political economy, governance problems, and the role and functioning of social norms. It represented the maturation of Stage 2 research in the field.

This enabled Stage 3 to commence. As a backdrop to this it is worth mentioning changes to mainstream theory that had also occurred during the 1970s and 80s. It could now accommodate a far broader range of phenomena, with the increasing incorporation of a game theoretic tool. But this also meant that the Walrasian paradigm, a single overarching unified framework that had dominated economics for almost a century or more, was giving way to a fragmented collection of disparate models designed to explain disparate phenomena. Replacing price theory by noncooperative game theory meant there was now scope for great arbitrariness in the formulation of the institutional setting: who are the players, what are their strategy sets, who moves when, knows what and so on. Added arbitrariness is introduced by a proliferation of equilibrium solution concepts in the presence of dynamics and imperfect information. More recently game theorists have been exploring yet other variations in terms of limited rationality and alternatives to common knowledge assumptions. The result is an embarrassment of riches when it comes to choice of a theoretical model for almost any phenomenon.

This paradigm shift has of course occasioned many other methodological debates within the profession, most notable of which is the interchange between Carl Shapiro and Frank Fisher concerning models of industrial organization. Their debate highlights the strength and weakness of the 'new institutional economics' grounded in game theory. On the one hand one can now more easily formulate theoretical models of a much large ranger of phenomena; on the other one can find a profusion of very distinct models for the same phenomenon, which are empirically difficult to distinguish. While Fisher laments that 'there is no theory of oligopoly', Shapiro hails the ability of the approach to capturing the richness of forms of oligopolistic interaction and business strategy, analogous to theories of evolutionary biology grounded in general principles (of adaptation and survival) that yield disparate range of behavior and strategy in different environments.

Shapiro's view is consistent with the now widely accepted view in development economics that 'institutions matter'. But for the further progress of research, the profusion of theories for any given pheneomenon that are difficult to distinguish empirically, is a bewildering problem. What agents care about, what they can do, when do they move, do they interact repeatedly, are there important state variables or is the interaction represented by a repeated game, how patient they are, what can they contract over — these are all choices which theoretical models today must confront, with very little guidance from empirical facts. So while the new theoretical developments provided a language to discuss many classic developmental issues, unlike the Walrasian paradign, they raised at least as many new questions as they resolved. Attempts to extend the

Walrasian paradigm to contexts of asymmetric information have similarly run into the problem of many competing formulations with diverging implications for inferences concerning market failure, and the role of the state. An instance of this is the absence of any single competitive theory of moral hazard, with Prescott and Townsend constructing one such theory where the classical Arrow Debreu theorems extend, while Stiglitz and his various coauthors construct alternative competitive models where they do not. These competing extensions vary with respect to formulation of commodities that are traded, and of the agents in the economy, issues so fundamental that they cannot be empirically distinguished. Nor can they settle on theoretical grounds either, leaving economists with trusting their own subjective judgment for the most appropriate formulation in any given setting.

Back now to Stage 3 of the progress of the research agenda in development economics, which can be said to be well under way over the past decade. The typical paper at any leading conference or journal in development economics is now of this *genre*. It will typically focus on an issue or phenomenon on which the authors have gathered some empirical data, frame a theoretical hypothesis which can be 'taken to the data', followed by econometric estimation and testing. Even theoretical papers are pressed to refer more to documented empirical facts for purposes of motivation and justification. Increasingly scholars are going to the field to get a feel for ground level institutions, in order to decide on the most salient issues to focus on and the kind of theoretical formulation that is best suited to the task, then collect their own data, before proceeding to the econometric analysis. The theoretical model helps identify the relevant variables, ways to measure them, identify potential econometric problems such as endogeneity bias, measurement error, selection bias and so on, and then the best ways of testing for these biases. The empirical methodology is quite close to those pursued in other fields of economics, most notably labour economics. This is pretty much the kind of research that Koopmans had in mind while criticizing the Burns and Mitchell statistical compendium of business cycles. To my mind this kind of empirical work represents an important stage of maturation of the field, an important progression from Stages 1 and 2 to Stage 3.

The key problems confronted by a typical empirical paper today concern the seriousness of the various possible econometric biases. The skill and quality of the paper is related to the degree of persuasiveness of the inferences made by the analysis, in terms of its vulnerability to inferential errors. Most of these problems can be confronted with appropriate econometric tools, but ultimately with the availability of higher quality data sets, e.g., with better measured variables, longitudinal panels to control for unobserved heterogeneity, and availability of suitable 'instruments' for potentially endogenous regressors and selection biases. These econometric concerns are important and substantive, and lie at the heart of Keynes' "slippery problem of passing from statistical description to inductive generalization", or going from observed correlations to inferences concerning causation.

Not surprisingly, all this comes at a price. Research papers tend to get evaluated almost exclusively in terms of their success in combating the econometric problems, often to the exclusion of the importance of the context or issues addressed by the analysis, the imaginativeness of the underlying hypotheses formulated or tested, or the importance of the findings from a wider standpoint. A well executed paper goes into a particular phenomenon in a particular location in considerable depth, data permitting. The research is consequently increasingly microscopic in character. We have very little sense of the value of what we have learned for any specific location to other locations. If suitable data does not exist to address a given topic in an econometrically satisfactory manner, then the research project is dropped, even though some aspects of the data would be of wider interest.

The concern to minimize econometric bias is increasingly motivating the discipline to study randomized experiments, either natural or controlled. In such experiments the treatment of the key explanatory variable of interest is randomized by design, much like the statistical experiments initiated and applied to the context of agriculture crop experiments and more recently, clinical trials of drugs in medicine. This is a way of ensuring the observed treatment effects are entirely uncontaminated by any kind of bias, either owing to measurement error, exclusion of omitted variables or reverse causality. More often than not the exercise concerns the effects of some policy intervention on an outcome of intrinsic interest to policy makers. In order to avoid the problem of vulnerability to any kind of arbitrariness with respect to theoretical formulation of structural relationships, only 'reduced form' relationships connecting the treatment variables to outcome variables are estimated. The result is akin to clinical trials concerning a particular medical treatment, the effect of which on some dimension of health outcomes of patients is sought to be estimated. Once the relevant 'experiment' is set up — i.e., the treatment and outcome variables identified, and the randomized selection of treatment and control groups implemented, all that remains to be done is a statistical comparison of corresponding averages of the outcome variables across the two groups. The purpose is not to understand the underlying structure of the system of relationships generating the outcomes, only the statistical outcome impact of certain policy treatments. Indeed, the only knowledge of structure required is that involved in designing the experiment. To this extent it responds to Koopmans' first critique, and by its very nature also to the second, being concerned directly with policy evaluation, though it can be argued that greater use of theory could permit a wider range of policy assessments.

Controlled experiments of course can be used for other purposes as well, such as in testing theories, as they are used frequently in the natural sciences. With few exceptions, the wave of recent randomized evaluations in development economics are not designed to test theories, but proceed directly to the question of policy evaluation that constitutes Stage 4 research. In particular, these represent an approach to evaluate policies with minimal knowledge or interest in structure. It is in this sense that there is little theory at the frontier of development economics today; this seems to be reflected in the curricula and training of graduate students at leading universities. Whether it is 'too little' or 'enough' is the question we want to finally address.

'Too Little' or 'Enough' Theory?

Let me now put forward the set of reasons why we feel that it is 'too little'. First, there are still many important and interesting theoretical questions still waiting to be addressed. These include dynamic implications of factor market imperfections for individual agents, for their investment decisions that affect the evolution of their families' future assets and occupations, and how these would be affected by external shocks or policy interventions. The interaction of economic processes with political institutions and social norms is another important area where many interesting theoretical possibilities remain to be explored. The implications of replacing traditional assumptions of rationality by behavioural models, and endogenous evolution of preferences for many key policy issues in development are just beginning to be explored.

Second, even within the context of randomized policy experiments, there is considerable scope for enlarging the scope and precision of inferences if they were combined with an effort to test for alternative theories of the structure of underlying relationships generating observed outcomes. There are a variety of reasons for this. For one, observed outcomes do not tell us what it is that economic agents really care about, i.e., the nature of their preferences. From a policy standpoint, eventually, welfare effects should be what really matter. How can we ascertain which kinds of interventions that members of any given community really care about? Social scientists risk imposing their own judgments regarding this matter, given the fact that due to their expense and organizational difficulty they have to choose only a few interventions to evaluate. In the

1970s and 1980s the main issues that development economists used to address in the context of rural areas of underdeveloped countries were imperfections in land and credit, issues that have since been superceded by the delivery of education and health services in contemporary research. There is relatively little attention to the comparative significance of investments in rural infrastructure, such as roads, irrigation and marketing arrangements, which may well be more fundamental. One accordingly needs a theory concerning the objective functions of agents, concerning their own evaluation of alternative public interventions, which needs to be tested.

Moreover, by their very nature (similar to many clinical drug trials) the scope of randomized experiments are limited to assessment of short-term effects, to ignoring possible side effects or general equilibrium responses, and of a narrow range of policy interventions. Wider assessments would be possible in the presence of better knowledge of the underlying behavioural and structural relationships. For instance, theories about the payoffs of agents, or the nature of technology and costs, will permit simulation of the effects of an alternative range of policies. One could enlarge the scope of randomized experiments to allow testing or calibration of structural models that would enable such simulations to be carried out.

Finally, we have now come to expect that institutions matter, and that institutions vary greatly across communities, regions and countries. If so, what we learn about the effects of a given policy intervention in a given context may not apply to other contexts as well. The problem is obviously far more serious for economics than in clinical drug trials, since heterogeneity in human physiology is undoubtedly far less significant compared to economic and social institutions. Theories of institutions that relate them to observable community characteristics could help us understand how context specific the results of specific experiments are.

We should reiterate that my argument is not that randomized experiments do not represent a major step forward in the methodology of economists. Instead, it is that they tend to be conducted in a manner to minimize the use or testing of theoretical hypotheses. They could be substantially enriched if they were also used as a tool for testing theoretical hypotheses, or at least maximizing the information that could be extracted from such experiments. In this respect they are still subject to Koopmans' third critique. We would add to this that understanding the structure of economic relationships is an objective of innate intrinsic importance in social science, quite apart from their usefulness in prediction and policy evaluation.

In summary, we are not quite sure that we have made sufficient progress in Stage 3 to proceed comfortably to Stage 4. Experimental evaluations represent an exciting new innovation in research methodology, but they could be designed to also test theories instead of just measuring the impact of specific policy interventions. Besides the prospect of greater interaction with empirical and experimental methods, investing in theoretical research is desirable for the sake of posing new questions and hypotheses that are bound to generate interesting spin-offs for future empirical and policy analyses. So my hope is that the field of development economics will pursue a more balanced portfolio of research methodologies in the future, with a little more emphasis on theory than is the current norm.

CHALLENGE TO THEORY IN NEW DEVELOPMENT ECONOMICS

If we take the list of papers cited by BBM (Professors Bardhan, Basu and Mookherjee, all in this issue) as representative of what they call "New Development Economics", what is striking is how old-fashioned it all sounds. The topics, for the most part, are the familiar ones: education, health, credit, technology, land, migration. Even institutions, which sound a bit more novel, were being discussed and debated by North and his colleagues more than twenty years ago. It is true that agriculture is a bit less in fashion now than it was twenty-five years ago, and there is, to my taste, a bit too much about human capital, but relative to many other fields (think of macroeconomics) the picture is one of remarkable stability.

In terms of empirical methodology, while there is heightened emphasis on running well-identified regressions, the basic concern with distinguishing causation from mere correlation, that it reflects, obviously goes back a long way. The seemingly unending debate among development economists of the 1960s and 70s about whether bigger farms were less productive (the so-called size-productivity debate), was ultimately a debate about causation—about whether it was really size that was doing the damage or something associated with size.

What has changed since then is that development economists have now embraced all the strategies that have been developed in the last two decades, mostly by labor economists, for dealing with identification issues—difference-in-difference, regression discontinuity designs, randomized experiments, etc—and have access to the kind of data that is needed to make of use these techniques.

In other words, these papers reflect, more than anything else, the mainstreaming of empirical work in development economics. The field, as Professor Mookherjee explicitly recognizes, has matured.

In Defense of Experiential Method

BBM share a feeling that in the process of maturing things have gone a bit awry. Their main complaint, though none of them quite puts it this way, is that empirical standards are now unrealistically high, with the consequence that the top journals are now filled with well-identified but uninteresting papers.

To some extent this has to be right. To accept something that obviously does not meet the standards of the profession because the subject is interesting, editors have to exercise judgment, and exercising judgment is never easy, especially once you recognize that this will expose you to the charge of favouring certain people and/or ideas. There are certainly interesting papers that shed important light onto questions we know little about that do not get published because they do not quite make it on some methodological imperative.

Would we therefore rather that we had not come to a point where development economists are at the cutting edge of empirical techniques? Absolutely not! we think the fact that there is no special pleading for empirical work using developing country data is the reason why so many of the brightest and the best among economics graduate students are coming into the field now. When I was a graduate student, everyone always said that development economics was very important but no one actually did it: The problem was that if you were a top student you wanted to be where people appreciate your mastery of everything that was clever and new (I, for example, did theory, which was very much in fashion then). Now it is development economics that is in fashion.

As far as I am concerned this alone is enough compensation for the sacrifices that we have to make to the harsh god of identification. But I am also convinced that the danger of unwarranted rejections is nowhere as serious as the danger of publishing spurious results. As we have argued elsewhere, there is no dearth of ideas in the world of development practitioners today. What is missing is discrimination: There is no rigorous process by which bad ideas get dropped and good ideas are identified and made better.

A World Bank publication from few years ago provides an excellent example of the attitude towards evidence in the development community outside academia. The Sourcebook is meant to be a catalogue of what, according to the Bank, are the right strategies for poverty reduction. These are also, we presume, strategies into which the Bank is prepared to put its money. It provides a very long list of recommended projects, which include: computer kiosks in villages; cell phones for rent in rural areas; scholarships targeted toward girls who go to secondary school; schooling voucher programs for poor children; joint forest management programs; water users groups; citizen report cards for public services; participatory poverty assessments; internet access for tiny firms; land titling; legal reform; micro-credit based on group lending; and many, many, others.

While many of these are surely good ideas, the book does not tell us how we know that they work. Indeed, one memorable example makes clear that this is not a primary concern of the authors. The book describes a program called the *Gyandoot* program which is based in Madhya Pradesh in India and provides computer kiosks in rural areas. The Sourcebook acknowledges that this project was hit hard by lack of electricity and poor connectivity and that "Currently only a few of the Kiosks have proved to be commercially viable". It then goes on to say, entirely without irony, "Following the success of the initiative....".

The most useful thing a development economist can do in this environment is to stand up for hard evidence and to be demanding about the kind of empirical work that gets into the better journals. Regressions published in the top places have a way of filtering into policy conversations—the power of statistics combined with the imprimatur of a top journal can be irresistible. A recent example is the work by Burnside and Dollar on the impact of aid on growth: In a paper published in the *American Economic Review* (2000), they showed results suggesting that aid does help growth but only when it is given to countries that pursue the "right" policies. This is, of course, also the idea behind President Bush's Millennium Challenge Account (MCA), and while we do not have any direct evidence of a causal connection between the two, the Burnside-Dollar work is frequently cited as a part of case for the MCA (including by the United States Congress Research Services). Yet there are multiple reasons why we (and especially the editors of the *AER*) should have been more skeptical of the Burnside and Dollar results. First, because policies are not exogenous: They reflect other things that are right about the country. Second, aid is not exogenous either—countries with bad policies that received a lot of aid may have other problems (for example, dictatorships that are aligned with the U.S. tended to get a lot of aid in the old days), which makes it hard to compare them with other countries. In any case, a later paper by Easterly, Levine and Roodman (2003) showed that the result in the

Burnside and Dollar paper disappears when they update the data. William Easterly, Ross Levine and David Roodman, "

But how do we know that well-identified regressions are any better? For one, as Professor Basu points out, there is the very real risk of reporting bias: To get published it helps to have the kind of results that the editors or referees want. Professor Basu is worried that this favours papers with unexpected results, but it could also favour results of a particular political bent.

Note, however, that this is potentially just as true of ill-identified regressions as it is of well-identified ones. Indeed, the fact that papers these days are getting published because they have a clever identification strategy, something that Professors Mookherjee and Bardhan deplore, has the advantage of reducing the emphasis on results. The main contribution of a number of the papers that BBM cite as examples of new development economics (Acemoglu, Johnson and Robinson (2001); Munshi (2003); etc.) was to provide credible evidence for what many others before them have claimed ("institutions matter", "social networks are important", etc.).

That being said, we think there is a widely shared feeling that we need to do more about this problem. In particular, we support an initiative to set up a website where every randomized evaluation has to be registered before it gets launched. At the time of registration, the principals of the study will be required to list the outcomes of interest and their predictions regarding each of them (just the direction, not the magnitudes), as well as a reasonable study completion date. They will then be required to report whatever results they have, on or before the announced date. This would guarantee that all studies (including the ones that fail and the ones that have boring results) get recorded, that the authors cannot decide *ex post* to emphasize interesting outcomes that they never thought of when they started the work, and that the experiment does not continue until it yields the desired result. Doing something like this for non-experimental work would be harder: While experiments tend to be very visible, there is no way to know all the failed regressions that get run—unless the authors want to report them. One thing that might help is to set up a web-space where people can report their failed regressions (just a paragraph... we ran this regression in this data set and found the wrong answer or no answer), and then editors can require all future published authors on the same subject to cite these failed studies. In the end, however, this remains another point in favour of randomized experiments over more traditional empirical exercises.

On the other hand, it is true, as Professor Bardhan points out, that randomized evaluations typically give us only the short-term impact of a particular intervention. However, the main reason for this is that the authors of the study want to be able to report some results without having to wait forever, though in many there is nothing, in principle, to stop them from continuing to follow the treatment and control groups after the first round results have been reported. For example, consider Miguel-Kremer's work on de-worming cited by Professor Basu. In that study, they randomly assigned a program of giving free de-worming medicine to children across a set of schools in Busia District in Western Kenya and found that the children in the schools where the medicine was given came to school much more regularly. While that paper is published, the study continues: The goal is to discover whether the fact that they came to school more often helps these children in their future life. To do so they will need to follow the children in both the treatment and control groups as they grow older. This is possible because even though the control schools may now be treated, the children who graduated from those schools before the medicine was introduced there continue to be a valid control group for the corresponding cohorts in the treatment schools.

The point is that there is no necessary conflict between the goals of extending the treatment to the control group (assuming it works) and studying the long-term impact of the treatment. There are cases where this will not work—these are programs where literally every group will end up treated once the program is expanded—but these are more the exception than the rule.

The bigger constraint, it seems to me, is the sheer effort that goes into following people into the future, but if the stakes are high enough, it will be done.

Among the various concerns raised by BBM, the two most important are what we would call the problem of scope and the problem of size. The problem of scope comes from the fact, emphasized by Professors Bardhan and Mookherjee, that most well-identified empirical exercises tend to be relatively localized: This is what makes it possible to rule out other conflating factors (the extreme case of this is a randomized experiment where we deliberately restrict the domain in order to have full control over the program placement). This, they suggest, compromises the external validity of these results—how can we draw general lessons from something so limited?

Professor Basu takes this argument a step further. The external validity of a piece of empirical research, however carefully done he argues, cannot be entirely derived from something internal to that work. To apply these results, we need to have a theory that helps us decide whether a particular location (in space, or Professor Basu emphasizes, in time) is sufficiently similar to the location from where the results came. And in most cases this theory would not come close to meeting the standards of evidence that development economics today aspires to, and even if it did, the problem of external validity would remain, just shifted back a layer.

This is obviously correct. Indeed it seems to me to be a version of David Hume's justly famous demonstration of the lack of a rational basis for induction. But at this point Professor Basu makes a curious leap into what reads like radical skepticism. As he puts it, "Two correctly done empirical results may have the property that one resonates with our intuition—we simply feel that if it was true in the past it has a reasonable chance of being true in the future—and the other does not. My inclination would be to go along with the intuition (while admitting that intuitions often go haywire)." This seems to imply (by continuity) that if one empirical conclusion accorded less well with his intuition than another, but was somewhat more "correctly done", would he still go with the latter? In other words, he denies the primacy of empirical methods over his intuition.

We must confess that we do not understand this position. To take an example, one of the early randomized experiments in Busia District of Kenya looked at the effect of having flip charts in the classroom on the performance of children. It found that the children in the schools that were randomly chosen to get a flipchart do not do any better. The study then looks at what it would have found if it had tried to answer the same question based on running a retrospective cross-section regression using data from other schools in the same part of Kenya. In other words, they ran a simple regression of the test scores on whether the school had flip-charts in this other sample of schools. They found that having flip-chart raises student performance about 0.2 standard deviations.

My inclination, faced with this evidence, is to assume that the experiment gave more or less the right answer for what would happen in an average school. We start from the fact that the experiment was correctly done: The experimental result is therefore the right conclusion for those particular schools. The question then is whether this also the correct result for other schools of this type in the area, including the ones in the retrospective study. To believe this, we would need to believe: (a) that the cross-section study is biased; and, (b) that the treatment effect does not vary across the two populations.

Say that Professor Basu, on the other hand, believes that the retrospective result is the correct generalizeable prediction because it fits better with his prior intuition (this is entirely hypothetical and almost surely unfair to him, but it helps to set out the structure of our disagreement). He therefore believes that: (a) the retrospective result is unbiased; and, (b) that the treatment effect is not the same in these two populations.

These two sets of beliefs (his and mine) are, however, not symmetrical. The fact that the treatment effect varies in this way is not something that he has any independent reason to believe: The study which (I assume) summarizes everything either of us knows about the area, suggests that the populations are in fact quite similar. Or to put it differently, the only reason to suppose that the treatment effect is higher in one of these populations than the other is that this is what squares with his prior—this was not something that he learnt from the data generated by the retrospective study or any other study. My suspicion of the results from the retrospective study, on the other hand, stems from the standard observation, confirmed by any number of studies, that schools in developing countries that have more school inputs tend to be schools where parents are richer and/or care more about education and hence are schools where the children would have done better even without the extra inputs. We worry that the fact that children in schools with flipcharts do better than children in schools without flipcharts could be partly a result of this. In other words, we favour the experimental result mainly because we have an *independent* reason to suspect that the retrospective result is biased upwards.

Moreover, my assumption that the treatment effect is the same in the two populations, while not justified by any direct evidence, would seem to be the natural default assumption in the absence of any information to the contrary. It is clearly the way we are designed to function in the world—when we meet a new child our first instinct is to treat him like all the other children we know—though we would not know whether it is evolution that has made us so (as Professor Basu would have it), or our own experience with what is sometimes called the "uniformity of nature".

None of this, however, tells us exactly what to do when we expect there to be systematic differences between the two populations. If our only really reliable evidence was from India but we were interested in what might happen in Kenya, it probably does make sense to look at the available (low quality) evidence from East Africa. Moreover, if the two types of evidence disagree, we might even decide to put a substantial amount of weight on the less reliable evidence, if it turns out that it fits better with our prior beliefs. Nevertheless, there remains an essential asymmetry between the two: The well-identified regression does give us the "correct" estimate for at least one population, while the other may not be right for anyone. For this reason, even if we have many low quality regressions that say the same thing, there is no sense in which the high quality evidence becomes irrelevant—after all, the same source of bias could be afflicting all the low quality results. The evidence remains anchored by that one high quality result.

That being said, the only way to build trust in experimental and quasi-experimental results is to replicate them in several different locations. One of the strengths of the Miguel-Kremer work on de-worming cited by Professor Basu, is that it has now been reproduced in India (the original study was in Kenya) with very similar results. Moreover, Bleakley (2004), using quasi-experimental methods to estimate the effect of de-worming in the U.S. South also finds a structural estimate very similar to what these two other studies find. The randomized evaluation of the Balsakhi remedial education program in India was carried out simultaneously in two different locations (Mumbai and Vadodara) by two different implementing teams for exactly this reason, and, reassuringly, found more or less the same results in two locations. These results suggest that extrapolating these results across large distances may not always be as bad as it might seem, but clearly many more replications need to happen.

The problem of size arises because randomized experiments in particular tend to be relatively small-scale, partly due to practical and financial constraints, but also in part because we want the experimental results *before* scaling up the program. Other careful micro studies are less constrained, but the need to know exactly what is going on, which underlies good identification strategies, tends to limit the scope of these studies as well. Size is important for two reasons: One, which applies only to randomized evaluations, is that small programs are easy to monitor carefully and therefore are not run like real programs. While this is a concern, many of the more recent randomized evaluations are only small relative to nation-wide programs: The Balsakhi and de-worming studies mentioned above, for example, each involved collecting data from tens of thousands of children and a number of other recent studies are even bigger. Moreover there is a lot of emphasis on making sure that the programs that get evaluated are developed enough to be modular, in the sense that what gets implemented at every location is described by a simple and common protocol. This makes it easier to limit the involvement of the program's sponsors and the evaluators in the implementation process.

Size is also an issue because of what are often misleadingly, called general equilibrium effects: Educating some more children in Vadodara or Mumbai is not the same as raising educational standards in the country as a whole—presumably if the number of educated people in the country goes up enough all sorts of other things will change. Wages paid to educated people will fall; the political clout of educated people will rise; other might see them and also start demanding more education; etc.

This is a very real problem, though obviously the import we need to give it depends on the question we are asking. If we are interested in how to get children to come to school, we might be okay in ignoring the effect of increased enrolment on wages fifteen years hence, since parents probably do not think that far ahead. On the other hand, if we want to figure out how much we add to the future earnings of these children by making them go to school, it would be silly to not worry about what would happen to wages. Even the most committed experimentalist would want to do something.

THE CONFRONT TO THEORY

This is where, Professor Mookherjee argues, we ought to be using more theory. Theory helps because what we really need is to make an assumption, and theory tells us what the right assumption would be. For example, we know from market equilibrium theory that the one number we need in order to assess the effect of the increase in education on wages is the elasticity of demand for skilled labor. Armed with this knowledge, we could go looking for an estimate of the elasticity and having found one (hopefully from an experiment or a quasi-experiment), could use it to calculate the true benefits from getting children into school.

Theory can also help us in solving the problem of scope. The conventional structural approach, which Professor Mookherjee supports, involves fitting a model with a small number of unobserved parameters to the observed program effects, and then using this model to make out-of-sample predictions. Conceptually, given that parameters of the structural model are estimated using the fact that the program effect is different for people with different observables characteristics, this is not that different from a naïve approach, where we allow the program effect to depend on observables, and then extrapolate the results using what we know about the same observables in the new population. The advantage of the structural approach is that we have a theory to guide us about the kind of parametric restrictions we want to place on the data rather than having to guess at it. The disadvantage is that the theory may be wrong. The fallout of the behavioral economics revolution in economics is that we are no longer particularly sure of what the right theory ought to look like, especially in as much as decision problems are concerned. In particular, we are no longer secure in the presumption that utility functions and cost functions are somehow more stable and more universal than behavioral rules. Of course, as Professor Mookherjee notes, we could also structurally estimate behavior rules, but for that we would need a new body of theory. In the meanwhile it is not clear that using the existing theory always dominates simply assuming an ad hoc empirical specification, but perhaps it is best to use the two approaches in tandem, using one to check on the other.

The bigger challenge to theory however comes from a different direction. The most important role of theory in development economics, and indeed in all the rest of economics as well, is to help us understand what are the right questions. The formulation of a testable hypothesis is only the final stage of this process, and one that is often left for the empirical researchers to do, since it often depends on exact nature of the data. What is prior to that, and in some ways, even more important, is the ability of theory to locate the empirical results within a broader intellectual context and make us see why we ought to care. In this sense, a lot of the best empirical work of the last decade or so can be seen as a response to a body of theory developed in the previous decade that made us really understand the implications of living in a world where neither markets nor governments work perfectly.

What is unusual about the state of development economics today is not that there is too little theory, but that theory has lost its position at the vanguard: New questions are being asked by empirical researchers, but, for the most part, they are not coming from a prior body of worked-out theory. The most intriguing results from empirical research today, as we see it, are not the ones cited by BBM, but results like those of Bertrand-Karlan-Mullainathan-Shafir-Zinman (2004) (the decision to take a loan is at least as influenced by whose picture is on the offer letter as it is by large differences in the interest rate), Karlan-Zinman (2004)(moral hazard in credit markets is a problem for men and not women, while for adverse selection it is the other way around), Duflo-Kremer-Robinson(farmers say that they do not buy fertilizer because they have no money, and do buy fertilizer if it is brought to them while they have money in hand, but will not go and buy it at the local store), etc. It is not just that we do not have a theory within which these results can be interpreted—it is not even clear how we would begin to build that theory. Indeed, the same goes for some less exotic results like Michael Kremer's finding that teachers teach better when students are given an incentive to do well (2004), but not when teachers themselves are rewarded if their students do well (2001).

The point is not that these phenomena are more complex than what we are used to and therefore need a more sophisticated theory. The problem is precisely that the correct explanation may not be particularly interesting or illuminating:

Perhaps the borrowers in Bertrand-Karlan-Mullainathan just liked the picture and responded to it. Maybe the farmers in Duflo-Kremer-Robinson had never thought of the possibility of going to the store when they had the money (which is a few weeks before they need the fertilizer). Could it not simply be that the students in Kremer's study are better at getting the teacher to do what they want, than the teachers are in getting cooperation from the students?

The challenge is to turn these explanations into a theory—something that would have implications for other things that we care about and pose new questions for empirical research. We believe that it can be done, but to do this we need to give up trying to defend the existing theory (which has been incredibly successful in many ways) against an onslaught of seemingly random results that are coming out of the field experiments. In Haavelmo's terms (as described by Professor Mookherjee in the present issue) we are back at stage 1: We are gathering impressions that would eventually allow us to build a set of new theories that, one day, will define a "newer" development economics.

Theory versus Empirics?

The late David Champernowne, a British mathematical economist of rare distinction, was once asked how much mathematics is necessary in economics. "The amount of mathematics I know," was his answer. There was a time when "mathematics" was associated with "theory" in economics. This is no longer the case. Mathematical techniques are as used in theoretical as in empirical economics, the techniques of mathematical statistics being prominent in the latter. The ground has shifted, since significant proficiency in mathematics and statistics is now the requirement in the best graduate economics degree programs in the world. Rather, it would seem, the major divide is now between using these techniques in theoretical versus empirical exercises. "The amount of theory I do", might now be Champernowne's apocryphal answer to the analogous question for modern times.

In economics generally, the last fifteen years have seen a major shift away from the prominence that was accorded to theory in the preceding decade and a half. One indicator of this is the Clark medal of the American Economic Association, awarded every two years to the most outstanding American economist under the age of 40. Of the last seven awards, only one was awarded to a pure theorist. Of the seven before these, five were awarded to pure theorists. This shift is reflected in the shift in graduate programs, and appointments in top Universities.

Development economics, which has itself become more integrated into mainstream economics in the last thirty years, has also followed this trend. After a long period of concentration on theory, research in development economics entered a strongly empirical phase around ten to fifteen years ago. This coincided with greater and easier availability of data, and of computational power. To take just one example, in the mid 1980s there were only one or two African countries that had nationally representative household sample surveys. Now more than a dozen countries have such surveys, and there are several panel data sets covering households and firms for half a dozen or more countries.

The situation was always better in Asia and in Latin America, but there too there have been improvements, sometimes inadvertently so—for example, the opening up of China in the late 1970s and 1980s led to the generation of many micro data sets. Added to this is the continued improvement, or at least the easier availability, of cross country data sets for developing countries that are at last nominally comparable—a good example of this is the Deininger-Squire data set on income distribution, which was made available worldwide through the World Bank, allowing a whole industry of cross-country regressions on inequality and growth to develop. The same is true of many other types of macroeconomic data sets that are easily available and easily useable. This is what leads Dilip Mookherjee to say: "Development economics is increasingly becoming an empirical discipline today."

Mookherjee characterizes four stages of research: Stage 1 is empirical description, Stage 2 is formulation of theory, Stage 3 is testing and Stage 4 is prediction and policy evaluation. The focus in the last fifteen years has been on Stage 3. Following where mainstream economics has led, development economics these days focuses greatly on testing, in particular the difficulties of inferring causality from correlation. This is the stuff of classical debates, like that between Keynes and Tinbergen, highlighted by Mookherjee. Mookherjee thinks that this focus is now tending to dominate the development discourse, and Bardhan and Basu agree. This is particularly true for two strands of the empirical literature—that which focuses on the search for instrumental variables, and that which uses experimental design of randomized evaluation. These take us to the frontier of empirical methodology in economics, and according to Banerjee it is this that explains, partly, why development economics is respected within the discipline of economics: "I think the fact that there is no special pleading for empirical work using developing country data is the reason why the brightest and the best among graduate economics students are coming into the field now."

For both of these strands, it is not the fact of their existence that troubles Bardhan, Basu and Mookherjee, but rather its current preponderance in the journals. This attention to empirics may, according to Mookherjee and Bardhan, crowd out attention to a whole range of interesting theoretical phenomena, such as "...dynamic implications of factor market imperfections for individual agents...., interaction of economic processes with political institutions and social norms."(Mookherjee), or "...how we can go beyond existing partial-equilibrium models of oligopoly to generate a viable theory of factor prices and income distribution in a generally oligopolistic economy;...the nature of transitional dynamics (as opposed to comparative statics) as we move away from traditional low-level equilibrium; ....." (Bardhan).

In addition, and this is a charge particularly leveled against randomized experimental designs, that the very thing that makes inference "clean", namely a specific controlled setting, makes any generalization from this inference problematic. This is the line taken in particular by Basu in his contribution to this symposium. But in his defense of this empirical method, Banerjee sets up the choice between one piece of evidence where the inference is clean, compared to several, from different locations and places, where the inference is problematic, and there is no doubt as to where he comes out: "...even if we have many low quality regressions that say the same thing, there is no sense in which the high quality evidence becomes irrelevant—after all, the same source of bias could be affecting all the low quality results." Having said this, however, he does of course accept that having many randomized experiments in different locations and at different times is the way to build confidence in their results.

Overall, my own sense is that the protagonists in this debate are not that far apart. Nobody would argue that the use of simple correlation to infer causation should be the modus operandi of empirical development economics. On the other hand, there is a tradeoff encountered as the environment generating the data is sufficiently controlled to make clean inference possible—in the extreme, the inference is valid only for that environment and no other. The role of theory in helping to make the best of this tradeoff is not disputed either. Fifteen years ago, there was clearly too little empirical work in development economics that met the current frontier standards in establishing inference. Fifteen years on, as the fruits of this empirical excursion have begun to be gathered, there is equally a need for theoretical perspective to make the best use of the empirical results, and to continue working on unresolved theoretical issues. Good sense will surely prevail and we will have both more theory and more good empirical work—a goldilocks solution for development economics.

Timepiece Out for the Bears

But, in my view, the real problems for development economics, as for economics, lie somewhat at a tangent to the balance between theory and empirics. The "theory" in the theory/

empirics balance is none other than modern neoclassical economics, where there is recognition of various types of market and information failures, and outcomes and institutions are understood in terms of these imperfections. This is surely an advance on the general equilibrium theory of thirty years ago, which was not even thought to be of much relevance to development economics. The integration of development economics into mainstream economics has been helped by the direction in which mainstream economic theory has moved, and it has to be said that this move is itself related to the fact that for economists like Amartya Sen and Joseph Stiglitz, standard general equilibrium theory was very far removed from the realities of the developing countries.

However, there remain two basic problems with the current state of development economics—one is in the realm of theory, the other in the realm of policy. In the realm of theory, the basic formulation of individual behavior, even in "Stiglitzian" models with imperfect information and so on, is one that satisfies the text book axioms of "rational choice." The behavioral economics revolution in mainstream economics is bringing into question the empirical validity of these axioms, and thus raising questions for those sub-disciplines, like development economics, public economics or labor economics, that are heavily dependent on the framework of standard rational choice. These questions, raised originally by empirical research in behavioral economics, are now being asked anew as similar findings emerge from the empirical development economics. As Banerjee notes in his commentary : "The most intriguing results from empirical research today, as I see it, are not the ones cites by BBM, but results like those of Bertrand-Karlan-Mullainahan-Shafir-Zinman (2004) (the decision to take a loan is at least as influenced by those whose picture is on the offer letter as it is by large differences in the interest rate),......Duflo-Kremer-Robinson (farmers say that they do not buy fertilizer because they have no money, and do not buy fertilizer if it is brought to them while they have money in hand, but will not go and buy it at the local store), etc.....It is not just that we do not have a theory within which these results can be interpreted—it is not even clear how we could begin to build that theory." Bardhan, Basu and Mookherjee also highlight the need for new departures from the current centre of gravity of development economics theory when they raise the question of the important role of norms in economic and social behavior. Bardhan further emphasizes the point when he says, "Methodological individualism which undergirds most of economics (including) the recent attempts to depart from postulates of self-interested maximization) may not be an appropriate principle when issues of group dignity and autonomy supersede individual oriented motivations."

The second major problem is not so much with development economics theory as with development economics policy analysis. No matter how sophisticated our theory and empirics become, it seems that the in the debates on great policy issues of the day—on exchange rates, trade policy, labor market policy, deregulation etc—simple "ECON 101" economics is very important. For many if not most policy analysts, the basic competitive model (and a partial equilibrium one at that) is the workhorse tool—it is the framework that slips most easily into mind when thinking about economic policy. Even some of those who made their names developing the theory of economic policy in a world with imperfections, tend to fallback on the simple policy prescriptions of "ECON 101". The justification given is often of a political economy nature, that the more complex policies called for by modern theory (and empirics) are likely to be used and abused by special interest groups. At the very least one can say that this position needs to be tested in theory and in empirics.

Thus even as we grapple with the perennial question of the right balance between theory and empirics, we should also focus on the fundamentals of the development economics we teach our students, and how policy makers use (or do not use) the development economics we teach.

ASSUMPTION OR EMPIRICS IN EXPANSION ECONOMICS

In the last two decades there has been a rejuvenation of development economics, and in this the leadership has been provided by a group of empirical researchers mostly in the US. In this period there has been an easier availability of detailed disaggregated, often household-level, data (for example, LSMS data of the World Bank for several countries and Census data in many countries, apart from the Indian N.S.S., ICRISAT, and NCAER data). Large memory capacities in our desk computers and sophisticated statistical analysis software have made the handling of gigantic datasets easily manageable, with a speed that still amazes some of us who, when we started our own empirical work, had small Facit machines to be hand-cranked for calculations (including inverting reasonable-sized matrices in the most labour-intensive way), and for large jobs had to wait for days in the queue in the main large-frame computer for the whole campus.

Also the influence of Labour Economics, where applied econometrics had advanced in a major way a few years earlier, has been substantial in allied fields like development. Much more meticulous attention is now paid to finding appropriate identification strategy in our econometric analysis of causal explanations in a way that makes some of the earlier empirical work in development (including my own) look more cavalier.

As empirical work has become more respectable in development economics, and sophisticated empirical strategies (including that of random evaluation) explore new horizons, whole armies of graduate students and young faculty are now excited by the field, and nearly 90 per cent of the papers presented in Development Seminars in the US (including mine at Berkeley) are now mainly, and proudly, empirical.

This is a big change from the days when the brighter students in development would not dirty their hands with the (inevitably messy) data, when the intricate theorems in optimum growth, general equilibrium, imperfect information, or game theory beckoned alluringly. The question that Mookherjee posits suggests that the pendulum may now have swung too much in the other direction. As someone who has dabbled both in theory and empirical work, my inclination is to agree with him and also point, as Mookherjee does, to some of the limitations of the newly fashionable empirical approach, without doubting its valuable contributions. I shall, however, qualify this with some special remarks on the empirical work on Indian development at the end.

In order to slay the dragons of 'endogeneity' and 'reverse causality' that threaten the validity of inference in many of the empirical exercises researchers are forever in search of clever 'instrumental variables'. Once one hits upon a clever 'instrument', then the rest is considered relatively secondary, and you crank out your triumphant causal explanation from the two-stage regressions. In this we are often careless about the many pitfalls of instrumental variables, fail to examine the larger meaning of the identifying assumptions, and jump to conclusions. We forget that an instrumental variable even if it has satisfactory statistical properties does not by itself give us an adequate causal explanation or a satisfactory testing of a theory. Let me take the example of an article which is probably the most widely cited in the recent literature on how development depends on institutional quality: Acemoglu, Johnson, and Robinson, AJR (2001). It so happens that I am often on the same side as these authors when it comes to underlining the importance of institutions in development economics, but I cannot go along with the way the profession seems to have lapped up their results as authoritative in quantifying the effect of institutions, and over-interpreted their significance. In their search for an instrumental variable that exogenously affects institutions but not income directly, they imaginatively picked a historical variable, colonial settler mortality, and used it in their first-stage regressions, and the predicted institutions then explained inter-country differences in per capita income in an econometrically cleaner way than has been the case before in this literature. Their presumption is that the mortality rates among early European settlers in a colony determined whether the Europeans decided to install resource-extractive or –plundering institutions there or to settle and build European institutions, like those protecting property rights which help long-run investment and development.

Even ignoring the usual questions about the quality and comparability of data that afflict such cross-country empirical exercises, the fact that some of the early colonies (say in Latin America) were run by Europeans (from Spain and Portugal) at a time when they did not have those property rights institutions quite in place even at home, and the fact that there are many developing countries which largely avoided colonisation (for example, China, Thailand, Mongolia, Ethiopia), this particular exercise has many substantive and methodological problems:

(a) Are property rights institutions the only type of institutions that matter for development? What about participatory and accountability institutions, or institutions of investment co-ordination? Bardhan (2005) quantifies the effect of some participatory and accountability institutions in explaining the cross-country differences in human development indicators.

(b) As Przeworski (2004) points out, the procedure of instrumenting recent institutions by referring to some old historical fact is flawed because institutions change over time. An instrument for the initial institutions need not be a valid instrument for the current ones. If good institutions are more likely to survive in more affluent countries, then institutional quality today is still endogenous with respect to income.

(c) Albouy (2004) corrects some flaws in the AJR settler mortality measure and shows that when the revised data are used, the AJR analysis suffers from a 'weak instrument' problem. (In general in some of the recent use of the instrumental variable approach it is often ignored that a weak instrument can be worse than no instrument). AJR, however, has contested Albouy's corrections.

(d) The disease environment in the 18th or 19th century may be correlated with that today, and the latter affects current incomes directly as well as through its effect on institutions.

An econometrically cleaner method of establishing causality is through random evaluation, which, borrowing a method from medical experiments, has become increasingly popular in development economics, as Mookherjee has noted. This is a very promising development and some researchers have made a creative use of this, including getting involved with NGO's in the field, as participant observer/researcher and influencing their survey design to generate robust statistical estimates. One of the best examples of work in this genre is Miguel and Kremer (2004), on the impact of deworming drugs among Kenyan school children; this is one of the cleanest empirical assessments of externalities, which development economists always talk about but find hard to measure. But I share some of the general doubts expressed by Mookherjee on the methodology in general. By nature these experiments are much too microscopic, and there is a danger of missing 'the forest for the trees'. A rush to generalizations from these experimental results will be unwarranted, as they ignore macro or political-economy or general-equilibrium effects of a programme when they are extended to a larger scale, and the whole is usually more than a sum of the parts. How reliable will it be to generalize the treatment effects of an NGO or government programme, when it is implemented nation-wide (as in the case of PROGRESA in Mexico, Grameen Bank in Bangladesh, or Self-Help Groups in micro-finance in India)?

And after all there is more to development economics than more precise programme evaluation or the impact study of a particular intervention. I can see that the latter is particularly important for some administrators and loan givers; I can also see why international financial institutions (like the World Bank) can benefit from the results of these studies on their many projects, which are currently often crudely evaluated. But the task of development economists is beyond writing more effective policy manuals; at least some of them should think about larger structural and conceptual issues. Our improved identifying strategies and controlled experiments have not made us any wiser in deciphering the mechanisms through which certain outcomes are generated (the 'why' and the 'how') and the social dynamics that are involved, and without these our causal explanations are weak, for all the precision of our tools or the statistical significance of our estimates. In fact we are sometimes so obsessed with the precision of these tools, that we dismiss potentially insightful exercises that do not pass the standards of our econometric vice squads, and we often let the best be the enemy of the good.

In fact our preoccupation with accurate quantification often takes us away from the more important causes of a phenomenon and we concentrate on variables that are better measured but may be socially and economically less significant, reminding one of the oft-repeated charge against economists, who look for the missing keys not in the dark place where they lost them but where there is more light. We tend to work with a thin conceptual menu and a large box of precision instruments. In contrast sociologists and anthropologists spend much less time on honing these instruments, and more on a richer understanding of the processes, relations and dynamics.

In calling for a more balanced portfolio of research Mookherjee has briefly cited some of the directions which theoretical research can fruitfully take. Let me add a few more to his list. We don't know enough about the relationship between factor market imperfections and the social norms, and how this relationship evolves with changing demographic and technological circumstances; how economic processes and community institutions interact; how we can go beyond the existing partial-equilibrium models of oligopoly to generate a viable theory of factor prices and income distribution in a generally oligopolistic economy; an integrated theory of vertical product differentiation, firm heterogeneity, marketing economies of scale and international competition; the nature of transitional dynamics (as opposed to comparative statics) as we move away from a traditional low-level equilibrium; how economic processes get moulded when the state is weak and distant, the legal system is poorly enforced, and there is an 'oligopoly' of violence (as opposed to the 'monopoly of violence' that Max Weber ascribed to the state); and so on. Also, in the recent theoretical and experimental work in economics on departures from self-interested maximising behaviour not enough attention has been paid to special behavioural issues that arise in poor countries.

For example, the ideas emanating from the growing literature on fairness and reciprocity in individual economic behaviour need to be integrated with the idea of 'moral economy' that historians and sociologists have talked about both with respect to European and Asian cases: for example, Rudé (1964) and Thompson (1963) cite cases of peasant *jacqueries* where peasants in their rage against high prices sometimes looted the granary of a merchant but then paid him what they considered a 'fair' price; Scott (1976) has cited cases in colonial Vietnam when peasants rebelling against landlords seized the harvest but paid the landlord what they considered a 'fair' cropshare. The interesting angle from the anthropological literature on this is that traditional notions of fairness are often asymmetric: (a) in acts of reciprocity or gift-exchanges between two parties payments are not supposed to balance, and (b) moral economies often have double standards depending on the domain of the moral community (a peasant who is meticulously fair-minded in his transactions with fellow members of the community has no scruple in cheating people whom he considers outsiders). Our theoretical literature, while beginning to handle normative and weak-willed or time-inconsistent behaviour, is yet ill-equipped to tackle another type of social action which sociologists have pointed attention to: problem-solving interaction with others in which our ends and means co-evolve, with ends discovered and transformed in the process.

The psychological literature on cognitive dissonance and internalization of severe constraints has obvious relevance to the way the poor behave: as Sen (1984) reminds us, 'many of the inequities of the world survive by making allies out of the deprived and the abused', and as Appadurai (2004) reminds us, the poor may lack "the aspirational resources to contest and alter the conditions of their own poverty". The constraints they internalize are not just the ones they themselves face, but their parents, peers and neighbours have faced. There is much to draw here from the sociological literature on role models and peer effects and the growing socio-economic literature on neighbourhood effects (mostly relating to poverty traps in US inner-city ghettos). This also relates to the role of group pride, group anxiety, and other culturally sanctioned collective processes which deeply affect our preferences (particularly in developing countries suffused with ethnic, caste, or religious affinities), and are yet largely ignored by economists. This has implications for incentives and organizations in labour markets—as Akerlof and Kranton (2005) have emphasized, but also for our theories of collective action (which are dominated by simplistic free-rider presumptions). It raises a larger methodological issue as well. Methodological individualism which undergirds most of economics (including the recent attempts to depart from postulates of self-interested maximisation) may not be an appropriate principle when issues of group dignity and autonomy supersede individual-oriented motivations.

Finally, while we may agree that there is too little emphasis on theory compared to the newly fashionable, though highly valuable, empirical exercises, this is mostly in relation to development economics as practiced in the West. We have to qualify my agreement in relation to development economics as practiced in India, where I believe the old Brahminical tradition of high premium on theory still persists. We have a fascination for the esoteric intricacies of a theoretical problem, much less for the sweat, toil, and tears involved in grubby empirical work. In particular, there is a dearth of careful empirical work on many vital issues of the Indian economy. While there is a massive amount of largely descriptive empirical work published every year (including in the pages of the EPW), a great deal of it would have improved in explanatory power if more attention were paid to the identification strategies and selection issues that worry econometricians. This also would have stimulated the need for better data collection and for trying out experimental methods in the field, involving real farmers, real workers, real entrepreneurs. There is a great need for more empirical work in India on the structure and practices of enterprises in the vast informal sector (more than 80 per cent of even the non-agricultural labor force is employed there), on inter-relationships among firms in a given industry, patterns of industrial evolution with the use of firm-level data, on how our marketing and informal insurance institutions work both in agriculture and outside, work place practices, recruitment mechanisms and wage-setting institutions in industry, trade, and the service sectors, on patterns of technology diffusion, etc. We have a relative abundance of household data on consumption and employment. This has fuelled the endless debates on measurement of poverty and inequality over the last four decades. Yet to this day we know very little on inter-generational mobility, which is probably the most important aspect of inequality in an extremely hierarchical society like ours, and there are very few attempts at collecting the requisite longitudinal surveys of families. Compared to other countries, we have much less solid empirical work on the necessary restructuring of our pension system or the building of a comprehensive health insurance system outside the formal sector. Fewer good economists are now working on Indian economic history.

EMPIRICAL DEVELOPMENT ECONOMICS

The methodology of scientific research is largely a matter of intuition and knack. As a consequence it is hard to think of formal criteria for evaluating methodology. This must be one reason why the philosophy of science has made so little progress compared to science. The same is true of economics. The subject has made huge gains. But the skirmishes that have been fought about its methodology—for instance, the debate based on Friedman's famous paper (1953)—have done little to enlighten us. Nevertheless, there is value in occasionally pulling ourselves back and asking whether the method that we use to advance knowledge in a particular discipline is right. Dilip Mookherjee's masterly essay, based on a symposium at Cornell University, does precisely that. It is an exercise in introspection and an invitation to practitioners to take stock of the methodology of development economics.

There may be special value in taking up this invitation because development economics has witnessed an upsurge in innovative empirical research. The new empirical development economics is a remarkable achievement. It is not surprising that, once its method was properly understood, there was an explosion of research using its techniques (by, for instance, Esther Duflo, Raghabendra Chattopadhyay, Edward Miguel, Simon Johnson, Michael Kremer, Daron Acemoglu, James Robinson, Kaivan Munshi, Rohini Pande). But I have some critiques to offer of this method, which overlap partly with the criticisms put forth by Bardhan (2005) and Mookherjee (2005), and goes beyond to some rather philosophical matters. I shall in this essay concentrate on what, in Dilip Mookherjee's paper, is described as Stage 4 research and a little on his late stage-3 research.

One reason for the popularity of this new method is the precision of its findings and because, once a result is discovered by this method, we fully understand what it is that has been discovered. Let me consider here one particularly elegant paper written in this mode, namely, Chattopadhyay and Duflo (2004). One of the results reported in this paper is the following: In West Bengal, having a woman head a panchayat has made a difference to what the panchayat does; it leads, for instance, to the better provisioning of water in the village.

In a lot of empirical research, there is the risk that reality may be the reverse of what is being claimed. For example, suppose that in areas with poor water-supply, women (whose traditional job is to fend for the household's water supply) are so preoccupied with the task of fetching water that they cannot participate in local panchayat politics. This could easily create the impression that if women participate in panchayat politics then *this leads to* the better provision of water. In this case the deduction would be wrong; the causality runs the other way around. What is remarkable about this new empirical development economics is that by using the fact of an exogenous randomization or the method of carefully-selected instrumental variable it has found a way to get around this problem.

Findings like the above one are extremely valuable; they tell us important things about the way the world is. A popular view, often encountered in newspapers, is that, in a traditional society like India's, having a woman head a panchayat is of no real consequence because she would invariably do her husband's bidding or be bull-dozed by the male members of the panchayat. The study by Chattopadhyay and Duflo tells us, compellingly, that that is not so. The new empirical development economics aspires to results of this kind. Where this method applies (and as Mookherjee reminds us, it does not apply everywhere) it is an excellent method to use.

If despite this, I have criticisms of the new empirical development economics, it is clearly not about the method itself but about what we do with it and how we interpret it. And on this there are many popular misconceptions that need to be countered.

Furthermore, it should be stated at the outset that I have some skepticism about all human endeavour to acquire knowledge. Hence, the limitations that I point to here apply much more widely than my focus of attention in this essay, to wit, development economics. I use the new empirical economics as a peg for my argument precisely because it constitutes some of the best research going on in the field.

Forecast and Policy

First, it must be recognized that the new method, at least by its own criterion of what constitutes correct inference, does not help us predict the future. Put differently, suppose we apply the strictness of criterion that this new method demands of empirical work, and then ask what we can predict based on this new method? It is important to understand that the answer is "very little".

Suppose a researcher, studying the effect of aspirin, administers a very low dose of the medicine (150 mgs, say) to a random sample of people found walking in the streets of Delhi and finds that, if a person with a headache takes aspirin, he typically (meaning, let us say, in 90% of the cases) benefits from it. Let me call this the "research result" (RR). Now suppose you are asked what would have been the effect of giving 150 mgs of aspirin to a random selection of people in Delhi who were lying down with a headache? Based on the RR could you say that they would have benefited from it? The answer clearly is no; you can not say much, since this sample does not belong to the population on which the original study was done.

Let us now consider how we may use the RR for forecasting. If we next year give the people of Delhi, who are walking around, 150 mgs of aspirin, could we expect that those with a headache would benefit from this? Strictly speaking, the answer is no. The people of next year's Delhi are not the population from which the RR was derived. Also the state variables may be different. The weather may be warmer; there may be more suspended particulate matter in the air, and so on. So to use the RR and to predict the future is like doing a study of the effects of administering aspirin to people who are walking and then presuming that it will apply to those who are lying. If we are fussy about proper randomization for our study and take the view that we should not accept the wisdom of samples drawn in a biased manner or from the wrong population, we should also take the view that we cannot say anything about the future.

This, in turn, means that we cannot make policy prescriptions, since those are always recommendations for the future. This does not mean that the initial RR is useless. If a person told you that he had (at the same time that the aspirin research was being done in Delhi) selected people randomly from those walking in Delhi and given them 150 mgs of aspirin, you would rightly be able to guess that 90% of those with a headache would have benefited from this. The trouble arises with going over from yesterday's population to tomorrows.

One may try to counter this by arguing that between yesterday and tomorrow there is no fundamental difference and so no reason to expect a relation that was true yesterday to be not true tomorrow. But the difference between yesterday and tomorrow is not just a matter of time. Between yesterday and tomorrow there can be war and pestilence; between yesterday and tomorrow can be 9/11, altering the way world politics in conducted; between yesterday and tomorrow we can have a warmer globe.

One may respond to this further by saying that wars and pestilence do not make a difference to the human physical constitution and so we would expect the aspirin result to carry over from yesteryear to the future. This is perfectly reasonable but in making this argument we are immediately conceding the role of intuition. We are combining our statistical finding with our prior 'knowledge' that, for matters of health, knowledge acquired from one population can be carried over to another. We may hesitate to do this about the role of women in panchayats but feel confident about aspirins. This brings us to precisely the point I would endorse: These statistical findings are not useless for prediction but they have to be combined with unscientific intuition for them to be considered useful. We cannot reject the unscientific *and* claim that our method has predictive power.

Our intuition or our unscientific judgment comes in gradations. Before aspirin is tried on anyone, we may have no faith in aspirin; once we know it has worked on people last year we have more faith in it next year. And the faith grows inductively. For that matter the fact that it has worked on people walking may make us inclined to believe somewhat that it will work on people lying down. But note that there is nothing objective about these beliefs. As I will argue later, what we so often take to be features of the world are actually propensities of the mind.

Let me move on from the subject of prediction and *assume* (maybe for reasons of intuition just discussed) that time cannot make a difference to the subject matter that is being researched.

So a relation found to be valid today will be valid tomorrow—this is an axiom. In that case we can of course predict the future but there remains another fallacy that we can fall into if we are not careful in interpreting the results of the new empirical development economics.

Notice that, if we draw a person at random from among the Japanese who happen to be walking in Delhi, can we then use the above research result and say that he will benefit (meaning with 90% probability) from 150 mgs of aspirin in case he has a headache? The answer is no, because this person was not drawn at random from the same population as the original research. He was drawn from the *Japanese* walkers in Delhi, which is different from the walkers in Delhi. The stark case where this would be so is if 10% of Delhi's walking population was Japanese, and it was the case that 150 mgs of aspirin helped a walking person if and only if he or she was not Japanese. In this case the RR would be true and, at the same time, a randomly-chosen Japanese person would not benefit from aspirin.

This in turn leads us to the following troublesome question. Suppose you know of the RR (and this is guaranteed to hold over time). Now you are walking down Janpath in New Delhi with a headache, and wondering if you will benefit from 150 mgs of aspirin. The answer depends on whether you can be thought of as a random draw of a person from the walking population of Delhi. It seems reasonable to me to treat the answer to be no. For one, you could be a Japanese in which case you are drawn from the population of Japanese walkers in Delhi. Hence, you cannot draw any policy lesson for yourself from the research result. This is a rather worrying predicament. It means that whenever I want to use a research finding (based on proper controlled experiments) for my own treatment, strictly speaking, there is little reason for me to have faith in the result, since I am not a random draw from the population.

Am I using too demanding a criterion for what constitutes knowledge? Maybe, but since this new method in development economics is itself based on a very strict criterion of what is statistically correct, therefore those who view this kind of correctness as essential should go along with my skepticism.

Information and Evolution

The skepticism about the acquisition of knowledge expressed in the above section is troublesome. Despite my own inclination towards skepticism, I am aware that one must not have an unbending adherence to it (that would be a contradiction anyway for a skeptic). One possible mistake that both the skeptic and the practitioner of the new development economics have to guard against is that of denying that there may be other modes of acquiring knowledge.

To understand this, consider the number of things that we learn from poorly-controlled experiments or, for that matter, no experiments. A growing child learns soon enough that a frown implies displeasure and a smile implies approval that a slap hurts and a massage soothes (especially neck massage), that when a person cries she is sad and when she laughs she is happy.

Suppose this child's father stops the child each time she makes an inference, by asking whether she was sure that she was making the deduction from a proper random sample and not merely from her experience with those she happens to bump into in her everyday life. And suppose he asks her to discard any knowledge not picked up from properly randomized experiments. Surely this child will turn out to be a very ill-informed adult. The fact of the matter is that the knowledge that we human beings carry in our heads is disproportionately from wrongly conducted experiments and from biased samples. The knowledge that we have from scientifically-conducted studies—things like, 80 mgs of aspirin a day can cut the risk of a heart attack by half and oatmeal reduces cholesterol—are a tiny fraction of what we know.

This is indeed a puzzle: How *do* we know so much given the atrociously-biased methods we use through life to collect information? Of course, we make errors. My son, whose first experience of the world outside of India was Belgium, for a long time after our return used to point to any White person he saw in Delhi and say confidently, "Belgian." It took considerable effort on my part to persuade him of the sampling bias that underlay his deduction.

There are three responses we can have to this puzzle. One is to try to show how, even if each person uses a biased sample, by the act of pooling our individual information, as we human beings do, the biases tend to cancel out and for the large part correct itself. This would be an interesting research agenda in probability and information theory (even though it would still leave open the question of how we can predict about tomorrow from our information of yesterday).

But if this theoretical exercise turns out to be futile (and till such a result is proved it seems reasonable to proceed as if it were not true), then there are two possible positions that we can take. One is to claim that we human beings actually do not know much. Much of our knowledge is chimera—a mere illusion of knowledge. Many religious traditions and also some irreligious philosophers take such a view. There is a long Greek tradition of this. Historically, the most famous is the philosopher, Pyrrho (4th century BC). Pyrrho did not write down any of his philosophy because he was skeptical about its value (though, of course, he could have been equally skeptical about the value of not writing and written a lot, like Bertrand Russell, also a skeptic, did).

It is believed that he went with Alexander's army to India and returned humbled because in India he had met *sadhus* who not only did not write but did not even speak. Legend has it that he heard one of his teachers asking for help, having fallen into a ditch; but he walked away calmly because he could not be sure that the teacher would be better off outside the ditch than in it. The teacher in this case happened to be Anaxarchus, a philosopher who held many similar views to those of Pyrrho. After he was heaved out of the ditch by some others and safe, it is believed that his greatest praise was for Pyrrho whom he had seen walk past with complete sang-froid (Diogenes Laertius, 1925).

Maybe it was to counter these extreme versions that the later Greek philosopher, Carneades (2nd Century BC), stressed that, *behaviorally*, a skeptic need not be any different from a non-skeptic. It may however be recalled that Carneades himself caused some comical problems by arguing one day in favour of justice and another day against it, since he felt committed to neither view. In fact, the Greek physician and philosopher, Sextus Empiricus (2nd century AD), took the view that the main consequence of skepticism was the tranquility of mind achieved from resigning oneself to the futility of the quest for knowledge.

A second position, which is not incompatible with the above one, is to take an evolutionary view of knowledge. This is to admit that we do not know how we know things but, if it is the case that a person's knowledge or (at a more meta level) the facility for acquiring knowledge is inheritable, then the people who have wrong beliefs or knowledge about the way the world works (those, for instance, who think that the frown on the face of the person approaching them menacingly, knife in hand, indicates friendliness) would perish in the long run. So the people we see around know that an apple released in the air will fall downwards and know that the knife being brought down on a person will kill him. The fact of these people being around means that they and their ancestors have survived the weeding process of evolution. The ones who knew the wrong things or did not have the facility for learning correctly from nature are just not around anymore. By this theory, there is no right way to acquire knowledge. Nature is too idiosyncratic for that. But some minds are synchronized with our idiosyncratic nature and some minds are not. The people we see around us, by virtue of the fact that they exist, have minds that are in synchrony with nature.

My own belief about the puzzle of knowledge lies somewhere between the skeptical and the evolutionary claims. The trouble with this is that unlike others, who have strong views on what is the right method, I do not have any. I therefore find it difficult to take a clear position on debates like whether we need more theory or more empirics. I have some faith in our intuition. Two correctly done empirical results may have the property that one resonates with our intuition—we simply feel that if it was true in the past it has a reasonable chance of being true in the future—and the other does not. My inclination would be to go along with the intuition (while admitting that intuitions often go haywire). And the same is true with theoretically-derived results. Some feel right; some do not. I would be tempted to give in to the feeling. Hence, the issue is not between theory and empirics. We need to do both as correctly as we can and then use our intuition to select the ones we want to live by and base our policy recommendations on those and, most importantly, keep our fingers crossed behind our backs, when doing so.

A Remark on Causality

Economists have a propensity to find the lack of evidence of causality in other people's research. We complain about how other people's empirical papers demonstrate correlation but not causality. Such language is fine, as long as we realize that there is no real way for demonstrating causality. Indeed, there is no reason to believe that there *is* anything objective in nature called causality.

It may sound baffling at first sight but it is much more robust to maintain that causality lies in the eyes of the beholder. That is, we human beings have it hardwired in us to *think* in terms of causality. This can be a useful feature of our mind. It allows us to be more sure-footed than we would be if we could not live *as if* causality existed. There is reason to believe that what our mind takes to be causal is reasonably dependable because it has come to be reasonably well synchronized with the way nature actually works, thanks to thousands of years of human evolution. Hence, it is useful for us to feel that a particular relation is causal (and hence dependable in the future) and not merely a matter of correlation. But even on this we can make large mistakes. We will end on this cautionary note by constructing an example of how we can be led astray in our interpretation of probabilities.

Suppose that there was a ritual in the world whereby in each city the mayor tosses a coin 20 times at the start of each millennium. So the last time this was done was on January 1, 2000. Let us suppose in Washington a researcher wanted to see if there was reason to believe that there was a particular bias in coin tosses in Washington and he discovered that in fact all the 20 tosses had yielded heads.

He would be tempted to publish a paper entitled, "Heads Bias in Washington," and may have speculated if having too many senators or too many lobbyists caused this. In case he had no experience of the rest of the world but had experience of coin tosses by others in Washington, he may have thought he had made the discovery of how the city's mayor is head prone. It is indeed very surprising to get 20 heads in a row. It does seem to say something to us.

Now return to the problem and think of the larger picture. Given that this ritual is followed in thousands and thousands of cities, the probability is very high that a sequence of 20 heads will occur somewhere. So the fact that this *has* occurred somewhere is of no interest whatsoever. It reveals nothing beyond what we already knew from our rudimentary knowledge of probabilities.

Let me digress for a moment to deal with a possible technical objection. A critic may say that before publishing the paper the author should have collected more information so as to decide if what happened was just pure chance. He may for instance collect data on another 20 tosses of the coin in Washington. But surely that will not change anything because we can pretend that this has already been done. It could, for instance, be that he had first collected information on the mayor's first 10 tosses and, seeing that all were heads, asked the mayoral office to send him the data on the next 10 tosses. He was then astounded to find that the next 10 were also heads and therefore wrote the paper. Therefore, we can think of larger and larger number of tosses. As long as there are more and more cities where the experiment can be done, we can construct the same, logically-equivalent story.

To return to the example, what we have are two propositions. The Washington researcher's feeling that he is onto something interesting seems justified. The outcome that he has seen has too small a probability if the probability of each coin toss by the mayor of Washington landing a head is half. So he is right in concluding that the probability of a head is much more than half. On the other hand, we also know from our larger global perspective that there is actually no special information in what happened in Washington. A string of successive heads occurring somewhere is very high, even if each coin toss has a probability half of getting a head.

The analogue of this problem is that researchers the world over are studying different phenomena. They publish only what seems unexpected. Since the expected does not get published, we never get the larger global picture (like the data on coin tosses from across the world) and so *think* we have stumbled upon knowledge when, in fact, we have not.

3

Defence Economics: Its Contribution and New Developments

Defence economics is defined to embrace all aspects of the economics of defence, disarmament, conversion and peace. This definition needs to be modified to include the economics of wars, conflict and non-conventional conflicts.

DEFENCE ECONOMICS : CORE ISSUES AND CONCERNS

Defence economics is essentially the application of economic principles and analysis to defence issues, including formulation of defence policy. Contributions to the field of defence studies have historically brought analysis and expertise to bear on strategic concerns, international relations and issues relating to the organisation of the military. Only very recently has an attempt been made to systematically encourage discussion of defence economics. The public and the political leadership in India and most other countries by and large subscribe to a "holy cow" status of matters relating to defence. There is a presumption that the needs of defence must be met, and these needs are generally met without serious political debate. Defence budgets attact limited scrutiny even in advanced countries like the USA.

The accurate measurement of defence expenditures is also notoriously difficult. For example, paramilitary forces in a military role not being accounted for; merging defence pensions in the civilian budget; and intelligence gathering. With all these hurdles, it is reasonable to ask whether it is worthwhile delving into defence economics in India at all.

Size of economy : The sheer size and scale of the defence sector and its significant share in world economy and trade compel attention.

The world spent more than a trillion (1000 billion) US dollars on military expenditures in 2005. Nearly half of this was spent by the USA alone. Globally, arms sales (defence production) were of the order of $ 268 billion in 2004, of which about $ 170 billion was accounted by the USA. In international arms trade in 2004, the top exporting countries were Russia and the USA, and the top two importers were China and India. Arms imports by India in the 2001-05 period are estimated at over $ 9 billion at constant 1990 prices.

For a developing country like India, the opportunity cost (in terms of alternatives foregone) of the marginal defence rupee would tend to be greater than it may be for relatively more developed countries, and the imperative to seek its optimal utilisation accordingly greater.

Core issues : Defence economics has been emerging, mainly in the USA and UK, as a distinct branch of economics since the Second World War. While there are many studies on developing countries, rarely do these contain developing country perspectives.

The five sets of issues are as under:

- The Demand for Defence (expenditure), encompassing the "Guns versus Butter" debate, and arms races
- Defence and Economic Growth, including issues of impact and sustainability
- Military Manpower
- Arms Procurement and Trade
- Defence Industry, including "Make versus Buy" issues, and those related to Research and Development.

The Demand for Defence (expenditure): National security is highly valued by most populations, judging by the sacrifices that many countries seem willing to make when territorial integrity is threatened. Perceptions are important in determining the demand. India is no exception to this phenomenon. We have seen that the biggest spikes in defence expenditure tend to occur after a major conflict e.g., 1962 war. Some determinants of demand that may be relevant for India:

- Confrontations with neighbours due to territorial and sovereignty disputes, instability of a neighbouring country, hostile trans-border infiltration, managing bordering ethnic peoples.
- Multilateral and treaty obligations, cooperative efforts with the United Nations and other coalitions and countries, including peacekeeping operations, humanitarian assistance, and disaster relief.
- Impact of trans-national issues such as terrorism, drug-trafficking, and environmental issues.
- Protection of coastal fisheries, marine resources, and Exclusive Economic Zones (EEZs).
- Protection of market access to trade, investment, energy, food, and other vital resources.
- Maintaining domestic law and order, counter-insurgency.

In order to assess demand, we need to have clarity on objectives. In India, there has traditionally been a reluctance to define the country's vital long-term security interests and/ or threat perceptions in any formal way. These objectives, defined in terms of global, regional and internal security interests, could form a sound basis for projecting demand and planning for optimum levels of defence expenditure.

Secrecy requirements should not get in the way. Other countries have found ways to set out their objectives. For example, the UK's Defence White Paper of 2003. France's Law on Military Planning 2003-08. China's Defence White Papers 1998-2004. Canada's Strategy 2020. Most well organised countries attempt to set out their defence objectives and the means to be employed to achieve these objectives.

Given that the demand has been determined, by whichever manner, there is the issue of meeting the demand. Typically, there would be competing claims for funds, and inevitably resource constraints. Development programmes in social sectors such as education and health have highly valued ends. If a country has 'too much' defence, it is wasting its resources, and if it has 'too little' defence, its security is at risk. India's defence budget is a substantial Rs 89,000 crores. Another estimate puts it at Rs 104,000 crores, representing a 40 per cent real increase since 2002.

Because the numbers are big, the potential allocation trade-offs are also substantial. For example, just one-third of the \$3.5 billion (approx Rs 16,000 crores) proposed to be spent on procuring and building advanced Scorpene submarines from France would be enough to obviate the need for the Government to seek a \$1 billion loan from the World Bank to help finance the Bharat Nirman programme aimed at upgrading rural infrastructure. It has proved difficult in practice even to finalize a five-year defence plan before the end of the plan period. The historical resource allocation strategy has appeared to be incremental, driven and dominated by the felt need by the individual services. It is interesting to note that despite its maritime presence and ambitions, China is managing without an aircraft carrier even today.

Defence and Economic Growth: The defence sector has a major share of the budget in most countries. The perceived adverse effects of higher defence spending on economic growth are due to the following:

- Purchase by the defence sector of domestic goods, or the use of foreign exchange to purchase imported goods.
- The government sector shows no measurable productivity increases. Thus, an enlargement in defence spending shifts resources from the productive sector to the non-productive sector.

- A shift of resources to defence reduces the resources available for the rest of the economy and in particular "crowds out" private investment as well as diverts skilled workers from civilian sectors.

The dominant view among economists has been that defence is a drag on economic growth. A contrary view was brought out strongly for the first time in a study of developing countries on this topic by Benoit in 1973. Of the favourable effects of defence spending, Benoit lists many, of which the following seem relevant for the Indian situation: Security effects—To the extent that the military provides security to the country, it enables an atmosphere conducive to investment and long-term planning decisions.

Training effects—Military manpower receives training even at the rudimentary level and this can be beneficial if the recruits come in substantial numbers from the subsistence economy and if the military programmes introduce people to 'modern' methods and social skills and general inculcation of 'national' values.

Infrastructure effects—The military may create infrastructure, such as roads, airports, docks and communications, which can be used by the civilian sector, especially 'up country'.

Consumable effects—The services provide substantial numbers of people with food, clothing, shelter and medicines. They also engage in 'civic action' programmes and in 'hearts and minds' campaigns. The existing research by and large seems to indicate that certain groups of developing countries derive positive benefits from military spending.

The sustainability of the defence budget is a function of the health of the economy. A glaring example of this in recent times has been the inability of the Soviet Union to sustain high levels of defence spending in superpower competition with the USA, in the face of a faltering economy. Defence expenditure in India has benefited from higher growth rates in the recent past. In real dollar terms, the Indian defence budget has more than doubled in the past decade. The ratio of defence expenditure to GDP is well below 3% today, which is a healthy sign.

On the flip side, internal security is adversely impacted by social and economic backwardness and regional balance issues seems to be needed for the sustainability both of growth-fostering reformist economic policies as well as a stronger defence.

Military Manpower: The human resource dimension of defence economics is a relatively neglected field. US studies dominate the theoretical, empirical, and policy literature on military manpower. Two issues have been pre-eminent. First, studies of conscription versus an all-volunteer force. Second, the concern with downsizing and its implications for military manpower.

In India, the structure of military manpower has changed little since British times. Reliance continues on a large, conventional force with over 1.3 million men in uniform in the armed forces and another nearly 1.7 million paramilitary personnel with about 400,000 of these in organisations directly performing a defence role. In addition, entities like the Border Roads Organization (employing about a lakh) and defence civilians (estimated to be of the order of another four lakhs) perform a support role. There probably is a case for looking at overall numbers in the context of modernization; even the Chinese People's Liberation Army has apparently made conscious manpower reductions in recent times. Putting a price to the manpower input into defence would also be instructive in taking a call on these issues.

Arms Procurement and Trade: Arms imports by India in the 2001-05 period are estimated at over $9 billion at constant 1990 prices. Defence markets are large, government regulated, and generally non-transparent in their functioning. Economic factors are relevant in understanding and dealing with defence markets. For example, the post-Cold War situation and disarmament in NATO and in the former Warsaw Pact countries has made their defence contractors seek export sales to compensate for declining domestic procurement. As a result, disarmament in one part of the world might actually promote arms exports, regional arms races, and possibly instability elsewhere in the world. Similarly, major technical advances result in new products and fuel demand from buyers who need to "catch up."

The Indian Context: Issues relating to arms imports are important for India, which has only a 30% rate of self-reliance in arms procurement, despite a sizable arms industry. By their very nature, arms import deals tend to involve large amounts of money, and are politically highly sensitive. It is possible to work out the costs and benefits of a procurement alternative in quantitative terms, and such exercises should be encouraged, so that better decisions are made. The putting in place a new, more transparent Defence Porcurement Procedure in India in 2006 has drawn attention to the issue of "offsets". As the arms trade takes place in a byuers' market, it follows that arms importing countries are in a dominant position to extract compensatory investment.

The new procedure in India requires direct offsets of 30% of the value of the contract to be made for all defence capital contracts of over Rs 300 crores. This is expected, according to the Defence Minister, to result in gains for the country of over Rs 45,000 crores ($10 billion) in investments over the Eleventh Plan period (2007-12). The limited international research on the subject, however, tends to cast doubt on the net benefits of defence offsets to national economies. As has been pointed out in this context, "there are no free lunches."

Defence Industry: Strategic motivations apart, indigenous arms production efforts have been justified on the economic grounds that (a) It will spur generalized industrialisation by means of spill-over or spin-off effects; and; (b) It will permit foreign-exchange earnings. The reference point for determining the value of any defence-industry relationship is its contribution to the ability of the defence forces to meet their key responsibilities. Joint production or collaborative ventures should be expected to lead to cost savings and greater scales of output. But international collaboration is only one form of work sharing: alternative forms are licensed production and offsets; these also need to be evaluated as alternatives.

Economics of Defence Production: A substantial defence production capability has been developed in India, and inevitably some of the issues that surround defence industries in other parts of the world are relevant for India. Efficiency issues exist. The recent award of two $20 million contracts for rocket launchers to be used in the Pinaka missile system to the Indian engineering companies Tata Power and Larsen & Toubro is noteworthy in this context, since it is the first time that private-sector Indian companies have been appointed as prime contractors on a defence project. We should also be concerned that while two decades back, an estimated 40% of weapons and equipment requirements was met by outright imports, today this figure is around 70%.

In the case of India's Defence Research and Development Organisation (DRDO), the development time taken is in many cases said to be so long that before an item reaches the prototype stage, the specifications and performance parameters aimed at are obsolete by contemporary standards. Such things are known to happen in more advanced countries also.

The Economics of Insurgency and Extremism: Left wing extremism in India happens to have arisen in the most backward regions of the country, lending support to the argument that economic solutions in terms of raising the levels of development and improving economic prospects for the unemployed have to be a major factor in arriving at long-term solutions to the conflict. At the same time, it has been estimated that "10-20% of development funds" in militancy affected areas in India end up in the hands of the insurgents. major investments committed to the resource-rich but less developed states of central India are at risk due to insurgent attacks on economic targets.

Technology: Technological advances occur today at a breathtaking pace. Economists can contribute in helping identify least cost solutions consistent with security imperatives, using the potential offered by technological changes. The trends outlined are part of the global landscape today, and for the Indian defence forces, it is only a question of whether they will allow the changes to pass them by or will seek to stay ahead of the curve by factoring them into defence strategies. We can begin here and now. The rapidly evolving global scenario will have no mercy on laggards. Would it be prudent to deny ourselves the benefit of information, techniques and analysis that are currently available? Don't we want to squeeze the maximum "bang for the buck", so that the best decisions on strengthening of national security can be made, for any given level of resources allocated? These are the questions that we need to reflect upon. In the answer to these questions lies the road ahead.

NEW CHALLENGES OF ARMED FORCES

There are many challenges for defence economists. Let me conclude with two 11 examples. First, the scope for modelling the Armed Forces and the example of joint forces. Second, questions about the future of the defence firm.

Armed Forces comprise military units, their commanders and bases. These form inputs into the military production function which provides various defence capabilities. Challenges arise in determining the efficiency of the various military units. One possibility is to create an internal market with the various military units regarded as firms which can be grouped together to form industries (eg. infantry units forming the infantry industry). Military commanders could be regarded as entrepreneurs subject to budget constraints and acting as profit-seekers. Consider how this model might be applied to the creation of joint military forces. The private sector offers some guidelines for the creation of joint military forces. Mergers are the obvious example. Mergers provide economic benefits in the form of cost savings, but there are economic costs from possible monopoly power. There are three types of mergers:

- *Horizontal mergers* which occur at the same stage of production. An example would be the merger of two or more infantry units.

- *Vertical mergers* which occur at different stages in the production process. For example, an infantry unit might acquire transport units and vehicle repair units as well as recruitment and training organisations.
- *Conglomerate mergers* which create diversified firms involved in a variety of products. An example, would be joint military forces involving air, land and sea units.

Whilst the private sector model appears attractive, it has its limitations when applied to the public sector. The private sector is characterised by a number of incentive mechanisms which are absent from the public sector, namely:

- Competition and rivalry
- The profit motive which offers rewards for success and penalties for poor performance
- The capital market which is a 'policing and monitoring' mechanism providing the threat of take-over and ultimately bankruptcy (with managers losing their jobs).

In the UK, following the 1998 Strategic Defence Review, there was renewed interest in joint military forces. This interest poses three policy questions. First, what do we know; second, what is not known; and third what do we need to know for sensible decisions on jointery? Some of the UK examples of joint forces appear impressive. However, there is little published evidence on the benefits and costs of jointery and the examples are often minor/insignificant elements of the defence budget.

Joint forces raise a more general question about the appropriate balance between joint and single service forces. What is the 'best' (least-cost) organisational arrangement and size of units in the Armed Forces (cf. private enterprise firms)? Here, one rule might be to aim for rivalry rather than jointery: let the Armed Forces compete to offer innovatory solutions to joint activities. This rivalry could be reinforced with 'competing for quality' allowing private firms to search and bid for economical jointery (eg. across each of the Armed Forces and not within each Service). Such rivalry would also be used to promote competition and substitution between each of the

Armed Forces (eg. close air support provided by Army helicopters or air force Harriers), the aim being to abolish the traditional monopoly property rights of each of the Armed Forces.

The Future Defence Firm

During the 1990s, defence firms had to adjust to the end of the Cold War. The result was job losses, plant closures, exits from the industry and major mergers creating larger defence firms. This raises the question of what will the defence firm of 2050 look like?

The general answer is that the firm of 2050 is likely to be as different from today's defence firm as today's defence firms are from those of 1950 and 1915. The characteristics of the future defence firm are likely to be:

- It will be radically different.
- It will focus on more profitable defence activities, such as systems integration.
- There will be new forms of industrial organisation. Firms will buy rather than make and they will be global with international supplier networks and international alliances (the Joint Strike Fighter consortium).
- There will be greater military outsourcing with defence firms involved in support activities for the Armed Forces.
- Electronics and IT companies are likely new entrants to form the next generation of prime contractors.
- Some major suppliers will become 'mini-primes' responsible for whole subsystems (including R&D) and absorbing greater risks.
- Firms will have a 'mix' of defence and civil business. Civil work will provide insurance against defence downturns; it will allow the transferability of human and physical capital; and it will facilitate dual-use of technology, products, management and production expertise (eg. lean manufacturing; Just-In-Time Inventory; partnership sourcing; e-commerce used in the civil sector will be transferred to defence work).

Defence economics is a relatively new branch of economics. Considerable progress has been made since the pioneering works in the 1960s but there remains a rich and challenging agenda for future research. There is scope for more theoretical and empirical work on such topics as wars and conflict, terrorism, peace-making and peace-keeping and the creation of a new world order offering both peace and security.

CHALLENGES TO INDIA'S CURRENT DEFENCE PRODUCTION

India's experience of developing its defence industry and research and development capability over the past decade has been mixed.

Ordnance Factories and PSUs

The country's ordnance factories are capable of providing the Indian military with a significant proportion of their ammunition and low level material needs. In the period 1992/93-1997/98, for example, India only imported 11 per cent of its total ammunition needs. India is also planning to open a 40th Ordnance factory in the near future. Furthermore, speaking in the Indian Parliament, the *Lok Sabha*, on 4 July 2000, George Fernandes, the Indian Defence Minister, stated that the country's ordnance factories recorded a surplus of Rs 780 crores (a crore is ten million rupees) during the period 1999-2000. In addition to this, Fennandes stated that due to last year's Kargil conflict, output increased from 33 per cent to 900 per cent for ammunition items; 20 per cent to 108 per cent for clothing items; and 76 to 233 per cent for cables. More generally, an overall increase in output value of 34.6 per cent in 1999-2000, as compared to the value of issue in 1998/99. The picture for the PSUs is similar. Output in the sector has been rising rapidly since the 1980s, and all the companies have started to move into profitability. According to the latest MOD, moreover, the value of production in 1998-1999 (Rs 7205.55 crore) registered growth of 15.57 per cent over that in 1997-1998 (Rs 6234.75 crore). In addition to this all the defence PSUs reportedly earned a profit in 1998-1999.

Set against that is the fact that these two elements of India's defence industrial base continue to receive large amounts of money from the government in the form of government loans. Between them they also employ in the region of 300000 people. The picture is further complicated by the fact that almost half the production of the PSUs goes to the civil sector; a small proportion of the Ordnance factory production also goes this way. (Put another way if is arguable that, certainly in the case of the PSUs, it is the production of equipment for civil use rather than for military use that is actually making money). Against this backdrop, questions have been raised about their efficiency and ability to meet production targets, as underscored by the fact that it has taken Garden Reach Shipbuilders 12 years to build the Indian Naval Ship (INS) Brhamaputra; three times longer than 't would take Russia's cash strapped shipbuilders to do.

Traditionally, the price of purchasing systems and platforms from the PSUs has also worked out more expensive than purchasing them from abroad. For example, back in 1956 it was estimated that the cost of independently producing under license the HS-78 plane would be in the region of US$320000; come the end of the 1970s it stood at $1.5 million per unit.

Indigenous R&D

The success of India's indigenous R&D efforts is even more questionable: despite considerable investment through the 1990s nearly all major programmes implemented in the 1980s are experiencing time and cost over-runs.

The IGMDP: Covering the Prithvi and Agni short and medium/long range ballistic missiles, the Nag anti tank missile, and the Akash and Trishul surface to air missile, this programme has scored a number of notable and high profile successes. For example, the Prithvi has been tested regularly since 1988 and three versions of the missile (150km, 250km, and 350km ranges) are now believed to be in (or close to) production. The Agni was first tested in 1994 and in a 1998 missile test the missile flew close to 2500km. According to some reports, moreover, the missile is now operational. The Aksah, Nag and Trishul, meanwhile, are expected to enter service soon. However, none of these missiles are entirely indigenous. Some reports suggest, for instance, that five to ten per cent of the technologies used in the Prithvi are imported from abroad

The Arjun: India's experience of designing an indigenous tank has been less successful. Take the example of the Arjun tank. Originally, expected to be in operation service by 1985 the tank has suffered from continued problems, such as problems with the engine overheating. Limited production of the tank has now started; however the Indian Army has cut back on the number of tanks that it is ordering.

The LCA The story of the LCA is almost identical to that of the Arjun tank. The programme has experienced delays since its inception in 1983 for a variety of reasons. And the first flight-test, originally scheduled for 1996, is now not expected to take place until some time in 2002. The cost of the programme, in the meantime, has increased from Rs560 crores. This increased to Rs2188 crores in 1993, when approval was given to enter the Full Scale Engineering Development Phase-1.

Other Programmes: The picture is much the same for a number of other less high profile programmes, such as the Pinaka, MBRL. This was initiated in 1986 with a budget of Rs25.6 crores. This was subsequently increased to 49 crores. The system underwent troop trials in October 1999, moreover, but is still waiting for acceptance by the Army before entering full production. A similar story emerges for products such as the Indian Small Arms System (ISAS). The only product deemed to have been a complete success is arguably the ALH. The failure of many of India's R&D programmes and its reliance on the outside world for key technologies is confirmed by a number of by external assessments, such as the United States government Military Critical Technologies List (MCTL). For example, India's capability to manufacture, gas turbine engines, and human crew systems (aeronautic systems technology) is not even considered worthy of a mention in the MCTL. Likewise, its ability to manufacture the systems necessary to ensure that a combat vehicle is superior to the technology that it is confronting. India scores a little better in the area of Marine Systems Technology, where it is rated to have limited Sub-surface and Deep Submergence Vehicle Capability. One area where India is deemed to have been successful is in the area of Means of Delivery Technology for nuclear and other non-conventional weapons, where it is rated as having a sufficient Theatre Ballistic Missile Capability (TBMC), some ICBM capability; and a sufficient Cruise Missile capability. By way of a comparison, outside the core-areas of competency that it has developed, India's defence production and R&D capabilities do not compare that favourably with other developing countries such as China, which has managed to develop its defence industry across a broader spectrum.

Consequences and Responses

India's inability to meet its top end defence needs have been compounded by the approaching obsolescence of a number of platform and systems; a problem that has been made even worse by the fact that Indian has not made any major defence purchases for the past ten years. Last year's crisis in Kargil has also impressed the need to introduce new equipment on the armed forces-according to the reports, for example, the Indian military assessed Pakistan's Ukranian T-80s as being 'almost a generation ahead of what we had'. In response, as far as major systems and high-technology products are concerned, the government has reversed the pattern of the 1990s and shifted the balance of procurement funding away from its home grown programmes and back towards external procurement. This re-evaluation started in the late 1990s and has progressed since there. Thus in 1996-97 and 1997-98 the DRDO's share of the defence budget decreased in real terms for the first time in that decade. At the same time, India announced its decision to purchase 40 SU-30MK fighter/bombers from Russia in India's largest ever defence deal. Likewise, even though India announced that it would increase its defence budget by 28 per cent to $13.94 billion (2.5 per cent of GDP) in 2000-2001 this March, funding for domestic R&D was only raised by 5.2 per cent; the percentage of the defence budget allocated to defence R&D has also slipped to 4.4 per cent of the total budget. At the same time, while this year's defence budget has seen the amount of money for R&D fall in relative terms, the funds for the purchase of defence equipment from abroad have been steadily increased since 1998.

Reviving the Russian Link

Despite the challenge to their defence relationship that occurred following the end of the Cold War and the economic crisis in India, Russia and India still managed to maintain close defence ties throughout the latter part of the 1990s. For example, the two countries signed a long-term defence cooperation programme in 1994; a number of agreements for the upgradation of Indian defence equipment were initialled; India also agreed to buy 40 SU-30MKs in 1997 ; and according to the Russian Vice Premier Liya Klebarov, defence sales to India account for between 20 and 25 per cent of the annual total export of Russian military goods, making it India's largest arms supplier.

It comes as little surprise to find, therefore, that much of the money allocated for procurement will be spent in Russia. Although many of the deals have been under negotiation for some time, the October visit of the Russian president, Vladimir Putin, appears to have broken the logjam.

Thus, although the details still have to be finalised, India and Russia officially agreed to extend their defence cooperation programme until 2010. Furthermore, India announced its intention to buy Russian arms worth more than $2 billion. Intended purchases include, additional Su-30 long range fighter bombers, a number of which will be made under license in India, more than 300 T-90 Main Battle Tanks (MBTS), one third of which will also be made in India, the ageing Soviet-era aircraft carrier, the Admiral Gorshkov, which will be provided for free but would cost $500 million to refurbish; an, as yet, unspecified number of MiG-29s for the ship; and a number of Smersh MRBLs.

European and Other Suppliers

India has also looked to solidify its links with European suppliers. For example, although the details of the deal have yet to be finalised the British based company BAE SYTEMS is also believed to have secured the deal to provide India with the Hawk advanced jet trainer aircraft. (India has been negotiating this purchase for over a decade). France has also been particularly successful, recently concluding an agreement to sell India additional Mirage 2000 fighters.

Outside Europe, India has established a close defence procurement relationship with Israel, which is thought to have provided it, among other things, with equipment suitable for border surveillance. Furthermore, reliable sources have suggested that the Phalcon early warning plane (AEW) that Israel was building for China but recently agreed not to sell to Beijing after pressure from the United States will be delivered to India. South African arms exports have also managed to carve out a small niche for themselves in the country. A number of Eastern European nations are also looking to provide India with new equipment and to help it upgrade its existing inventory. Quite simply, these purchases will fill those gaps that have appeared in India's armed forces in recent years.

INDIA'S CURRENT DEFENCE PRODUCTION CAPABILITY

The foundations for India's defence industry are widely believed to have been laid in 1801 with the establishment of the Gun Carriage Agency in Calcutta by the East India Company. Although historically true, the birth of India's current defence industrial really came during the Second World War, when the decision was taken to establish a limited defence production capability in the country, to support the British war effort in Asia and the Middle East. Before then, the British had decided against establishing a significant defence equipment manufacturing capability in India, for fear of 'giving the natives access to modern military industry'.

Ordnance Factories and Public Sector Undertakings

At the end of the WW2 India's defence industrial capacity amounted to 16 ordnance factories, a clothing establishment, and an aircraft production plant; and the new government subsequently inherited this capability. No new factories were built in the first years after independence. From 1958 onwards, however, the ordnance factories were steadily expanded. The war against China in 1962 (described by some as India's 'Pearl Harbour') prompted a further expansion in India's ordnance capability. By 1970, the number of ordnance factories had risen to 31 and by the 1980s the number had reached 35. Today the country has 39 ordnance factories. The Indian Ordnance Factories Organisation (OFO) is currently the largest departmentally run industrial undertaking in the country. In addition to its ordinance factors, India has eight defence focused public sector undertakings (PSUs). These are Bharat Electronics; Bharat Earth Movers; Mazagon Dockyards; Garden Reach Shipbuilders and Engineers; Goa Shipyard; Bharat Dynamics; Mishra Dhatu Nigam (Midhani); and Hindustan Aeronautics. The PSUs produce a range of defence equipment including helicopters, state of the art electronics, heavy trucks and tank transportation trailers, submarines, missile boats destroyers, frigates, corvettes, fast attack craft, guided missiles, and aeronautics. They also provide overhaul and maintenance facilities.

DEFENCE RESEARCH AND DEVELOPMENT

India also has a defence research and development capability: the Defence Research and Development Organisation (DRDO). The DRDO has its roots in the Technical Development Establishments (TDES) formed during the Second World War. These were amalgamated in 1959 to form the Defence Science Organisation (DSO). This, in turn, was amalgamated with the Defence Science Services in 1958, to form the DRDO. The organisation employs in the region of 25000 people (about 6000 of which are scientists and engineers and 10000 technicians). The DRDO draws on the work of 51 laboratories/establishments across the country, and (in theory at least) has close links with the eight PSUs. It also co-operates with 70 academic research institutions, 50 national science and technology centres, and some companies in the private sector.

The organisation really came into its own in the 1980s, under the leadership of Dr A.J.P Abdul Kalam, when a number of major programmes were launched. These were the: Integrated Guided Missile Development Project (1983); the Light Combat Aircraft (1983); the Advanced Light Helicopter; the Arjun Tank (first conceived in 1974); and a number of smaller projects, such as the Pinaka, a multiple barrel rocket launcher (MBRL).

Major Government Actors

India's defence planning system is centred on the Ministry of Defence (MOD), which uniquely, is manned only by civilians. In simple organisation terms, the Ministry of Defence (MOD) is the major coordinating body for defence production and R&D. It consists of three main departments: the Department of Defence; the Department of Defence Production and Supplies; and the Department of Defence R&D. In addition to this, there is the MOD Finance Division, which exists at the same level. The Department of Defence (DOD) is headed by the Secretary of State for Defence. He co-ordinates the activities of the other MOD Departments and the three armed services. The Department of Defence Production was established in 1962 after the war with China in order to create an indigenous defence production base, while the Department for Defence supplies was established in 1965, with a view to forging links between the civil industries and defence production units. The two departments were eventually merged into one 1984. The Department of Defence Research and Development, meanwhile, is headed by a secretary who is also Scientific Adviser to the Defence Minister. Its main responsibilities are R&D planning and advising the Defence Minister on scientific aspects of military equipment. Several committees are also involved in the defence planning process: The Defence Minister's Committee (now replaced by the Defence Minster's weekly morning meeting); the MOD production and supply committee, which deals with matters relating to import substitution, domestic arms production, and the operation of the ordnance factories; and the Defence R&D Council, which formulates and reviews R&D defence programmes, and brings together the Defence Minister and the Directors General of the Council for Scientific and Industrial Research. The Chiefs of Staff Committee, which comprises of the three Chiefs of the Armed Forces, provides a channel for providing military advice to the Prime Minister. A defence-planning cell, which was established in 1965 with a view to improving liaison between the National Planning Commission and other relevant Ministries to ensure that overall defence planning is integrated with overall economic planning, is rumoured not to have functioned as intended.

DEFENCE PRODUCTION IN PRIVATE SECTOR

The Government of India has been reiterating its commitment to achieve the much-publicised target of procuring 70 per cent of its defence requirements from indigenous sources by 2010. Despite its best efforts over the last two decades, India is nowhere near that figure as yet. The Government is well aware of the emergence of private sector as a vibrant and dynamic force, especially in information technology, service sector and manufacturing fields. It has come to realise that self reliance would remain a pipe dream if it continued to bank on public sector alone. One of the objectives mentioned in the new defence procurement procedure is to achieve self-reliance in defence equipment. But the whole procedure is silent about the role of the private sector and no worthwhile initiatives have been proposed to integrate its potential in India's quest for self reliance.

In addition to economic factors, defence industry is generally considered to be an instrument of national sovereignty and pride. Defence industry comprises of all industrial undertakings engaged in the production of hardware and services for use by the defence forces. The origin of the Indian defence industry can be traced to the establishment of Gun and Shell Factory at Cossipore in 1801. At the time of the Independence, India had 16 Ordnance Factories, established by the British to produce low tech items. Bharat Electronics Ltd was the first Defence Public Sector Undertaking (DPSU) established in 1954 to manufacture electronic equipment for the forces. Today, India has 39 Ordnance Factories and eight DPSU.

The Industrial Policy Resolution of 1956 divided industry into three parts:-

- Schedule A: Basic industries which are the preserve of the state, including defence and heavy engineering.
- Schedule B: Industries in which private industry was allowed to operate.
- Schedule C: All other industries.

Manufacture of components, assemblies and sub-assemblies was thrown open to the private sector in 1991. With a view to promote defence-industry partnership, the Ministry of Defence (MoD) constituted six Joint Task Forces in collaboration with Confederation of Indian Industry in 1998. Consequent to their recommendations, the Government opened defence production to the private sector in January 2002. It allowed 100 percent private equity with 26 percent Foreign Direct Investment (FDI). It was a major policy change. Subsequently, the Department of Industrial Policy and Promotion issued detailed guidelines for the issuance of licence for the production of arms and ammunition.

The Kelkar Committee, constituted in 2004, made many radical recommendations. The Government has accepted a majority of them but their implementation has lacked earnestness and focus. The Department of Industrial Policy & Promotion (DIPP), in consultation with Ministry of Defence, has so far issued 37 letters of intent for the manufacture of various types of defence hardware which include armoured and combat vehicles, radars, electronic warfare equipment, warships, submarines, avionics, military aircraft, safety and ballistic products, armaments and ammunition.

Despite the above measures, there has been no discernible change in the ground situation. Only a handful of India's top companies are involved in small value defence contracts. The private sector has to remain content with the supply of some low-tech items to the public sector. Its supplies to DPSU and Ordnance Factories grossed over Rs. 1200 crores and Rs. 1900 crores respectively last year. Whereas these figures signify the contribution made by the private sector, they also highlight the fact that the private sector continues to be merely an outsourcing base for the public sector.

Privatization Sector

The private sector can replace inefficient, often subsidized, money-losing state enterprises with modern industrial plants that will serve the needs of the consumer as well as relieve financial pressures on the government. The successful experiences of Britain and France in the recent past are good examples of how privatization has led to the resurgence of those economies and their staying competitive in the global marketplace. Liberalization measures introduced by the Indian government in the 1991-94 period were also in the right direction, but subsequent economic reforms for the most part have only been marginal, lacking any bold initiatives. In order to accomplish successful privatization, issues such as the appropriate financial strategy in the sale/transfer to the private sector, property rights and law, tax structure specific to private ownership, and politics related to various interest groups need to be carefully addressed. However, until such time the government is prepared to recognize that it has no role to play as an inefficient and non-competitive employer for "social reasons," other obstacles cannot be overcome.

Privatization must be complete (no partial ownership by government), and should occur in practically all sectors of the economy, including transportation, financial, and even defense industries, and should be done in a manner that creates competition. The burden of proof must be reversed, that is, the government should be the one who has to give compelling reasons, if any, for its ownership of a particular industry or service.

Monopolistic practices are widespread in India, and they have led to inefficiencies, poor quality, and higher cost to consumer. Sheltered from internal and external competition, monopolies feel less compelled to improve their product's quality or offer superior services, and the forging of cost reductions in the production process is given only secondary importance. Rapid technological change is closely linked to competition. Competitive pressures compel firms to pay close attention to the value offered by their products and to production methods. It is apparent that the problem is best overcome by operating as far as possible on an international rather than a national scale in a competitive environment.

Adherence to the principle of economic self-reliance that is rooted in a profound mistrust of global economic forces is dangerously misguided. Globalization is essential for India's economic success in the next century, and this must happen all across the board — in manufacturing, service industries, and finance. This and this alone will assure continuous inflow of technology, efficient production processes, economies of scale, responsiveness to consumer needs, and fair pricing practices. In a competitive world, companies will learn to distil the essence of the various product, process and organizational innovations that are practiced in industrialized countries, and develop a unique synthesis of the most relevant factors applicable to the local situation for long term growth.

Small businesses are the bloodstream of any economy. The economic system must permit new ventures to compete and thrive amongst established firms. Small businesses that are constrained by their capital limitations must be given sufficient access to financing channels through such measures as government guarantees to support prudent private lending. When an industry consists of several large firms, each with its network of relatively smaller suppliers and subcontractors, and numerous other small to medium firms, all competing with each other to offer consumers superior products and services at the least cost, we assure ourselves a vibrant economy that is generally free of many of the constraints to its efficient functioning, such as price fixing, bribes, and fraudulent business practices. Ownership of land is one of the biggest aspirations and incentives for most people. The economic success of Australia in a few years following the arrival of convicts from England over one hundred years ago can be attributed to the fact that they were able to own property and make it productive. State governments in India still own large areas of land, and if ordinary citizens, especially the poor, can be offered ways to "purchase" them and make them productive, we will witness a major economic miracle in the country in a short time.

There is a high degree of cynicism over the transparency and accountability of the Indian government at practically all levels. Corruption in government, perceived by the people, lowers respect for constituted authority. With erosion of belief in the even-handedness of public officials comes the need to cultivate special contacts, to develop enough "pull" to offset the claims of others. The amount of time and energy devoted to making these contacts is immense. The opportunities for bureaucrat bribing are directly related to the scope of the government's intervention in transactions between private parties. Since such government policies as price controls, licensing restrictions, permits, subsidies, duties and other interventions in the way of socially beneficial exchange place burdens on transactions, they present clear opportunities for corruption by the granting authorities, and for businessmen to seek special favours.

Corruption usually results in closing competitive doors. When corruption is extended to judges and politicians, laws and judicial remedies are broken, threatening the very fabric of the society. If corruptive practices are to be reduced, their opportunities must be reduced through competition, less intervention by government, prompt judicial remedies, and effective enforcement of laws.

Restricting government activity to the enforcement of laws protecting the person and property of individuals, instead of trying to direct human activity, will not only get rid of many of the obstacles to economic growth but will also simultaneously eliminate the ability of political elite to manipulate markets for their own personal benefits. Provided there can be further relaxation of the bureaucratic and legal obstacles that clog India's commercial system, a class of entrepreneurs, designers, software engineers, consultants, lawyers and middlemen will emerge to play in the global marketplace and reap the benefits from the borderless world.

In addition to getting rid of unwanted regulations, there is a need to place checks on government agencies' ability to institute new regulations. A broad set of regulatory reforms must encompass paperwork reduction, elimination of unwanted regulations, and cost-risk justification before implementing new regulations. If a regulation is likely to result in a major increase in consumer costs or a significant adverse impact on competition, it should not be implemented. The uncertainty resulting from the discretionary authority of government officials and the arrogance often associated with it, as opposed to the clarity provided by purpose-independent laws, necessitates the diversion of effort from the economic function of production to the political function of influencing the decision-making process.

Similarly, the legal uncertainty created by purpose-directed legislation — laws to achieve certain social or economic goals — constitutes a serious impediment to economic growth. For example, when the status of property is uncertain, when individuals are never sure whether their property will be seized or their use will be restricted by the state for "social equality," they are reluctant to increase the value of their possessions through investment. Legal uncertainty regarding property rights (such as the ability to vacate a tenant at the end of a rental term) seriously impedes the emergence of the extended order, since it limits the scope of exchange to those one can trust from personal knowledge alone.

Efficient economic activity presupposes clear laws, their effective enforcement, and smooth and swift resolution of disputes. Government must create an environment of fair and prompt legal remedies within which individuals and enterprises can seek resolution of conflicts. When legal remedies cannot be sought to redress injustice or to attain rights, there is no chance for an orderly universe. Just laws and their fair and equal enforcement are a necessary condition for the smooth and efficient functioning of any economy.

Equally important is the ability to attain justice within a reasonable time; justice delayed is justice denied. The Indian legal system is clogged with delays caused by a host of factors such that commercial transactions cannot rely on their legal enforcement through contracts and agreements. The failure of the justice system to adequately meet the commercial needs of the society is a serious impediment to economic growth.

Infrastructure represents, if not the engine, then the wheels, of economic activity. Reliable energy and water supplies, transport and communications are essential to the development of an efficient industrial base. Agriculture employs over 70% of the nation's population, but is still at the mercy of good monsoons. Resources allocated to infrastructure have not been properly used in the past. For example, facilities are not maintained properly; unreliable and outdated systems burden users with extra costs and time; infrastructure has often been built in the wrong places or using the wrong techniques. Furthermore, infrastructure services have often been run with terrible inefficiency.

The root of the problem is the pervasive involvement of the government in the planning, execution and operation of public projects. Infrastructure throws up all the traditional excuses for state action and often ends up as "natural monopolies".

Lack of active private involvement, reduced competition and minimal consumer participation have all been the fundamental reasons for many of the failures in infrastructure development. Innovations in delivering infrastructure services, along with new technologies, point to solutions that can improve performance. This can be accomplished only through applying commercial principles of operation, increased competition, user involvement, and private industry participation. Removing barriers to cross-border flows of trade, technology and investment is probably the single best stimulant to developing good infrastructure.

Government has an important role to play in channeling adequate resources towards health and education. A majority of Indians still live below the real poverty level, with little or no access to proper health care. Preventive and primary health care, including adequate nutrition, is an essential service for all regardless of their income levels. While the nation attempts to generate employment mostly through the private sector, it must also address the basic needs of the disadvantaged that cannot still find a job. The concept of a "safety net" is still a social necessity, but it should not become a permanent feature in anyone's life, depriving the incentive to work and earn.

The literacy rate in India is presently below 50%. This explains only part of the problem; the labour force does not have the skill base to be productive workers in today's industries. Moreover, rural India is entirely dependent on agriculture, but their real incomes have not kept pace with those in the cities. As a result, more and more unskilled people are moving to cities from villages in search of job opportunities. The available labour force must be sufficiently educated and trained in those fields that are demanded by the private sector so that progress and employment are not constrained for want of knowledge and skills. It is not enough to have schools of higher learning, but basic quality education must be made accessible to all.

India possesses a potentially very rich resource: human capital. But the existence of masses of people becomes more useful economically when the society provides quality education to practically everyone, encourages experimentation and entrepreneurship, and consequently produces skilled workers, engineers, scientists, technologists and designers. In addition to colleges of higher learning, the educational system must provide more than the most rudimentary instruction offered in most villages; funds would be better employed in rigorous primary and secondary education, encouraging craft and technical subjects, and providing job-training programs more in line with the country's basic needs. An educational system that is marred by sub-standard quality, diffused focus, and uneven levels of access cannot generate the necessary human resources to equip a world class industrial base.

There is mounting evidence of the damage caused from population growth and modernization in India. Shortage of clean water, insufficient sewage facilities, toxic waste, and air pollution are few of the environmental problems facing India. There exists industrial regions whose air is so polluted that the visibility is poor even in cloudless weather; lakes and rivers are contaminated to the extent that the availability of safe drinking water supply is now threatened; millions of tons of topsoil are lost each year to erosion due to serious loss of forest cover; chemicals, trace and heavy metals and other pollutants have now entered the nation's food supply chain — all these are happening at an alarming rate and in dangerous proportions. Unless and until we are prepared to assign equal priority to the preservation of our environment, and remedy the damage already caused, all too soon we will not have livable cities, and for that matter, nothing worthwhile to leave for future generations.

CONTINUED NON-PARTICIPATION OF THE PRIVATE SECTOR

A number of defence-industry seminars, conferences and exhibitions have been held in the recent years. Given decades of insulation and prejudices, this was no small achievement. But old mindsets, complexity of procurement procedures and clout wielded by the public sector have been acting as major deterrents to any meaningful participation of the private sector. New aspirants, in particular, find the whole regime to be highly forbidding.

Policy and Procedural Issues

Decisions are taken by the Defence Acquisition Council to categorise a proposal as 'Buy' or 'Buy and Make' or 'Make' based on the advice given by Defence Research and Development Organisation and the public sector. No inputs are sought from the private sector. Its competence and potential are given no consideration. In all deals where transfer of technology is negotiated, the nominated recipient is always a DPSU, even if a private sector company is better placed in terms of infrastructure and know-how to absorb the technology. A DPSU may have to establish complete facilities ab initio, whereas a private sector company may need only incremental technology.

Requirements of the armed forces are not made known to the private sector sufficiently in advance, with the result that it does not get adequate time, either to scout for foreign tie-ups or to establish the necessary facilities. The time given for the submission of technical and commercial proposals is grossly inadequate for a new entrant in the field. Parameters for the equipment to be procured are formulated with foreign equipment in mind, after reading manufacturers' brochures. Private sector is not consulted in this process, whereas minor acceptable changes in parameters may make the Indian equipment eligible for consideration. As Requests for Proposals (RFP) are issued to foreign original equipment manufacturers as well, they prefer direct bidding. They decline joint ventures with Indian companies as it helps them to guard their technology and perpetuate their monopoly with consequent financial gains. All trials are carried out on 'No Cost No Commitment' basis. Whereas foreign vendors can incur the expenditure involved, many upcoming indigenous companies do not possess the necessary financial strength. This acts as a major disincentive.

Functional Issues

Due to the very nature of its usage, defence equipment has to meet highly exacting standards. There can be no failure in the face of the enemy. Regrettably, many Indian vendors have not fully grasped the import of this requirement and find the quality control regime to be extremely irksome. Every producer seeks economies of scale and assured continuous orders. Unfortunately, Indian procurement regime precludes both. RFPs are issued for one-time piecemeal quantities without indicating the envisaged total requirement over a period of time.

Additionally, no long term commitment is made regarding regular flow of orders. This deters Indian companies from committing resources for establishing production facilities as the venture can prove both expensive and risky.

Lack of Mutual Confidence

The Indian public sector has got used to a position of pre-eminence. Its hold over defence orders is total. It thrives because of its monopolistic clout and not because of any displayed excellence. It is fully aware of its weaknesses and knows that it cannot survive an open competition with the private sector. This sense of insecurity makes it wary of any move to facilitate the entry of the private sector and it tries all stratagems to block it. On the other hand, many functionaries feel that the private sector is out to make a quick buck and lacks required perseverance. They tend to view the private sector as traders rather than committed manufacturers who can endure the travails of long drawn procurement procedure. According to them, anyone desirous of entering defence industry has to be fully aware of the fact that defence orders take inordinately long to materialise and vacillation invariably proves unproductive.

The Communication Gap

There is a total absence of an effective institutionalised interface between the MoD, the services and the private sector for regular interaction at the policy making level. There are a number of 'groups' or 'partnership forums' in place, but their utility is limited to exchange of views only.

Procurement Agencies are Unaware of Industry's Potential : The procurement agencies are extremely keen to encourage indigenous production and limit imports to the minimum inescapable requirements. They, however, are unaware of the capabilities and potential of different private sector companies, as the competence of Indian companies has not been authentically catalogued as yet. They do not know whom to invite for submission of proposals. It is much easier to acquire details of numerous foreign producers.

There is no data bank of Indian industries available with the MoD. Requests for Proposals (RFPs) are issued only to a few highly visible companies, while many others lose by default. Although, the Acquisition Wing has been tasked to create the necessary data bank, the process has hardly taken off as yet.

Industry Lacks Knowledge of Defence Requirements and Procedures : On the other hand, many private sector companies have the capability to manufacture the whole range of defence requirements but do not know whom to approach to ascertain details.

They are ignorant of the procurement agencies, their policies and procedures. This ignorance makes them wary of dealing with the defence.

To compound the problem, there are over 150 different defence procurement agencies with different procedures. There is no system of centralised notification of requirements and vendor registration. Due to this lacuna, a new entrant finds the whole environment highly dissuasive.

The Way Forward

The present process of interaction between the Government, public sector and private enterprises should be continued, albeit with renewed vigour and purpose. All joint committees should be represented at the level of decision makers, so that follow up action can be taken in a time bound manner.

Structural Reforms

A representative of the designated industry association should be a permanent invitee to the Defence Acquisition Council, depending on the security sensitivity of agenda points. His inputs as regards the technical prowess of the private sector will prove invaluable while deciding whether to import technology or not. Similarly, selected agenda points of Defence Procurement Board, Defence Production Board and Defence Development Board should be circulated to the industry association for advice. These steps will go a long way in integrating the private sector.

DEFENCE PRODUCTION AND SUPPLY

The Defence Production Department created in 1962 and the Department of Defence Supply set up in 1965 were merged in 1984 to constitute the Department of Defence Production and Supplies. Presently, 39 Ordnance factories and eight Defence Public Sector Undertakings (DPSUs) come under this department. The Directorate of Quality Assurance, Air Technical Development and Production (Air), Standardisation, and Exhibition Organisation also form part of this Department. The Ordnance Factories produce more than 1,500 items of arms, ammunition, equipment and components. Most of these products constitute relatively low to medium technology items. Twenty per cent of the output goes to non-defence customers. Due to the very high cost of production, delivery delays and suspect quality, it has not been possible to meet export targets and, sometimes, even orders given by the Services. Ordnance factories as well as DPSUs need to shed the manufacture of low technology items to the private sector and focus on hi-tech products. They should also be in a position to take up substantial product improvement themselves and not be dependent on DRDO.

Defence Planning Tools

In recent years, defence economics and management techniques have made an important contribution to defence planning. A number of techniques such as Operational Research and Systems Analysis (ORSA), Planning Programming and Budgeting System have been developed to make the planning process more systematic and to maximise the benefits obtained from the given amount of resources. Systems Analysis can assist in developing rational procedures for procurement of new weapons systems. Systems performance at design stage can be evaluated through computer simulation. Planners all over the world are using computerised war-gaming techniques and structure analysis. Prospects exist for a more enlightened approach that can bring together military officers, historians, technologists and quantitative analysts. In many countries, there is a growing interest in analytical realism, operational relevance and integrated defence planning. In India the Services are far behind in introducing these aids in our defence planning system. The planning directorates in Service Headquarters do not even have data banks which can provide relevant information on a specified subject. Most of the planners have high combat and command qualifications but little clue of the modern techniques. There is an urgent need to introduce modern planning aids into our planning system. Defence planners should also learn the basic principles and techniques of economic analysis and not leave it to their 'Finance' colleagues.

Management of Defence Budget

A major lacuna in defence planning and implementation has been lack of financial commitment for the Plan period. Financially, the defence plans are treated more as annual plans rather than composite five years plan. There is a rush to spend the annual capital budget by the end of the financial year since the amount not spent has to be surrendered. In FY 2004-05, the previous government had proposed to institute a non-lapsable Defence Modernisation Fund of Rs 25,000 crore. This was a long awaited reform in the defence-finance mechanism as budgeted capital expenditure worth thousands of crores was surrendered year after year. However, the new government, being of the view that there are no provisions in the budgetary rules and regulations to carry forward unspent funds for three years, has done away with this reform. It needs to be pointed out that a similar procedure was being followed in the 1930s and 1940s. The provisions invoked at that time need to be studied carefully and could be used as a precedent. Action should be taken expeditiously to revive the Defence Modernization Fund.

Otherwise, funds earmarked for capital expenditure on an annual basis will continue to lapse, leading to lack of systematic defence preparedness. In the Revenue Budget, there is a need to include incentives to save and reduce annual maintenance expenditure without adversely affecting operational efficiency. It is also necessary to exploit the increasing domestic industrial capability to support the existing infrastructure and thus reduce maintenance costs and enhance the quality of maintenance.

Human Resources Management

The development of human resources must keep pace with the modernisation of the armed forces so that new, state-of-the-art equipment can be optimally exploited by well trained and motivated soldiers, sailors and airmen. The age profile of military personnel, particularly in the Army, and the age of commanders at battalion and brigade levels needs to be looked into. Currently, a soldier has to serve for 15 to 17 years to earn his pension. When he retires, besides the lifelong pension that has to be paid, a trained individual is lost to the nation. Similarly, while there is a shortage of approximately 14,000 officers, most officers retire in rank of Lieutenant Colonel or Colonel at the age of 52-54 years when they still have years of productive life ahead though they are no longer fit for active combat.

Innovative measures need to be adopted to reduce the effects of the current national loss on this account. The best method would be to institute a procedure of 'lateral induction" under which both officers and personnel below officer rank can be transferred to central police and paramilitary forces (CPMFs). The colour (active) service of jawans should be reduced to 7-10 years with no pension liability after which the volunteers are transferred to the BSF, CRPF, ITBP, CISF and other such forces. Similarly, the Shipping Corporation of India, National Port Trust and other such maritime organisations can fruitfully employ Naval personnel. Ex-servicemen will be expected to serve in these organisations till superannuation, after which they would be entitled to pension. This will improve the age profile of the Services, provide trained manpower to the CPMFs, ensure productive long-term employment for a large number of trained men till superannuation, and also reduce the pension bill of the Central Government. The Army should increase the recruitment of Short Service Officers to make up its shortfall. Induction of these officers to the CPMFs after five years of service will improve junior leadership and effectiveness of these forces in internal security and counter insurgency operations.

4

Defence Management in Economy Policy and Industry Development

Defence Management (DM) is a great concept to include different aspects from legal and conceptual ones through institution building and resource management to operations, international cooperation and civil control of defence. Defence management is closely related to good governance, especially when it comes to transparency, accountability, effectiveness and efficiency.

This document makes an effort to present defence management and civil society models as a first step in developing interaction model between them two in order to identify challenges and opportunities for good governance in the area from the prospective of cooperation between defence and civil society institutions. Idea is to stress the crucial role of this cooperation and the need to put at least as much effort in civil society institutions building as we put in defence institution building and even more in establishing of mature cooperation model on local, national, regional, Euroatlantic and global level. Main contributions in the chapter are focussed on development of:

- Reference model for effective defence management;
- Reference model for mature civil society environment around defence management system;

- Model of cooperation between defence establishment and civil society;
- Model of regional environment on civil society level in relation to defence management.

It is considered that enterprise architecture governance approach is one of the adequate ways to address change management challenge in the area of security/defence sector reform. Possible framework for implementation of such an approach is created by Geneva Center for Democratic Control of Armed Forces, SSR Working Group of the PfP Consortium of defence Academies and Security Study Institutes and the new established Human and Societal Dynamics Panel of NATO Science Committee.

Civil society measurement is extremely important and there is an opportunity to define the process of security sector reform/ transformation (SSR) as change management project around the concept of civil/societal security, facilitated and motivated by civil society institutions in cooperation with the administration. To hold up such a project there is a need for a network of academic Centers of Excellence (Coe) in SSR, cooperating between themselves on regional basis within the above mentioned framework.

In this context the paper covers general description of defence management model, defence related civil society model, cooperation model as well as regional dimensions in implementation of the change management project for the security/defence sector. Paper is based on assumption that analysis, assessment, planning of improvement and management of plan implementation could be achieved best way by using of enterprise architecture governance approach to the defence institutions and civil society relations.

REFERENCE MODEL OF DEFENCE MANAGEMENT

To analyze, compare, assess and plan improvements in more detailed level, there is a need of reference model/ architecture of the defence management system on several levels: Euroatlantic community, state/society, MoD, main structures in MoD. Euroatlantic level is a network of state/society level coordination bodies to harmonize security policy and its implementation. It is a result of state/society level elements and bellow, which are in the focus of this paper. General reference model for defence management could be described as a network of interrelated institutions as presented bellow. The National Assembly carries out the legislative foundations of Bulgaria's defence policy, including laws, budgets, ratification of international treaties, declaration of war, defence doctrines, regulations, etc.

Approves and leads the implementation of the plans and programs for the build up and development of the Armed Forces. Through its Parliamentary Commission on defence issues, and regular Parliamentary oversight sessions the National Assembly exercises an oversight of the Ministry of Defence and ensures the appropriate application of the system of legal and administrative provisions put in place by the NA. The President is the commander-in-chief of the armed forces. The President chairs the National Security Advisory Council, which includes among others the Minister of Defence and the Prime Minister. He signs decrees for the promotion and appointment of senior officers, including the Chief of Defence Staff. In time of armed conflict or war, the President leads the Supreme Command, which executes the war (in case of general war).

The Council of Ministers, as the executive branch of government, participates in the formulation and implementation of defence policy. In this function, the Council of Ministers is assisted by the Security Council, which might include among others the President's representative. It introduces to the NA for adoption the National Security Strategy, National Military Strategy and other legislation concerning national security. In time of war, the Council of Ministers assists the President in his functions as commander-in-chief. Security council is authorized to perform crisis management operations. The Minister of Defence is proposed by the Prime Minister and appointed by the National Assembly along with the rest of the cabinet members. The Minister of Defence leads and implements the state policy in the Ministry of Defence. He is the chief administrator of funds allocated to the Ministry of Defence.

Other Ministries and Agencies maintain legislatively prescribed relations with the Ministry of Defence, which provide for the proper peacetime functioning of the MoD and integrate the state institutions in the system of national security. International organizations (UN, NATO, EU, OSCE). As an element of integration policy in European and Euro-Atlantic security institutions, the Ministry of Defence interacts with international organizations and, when directed, participates in joint activities, during peacetime and during conflict.

Foreign Defence Ministries and Institutions. The Ministry of Defence maintains intensive relations with Foreign Defence Ministries and Institutions, on bilateral or multilateral level. Non-governmental Organizations. NGOs as part of civil society are a vital part of the civilian and democratic control of the Ministry of Defence. In addition, NGOs provide specialized expertise and stimulate the exchange of knowledge.

According to the Constitution, the institutions responsible for the national security and more specifically for the formulation of defence policy are the President, the National Assembly and the Council of Ministers. The National Assembly establishes the legislative basis of national defence and exercises an oversight of the Ministry of Defence. The Government and the Minister of Defence are accountable to the National Assembly for the leadership and management of the Armed Forces. In an annual report to the National Assembly, the Council of Minister identifies the risks and threats to the country and makes an assessment of the level of protection required to ensure the national interests. Accordingly, the Minister of Defence in coordination with the other institutions responsible for national security formulates the defence policy as an element of the system of national security. The Council of Ministers allocates the resources related to defence. In this process, the National Assembly, the Prime Minister and the Defence Minister are assisted by the exchange of information, views, and ideas at the National Security Advisory Council, chaired by the President. The permanent Security Council of the Council of Ministers and the Political Office of the Minister of Defence also assists the formulation of defence policy. The Security Council provides an information equal in volume and contents to the President, the Chairman of the National Assembly, and the Prime Minister Political Parties and Non-governmental Organizations participate in the formulation of defence policy by providing political and expert alternatives as well as democratic oversight of the Ministry of Defence.

The main functions of the Minister of Defence include:

a. Defence policy formulation. Assesses the defence and military capabilities of the country and formulates plans for the development of the Ministry of Defence in the context of the requirements of the Constitution, National Security Strategy, National Military Strategy and other relevant legislation in the national security system. Implements and controls the state policy in the Ministry of Defence. Coordinates and manages bilateral and multilateral relations with international organizations and states. In this function, the Minister is assisted by his Political Office.

b. Planning and conduct of operations. Organizing, joint training, and employing the Armed Forces to carry out the missions assigned to the Ministry of Defence. In this function, the Minister is assisted by the Joint Operations Headquarters.

c. Administering of defence policy implementation. In this function, the Minister is assisted by the General Administration of the Ministry. The General Administration supports the functions of the Civilian Administration and the Military Administration.

d. Control of implementation. In this function the Minister of Defence is assisted by the Inspectorate and the Office of Financial Comptroller.

The Defence Council is the principle advisory body to the Minister of Defence supplementary him in the administering of defence policy. It includes the Minister of Defence, Deputy Ministers, Parliamentary Secretary, Chief of Political Office, Chief Secretary, Chief of Defence, Chief of Joint Operations Headquarters, Chief of Joint Staff of Armed Forces, and Deputy Chief of Defence (Resources).

The Central Administration administers defence policy in the Ministry of Defence. Central Administration includes two branches—the Specialized (Civilian) Administration and the Joint Staff of Armed Forces (Military Administration), supported by third one – General Administration.

The functions of the Specialized (Civilian) Administration include the following:

a. Defence planning
b. Human resources planning
c. Materiel, infrastructure and financial resources planning

THEORETICAL STRUCTURE FOR DEFENCE MANAGEMENT

To produce these outputs, defence receives two main inputs. These are government policy and resources. Within the defence establishment, these inputs are converted to the outputs through a process of policy formulation, planning, programming and budgeting, execution of the plans and internal controls and corrective action. This process is shown schematically in the diagram opposite.

The diagram illustrate both the internal management processes of a defence organisation as well as the interaction of defence with government. Defence does not make national defence policy or the final strategic defence plan. It produces, through internal processes, policy options and advice to government as well as planning inputs into the national planning and budgeting processes of government. These inputs are considered at various government forums such as cabinet and parliament, and on approval become the official defence policy and plan. The defence department then converts these internally and executes the defence plan, in accordance with policy and the approved budget, to produce the desired outcomes.

Similarly there are internal control processes within defence departments, but there is also an external control and oversight process. Defence reports to government on its performance according to the plan by means of regular financial and other progress reports and government – by means of inspections and audits – maintains oversight of the defence function.

This process can only work and ensure appropriate, adequate, affordable and accountable defence for the nation if there is an open and mutually respectful relationship between government and the defence establishment. Government should respect the professional inputs from the defence establishment, ensure that it does not misuse defence for party political or personal reasons and ensure that defence is adequately resourced, equipped and financed to do its job. Defence leaders on the other hand must have respect for the constitution, the principles of democracy and the role of government in directing the defence function on behalf of the voting public. The South African White Paper on Defence (1996) states that "the Department of Defence respects the right and duty of Parliament to exercise independent and critical judgement on defence policy and practise" but goes on to say, "However, the government recognises that civil–military relations will only be stable if the requisite control is accompanied by the fulfilment of certain responsibilities towards the South African National Defence Force (SANDF) and its members".

These responsibilities, as described earlier in this paragraph, are elaborated upon in the White Paper.

CHALLENGES AND BEST PERFORM

Militaries in Africa are generally a power unto themselves, not transparent to civil society and inefficient. Defence budgets are closed to public scrutiny and very little control is exercised over defence expenditure. In general, defence management is not aligned with the principles of defence in a democracy. To change this situation and to align defence with modern best practice in democratic countries, African governments and defence establishments face some challenges, namely, to:

- establish good governance and ensure adherence to the constitution;
- establish democratic civil–military relations;
- establish defence policies aligned with the challenges facing the region, including a clear role definition for the military forces;
- improve efficiency in defence management;
- enhance the professionalism of the defence sector;
- further enhance collaborative security in the region; and
- institutionalise good planning, programming and budgeting practices in defence establishments.

GOVERNANCE IN DEFENCE MANAGEMENT

Good defence management and healthy civil–military relations are premised on the assumption of the existence of good governance of the state as a whole.

All too often in Africa, the problem with defence is not that the militaries are 'out of control' but rather that governments are misemploying their militaries for regime security, party political goals or the entrenchment of personal power. This often leads to an over-politicised military with the consequence of the military, having been invited in, eventually landing up running government.

It is therefore important that the roles and functions of the militaries as well as the rules and procedures for their employment be clearly established in law and that parliaments have a clear authority in vetoing the employment of the military. The employment of the military by the 'commander-in-chief' or president should be constitutionally subjected to parliamentary approval.

Self-governing Civil–military Relations

Africa has a bad record of military interventions in government and militaries that are not accountable to civil authority. This has led to the general situation where there are poor civil–military relations. Civil society does not trust or like the military and sees them as a power unto themselves, as not serving the national interest and as wasting scarce resources on 'toys for boys'. On the other hand, militaries in general think of civilians as ignorant of security matters and not trustworthy to share in 'the affairs of defence of the state'. The challenge to defence management is to break down these perceptions and barriers and to build mutual understanding, respect and trust.

The essential elements of good civil–military relations are:

- Effective and dynamic political oversight over defence establishments. This is best accomplished through the establishment and empowerment of parliamentary defence committees through the constitution or other legislation. Furthermore, the members of such committees need to be capacitated for the execution of their tasks by the provision of sufficient resources, access to military institutions and programmes designed to enhance their understanding of defence and security matters. Similarly political oversight requires the establishment of civilian defence ministries responsible for the political guidance and control of the military. Such ministries need to be equally capacitated especially by the provision of civilian staff members who have high-level qualifications in strategic and military studies as well as in public and defence management.
- Transparency and accountability in defence sector management. Transparency and accountability are crucial issues in the allocation and management of defence resources for all levels of planning, programming and budgeting. If defence resource allocation and management are not transparent, defence will never be able to achieve public support or the cooperation and

support of broader government. If not accountable to government and the people, defence becomes a cause unto its own and will not be aligned with national interests and priorities. It will easily be corrupted and decision making will be easily manipulated towards self-interests. Civil involvement and control of overall budget decisions, as well as careful auditing at all levels, can help ensure that resources are actually used to accomplish policy objectives. Nevertheless, the most effective solution to this problem is a commitment at all levels to national interests and objectives and the development of clear and transparent policy, planning, programming and budgetary processes and systems to implement them. These processes must of necessity be aligned with the national management framework. Transparency and accountability are enhanced through the system of performance agreements as this relies on the definition of clear output objectives and performance standards and the agreement as to the required resources. The system is also based on negotiation, ensuring better insight, understanding and co-operation.

- An informed civil society. Everybody cannot and does not want to be an expert on defence matters or even, for that matter, be involved in the defence debate. On the other hand, if civil society is ignorant of and uninterested in defence matters, it would not be possible to create healthy civil–military relations and defence would in fact have a licence to 'go its own way'. It is therefore imperative that academic institutions, non-governmental organisations (NGOs) and the media develop expertise in defence matters and defence management matters in order to inform broader society and also to influence governments in general and parliaments in particular. Such academic institutions and NGOs have the responsibility of doing research to bring to the table fresh and alternative options for improved defence policy and management.

INDIA'S DEFENCE INDUSTRY DEVELOPMENT

The pre-independence (pre-1947) defence-industrial infrastructure in India was limited. It generally catered to the lowest spectrum of defence production—repair and overhaul of imported weapons systems. The then ruling British followed a policy of retaining strategic capabilities for themselves while allowing the native Indians to assist in the tactical dimensions, confined to minor works in most endeavours. An example of this policy is evident from the fact that while the Royal Air Force retained the strategic elements like the bomber force and used their own formations, the Indian Air Force (IAF) was left with only tactical elements—supporting them with secondary and tertiary roles that mainly included repair and similar minor works. The Walchand Aircraft Factory (WAF) in Bangalore was wholly engaged in repair and maintenance of aircraft at that time. From March 1942 till the end of World War II, it was employed for the servicing of American aircraft and was managed, for part of this period, by the US Air Force.

Mazagaon Docks (Mumbai) and Garden Reach Shipyards (Calcutta) similarly existed prior to India's independence to repair warships. However, apart from such single air or ship industrial units, India's defence-industrial capacity during times of pre-independence mainly consisted of what is known as Ordnance Factories (OFs). These factories had been set up primarily to supplement land-based weapons and equipment produced in Britain. Before 1947, there were 16 OFs, all located on Indian territory.

The gun and shell factory at Cossipore (near Kolkata), established in 1801, an ammunition factory at Kirkee of 1889, a rifle factory at Ishapore of 1901, a gun carriage factory at Jabalpur of 1904, and others were built mainly to produce for the British forces. During World War II, possible threats to the sea lanes of communication in the Indian Ocean and requirements of the allied forces in the region, made it necessary to double the number of factories during this time. The filling factory at Khamara and the light machine gun factory at

Hyderabad were amongst such new factories. In brief, pre-partition Indian defence-industrial capacities were confined only to a supplementary role and were placed at the lowest end of the production spectrum.

Post-independence, the Indian leadership wanted self-sufficiency in every sphere of activity. This objective was obvious because India was never allowed to develop industrial competencies. The same objective was no different in the field of defence production. Right from the first Prime Minister Jawaharlal Nehru, every successive Indian leader sought self-sufficiency in defence production.

The need to establish a comprehensive defence-industrial infrastructure thus constituted a primary objective of the political leadership. Right from the beginning, India's industrial policies emphasised 'core' industries to be taken care of by the central government and others by the states. Defence industries, considered as critical national assets, obviously came under the exclusive control of the central government. The first Industrial Policy Resolution of 1948, consequently revised under the Second Five-Year Plan in 1956, made it clear that core industries, including munitions, aircraft, shipbuilding, iron and steel, heavy machine tools, heavy electrical plants, atomic energy and similar others were to be placed under exclusive central government control. During this period, many industrial units related to these fields were established under the strict supervision of the central government, known as 'basic' industries. The Defence Science Organisation was also established during this period to take up the challenge of undertaking R&D activities. As demands for defence R&D grew, this organisation paved the way for the creation of the Defence Research and Development Organisation (DRDO) in 1958, which to-date remains the most important contributor to India's defence R&D activities. It has got nearly 50 laboratories, spread all across the country, and other scientific establishments and institutions like the Council of Scientific and Industrial Research (CSIR).

At independence, India's defence-industrial production was mainly coming from the existing 16 OFs. These factories were engaged in the production of low technology items like small arms and ammunition, mines and other explosives. Their cumulative value of production was estimated at roughly US $7-8 million during the time of India's independence. Despite the first India-Pakistan War (1947/48) and the need to boost defence-industrial production, no new factory was built during the first decade (1950s). It was during the late 1950s that the need to construct more factories was contemplated. It is also during this time that peace time civilian production in defence industries was emphasised, especially by the then Defence Minister, V. K. Krishna Menon. The policy of production for civilian markets was primarily aimed at maintaining operational capacities during slack periods of demand as well as keeping the level of productivity high by the manufacturing units. By the end of the 1950s, the number of defence-industrial units almost remained the same. The production from these ordnance factories was still geared to low-technology items.

Apart from OFs, and various defence science and technology establishments, the Indian government also created a number of production establishments to take care of various productions in the field of defence. These, like others, were under the exclusive control of the government although they were created as corporations, commonly known as 'Defence Public Sector Units' (DPSUs). There are eight DPSUs in the country, devoted to the production of different military systems and components. They are: Hindustan Aeronautics Limited (HAL), Bharat Electronics Limited (BEL), Bharat Earth Movers Limited (BEML), Mazagaon Dockyard Limited (MDL), Garden Reach Shipbuilders and Engineers Limited, Goa Shipyard, Bharat Dynamics Limited (BDL) and Mishra Dhatu Nigam Limited (MDNL). Both, DPSUs and OFs, are administered by the Department of Defence Production under the Ministry of Defence. Both sets of industries have their own research and development units although the overall R&D activities are met by the DRDO. Bharat Electronics Limited (BEL) was the first DPSU, established in 1954, to manufacture electronic equipment primarily for the defence sector. Over the years, more than half of BEL's overall production has turned into products for the civilian market. And it is not the only production entity that has changed that way.

In the post-independence period, till the war with China in 1962, India's defence-industrial base was too weak to take the responsibility of all defence needs. The self-sufficiency model had been adopted since the beginning but as years passed and demands for security grew, India found it difficult to create an industrial base as it was hit primarily by two important factors – lack of sufficient funding and access to modern defence technologies. The Indian leadership was aware of these two problems but they also had a number of other issues to handle. The country was just independent, had already fought a war with Pakistan, did not even have a rudimentary industrial base, and faced numerous nation-building and socio-economic problems, independence, found it pragmatic to follow a policy of controlling critical industries, including defence, though this is widely debated now. Although both defence and non-defence critical industries were under exclusive state control, the former—due to their strategic importance—became a 'closed' sector.

The leadership also desired and pursued what is commonly known as comprehensive industrialisation. This meant that more and more big industries emerged to cater to needs that were vast, like steel, coal, mining, etc. Thus, big state-owned companies like the Steel Authority of India Limited (SAIL) was established. This was also evident in the defence sector where large industrial units were created to cater to the demands of the vast armed forces. As mentioned, the two problems of lack of investment and access to technologies became acute as the defence industries expanded, making many units perform below par. Also, investment pattern in this sector was not uniform. Critical establishments like the Hindustan Aeronautics Limited (HAL) and DRDO received more funds than others, such as OFs. The ever-growing demands of the armed forces and the problems in the defence sector in meeting those led many to criticise existing policies followed by the then ruling party. The government, in turn, was hard pressed for funds that were essential and was aware of long-term returns for investment in the defence sector. In brief, policies to maximise production in order to attain self-sufficiency in the defence sector although they were considered far-sighted, did not match expectations, thus leading to further constraints.

From Self-Sufficiency to Self-Reliance

The chimera of self-sufficiency in defence production was in fact realised from the beginning, and was complemented by the concept of self-reliance after a few years of persistence and failure. Self-reliance, as far as India was concerned, meant—apart from its own production base for support—a degree of dependence on reliable foreign sources for access to technologies, supply of components and complete systems. This, in turn, was debatable as foreign partners to achieve such long-term self-reliance were not forthcoming during the first few years as the West was considered to be unreliable both for military and political reasons. India tested self-reliance by meeting urgent and immediate demands through imports from abroad while simultaneously striving for indigenous capabilities in defence production. The west European weapons systems, primarily British, French and Swedish, were considered first choice in the Indian arsenal during the first few years; however, after the 1962 war with China, many western countries along with the United States were reluctant to co-operate with India which made a major adverse impact on India's defence production activities. The post-War scenario witnessed a slow entry of the Soviet Union as a major supplier, the position is still retained by its successor Russia.

The post-1962 scenario was marked by utter confusion in the decision-making circles, which in turn impinged the defence industry. India was humiliated in the war with China and thus started looking into its existent defence-industrial capabilities and found to its horror that all was not well. For example, the Indian Air Force (IAF) needed a high-altitude supersonic interceptor against the threat of the B-57 bomber of Pakistan (supplied by the United States) and the Tu-16 bomber of the

Chinese Air Force (supplied by the USSR). The requirement especially assumed a serious dimension after the war with China, when India looked outward and found out that only three fighter aircraft worth-considering were available in the market. India neither wanted to buy the British Lightning nor the Soviet MiG-21, and preferred the American F-104. This system was already supplied by the United States to Pakistan and despite repeated efforts India could not obtain it. India's effort to upgrade the existing HF-24 to supersonic capability was not considered by the Americans, either. It was at this time that the USSR came to India's rescue when they not only decided to supply the MiG-21 and other weapons but also gave a go-ahead for license production. India's quest for self-reliance got a major boost through this license production arrangement. This was indeed a turning point in India's self-reliance activities. The Soviets proved to be a trusted friend whose military supplies constitute more than 70 percent of India's total weapons acquisitions now. This friendship immensely benefited India's defence industry as it improved many notable weapons systems and components from this experience. In brief, India's self-reliance model in defence production was given a life lease by the Soviets.

After 1962, India sought to make up for the lacuna as well as boost defence production to match requirements. New ordnance factories were planned and established during the next three decades. The number of OFs thus grew to thirty-five by the mid-1980s. And, by the mid-1990s, it had reached thirty-nine. The fortieth ordnance factory (at Nalanda, in the state of Bihar), started in 1999/2000, is expected to be established by 2005/06. These OFs were established in different parts of the country: Ten of them cater to materials and components, ten for weapons, vehicles and equipment, ten for ammunition and explosives and five for other ordnance items. By the early 1990s, they were producing more than 1500 items of arms, ammunition, equipment and components. By the early 1990s, the OFs collectively reached place 45 on the list of the largest arms producing companies in the world, and were placed at 29 in 2000.

The OFs, with a cumulative work force of 1,75,000, have been engaged in various types of land-based weapons. During the period under examination, the bulk of the production, nonetheless, still constituted of large quantities of relatively low-to medium-technology items. These, among others, included small arms, anti-tank and anti-aircraft guns, mortars, associated ammunition, rocket projectiles, bombs, grenades, mines, transport vehicles, leather items, parachutes and ordnance clothing for the armed forces. The establishment of the Heavy Vehicle Factory at Avadi (in the state of Tamil Nadu) in the early 1960s was crucial for the production of tanks and combat vehicles. This is where the first series of tanks, called 'Vijayanta' were manufactured under license from the British firm Vickers. This was followed by the manufacture of the ex-Soviet T-72 'Ajeya' MBTs. Although this project was taken up during the 1970s, it finally rolled out in 1988. In some projects, however, the level of indigenization has been pretty high, for example, up to about 80 percent in the case of 'Sarath' infantry combat vehicles. The overall performance of the OFs during that period was modest, although a lot could have been done to improve the performance of many factories. Hindustan Aeronautics Limited performed modestly during this period. Created in 1964 through an amalgamation of two aircraft companies, Hindustan Aircraft Limited and Aeronautics India Limited, HAL has become the only major aerospace company. With a total work force of nearly 45,000, it stands as the 57th largest defence company in the world.

During the beginning, it was primarily catering to maintenance and overhaul but over a period of time has slowly developed itself to undertake assembly, license manufacture and indigenous design and development. During the 1960s and well beyond, it was engaged in various license manufacture projects, amongst others the MiG-21 series aircraft, HF-24 Marut transonic fighters, 'Kiran' HJT – 16 jet trainer.. Apart from this, it also undertook to license manufacture 'Cheetah' (Aerospatiale SA 315 B) and 'Chetak' (Aerospatiale SA 316 B) helicopters. Bharat Electronics, set up in 1954 to manufacture electronic equipment, was perhaps the only DPSU which showed positive production results during the same period. Other DPSUs such as BEML, BDL, MDL were engaged in production, which may again be termed as modest. Bharat Dynamics Limited, established in 1970, is the other DPSU, which was engaged in the production of missiles and associated products. Except during the 1990s, it had engaged in the past in license manufacture of some of the low range missile series. To sum up: While the Indian defence industry was expected to raise its production level during the half a century (1960s to mid-1980s), both its objectives of self-reliance through indigenous activity and more active collaborative activity, have brought very limited results. Some analysts even term this phase as an 'era of license-manufacture', nothing more. While plant utilisation capacities remained at the lower end, with around 40 to 50 percent, the quality, range and mode of production was modest and generally confined to low and medium technologies.

DEFENCE INDUSTRY AND THE ECONOMIC CHARACTER

The transformation of China's defence establishment into a system capable of independently sustaining modern armed forces was one of the major goals of the military modernization program. In the late 1970s and 1980s, defence spending remained relatively constant despite the shift in resources in favour of overall economic development. Reforms focused on reorganizing the defence research-and-development and industrial base, more closely integrating civilian and military science and industry, and selectively utilizing foreign technology. China sold arms for hard currency to provide additional funds for defence industries. The PLA continued to play its role in economic development by participating in selective construction projects, providing dual-use training, and producing most of its food needs.

Military Expenditures

In the 1980s Chinese statistics indicated that defence spending represented a decreasing percentage of government expenditures, falling from 16 percent in 1980 to 8.3 percent of the state budget in 1987. However, United States Department of Defence studies suggested that the published budget figures understated defence spending by about one-half. With the growth of the Chinese economy under the modernization program, defence spending also represented a smaller percentage of the gross domestic product (GDP) than previously. United States Central Intelligence Agency analysts estimated that defence expenditures in 1978 absorbed 8 to 10 percent of GDP; in 1986 United States Department of Defence analysts estimated that China's military expenses fell within the range of 6 to 8 percent of GDP. Comparison of indices of defence procurement spending and industrial production from 1971 to 1983 revealed that the former increased by 15 percent, whereas the latter rose by 170 percent. These studies indicated that Chinese leaders have indeed subordinated military modernization to economic development. United States Department of Defence officials in 1986 estimated Chinese defence spending by resources and force categories for the 1967 to 1983 period. Roughly 50 percent of defence expenditures were for weapons, equipment, and new facilities; 35 percent for operating costs; and 15 percent for research, development, and testing and evaluation.

By service, these costs broke down to 25 percent for the ground forces; 15 percent for the Navy; 15 percent for strategic air defenses; 5 percent for ballistic missile forces; 5 percent for tactical air forces; and about 35 percent for command, logistics, personnel, intelligence, medical care, administration, research, development, testing and evaluation, and other support. Beginning in the late 1970s, China devoted more resources to its Strategic Missile Force, indicating an effort to increase its strategic security while modernizing the economy, and to national command and support activities, reflecting an emphasis on modernization of the defence structure.

MILITARY R&D AND NDSTIC

The National Defence Science, Technology, and Industry Commission was the coordinating body for military research and development and industrial production. The NDSTIC reported to the party Central Military Commission's National Defence Industries Committee and the State Council's Leading Group for Science and Technology. The NDSTIC supervised weapons research and development, coordinated military production of defence industries, and controlled funding for weapons procurement. The establishment of the NDSTIC was a reform measure designed to break down the barriers between civilian and military research and development and industry. Military science and industry previously had been secretive, segregated, and privileged sectors, having material, financial, and personnel resources superior to those available to the civilian sector. The creation of the NDSTIC was one measure by which Chinese leaders hoped to facilitate the transfer of technology between the military and civilian sectors. The NDSTIC, in particular through its trading arm, China Xinshidai Corporation, coordinated procurement of foreign technology for military purposes.

Defence Industry

Beginning in 1978, Chinese leaders set out to transform the defence industries, which had a huge excess capacity and were criticized for having a "golden rice bowl" (rich but always begging for more). To utilize this excess capacity better and to break down the barriers between military and civilian industry, the machine-building ministries were reorganized, and civilians were appointed to manage them. The civilianized, renamed ministries and their responsibilities consisted of the Ministry of Nuclear Industry—nuclear weapons; Ministry of Aeronautics—aircraft; Ministry of Electronics Industry—electronics; Ministry of Ordnance Industry— munitions and armaments; Ministry of Astronautics—ballistic missiles and space systems; and China State Shipbuilding Corporation—naval construction. In 1986 the Ministry of Machine Building, which produced civilian heavy machinery and industrial equipment, and the Ministry of Ordnance Industry were consolidated into the new State Machine-Building Industry Commission as a way to strengthen the unified management of the national machine-building and weapons enterprises. In 1987 little information was available about this new commission or its relationship to the NDSTIC or to the State Economic Commission, whose Defence Bureau coordinated the civilian production of the defence industry. Further changes in defence industry structure occurred in 1986 and 1987, when inland defence enterprises were either relocated closer to transportation links or cities, closed down, or transferred to local civilian control and production.

Weapons Production

In 1987 China adopted a new contractual system for weapons research, development, and production. It was not clear from available information how this contract system would affect the role of the NDSTIC as the coordinating body for defence science and industry. Previously, the NDSTIC controlled procurement funding, reviewed proposals for weapons requirements funneled through the General Staff Department's Equipment Subdepartment, and coordinated with defence industries to produce the needed equipment.

Under the new system, the state divided defence research and development funds into three categories: military equipment research, basic and applied sciences research, and unidentified technological services. The first type of appropriation went to military arms and services, which signed contracts with research institutes or enterprises to develop and manufacture the required weapons.

The contract system involved the PLA, which had been removed to a large extent from such activities, in the development and manufacture of the weapons it would use. The second category of funds was devoted to basic research and applied science to help modernize the defence industry. The third category went to technological services necessary for research programs. This reform was another measure designed to integrate military and civilian industry by placing the military production of defence industries within the framework of the planned-commodity economy. The new system further sought to provide the military with better equipment at a minimum cost, to force the defence industry to upgrade weapons designs and improve production, to improve the management of weapons research and development through state application of economic levers, to promote cooperation between research institutes and factories, and to increase the decision-making powers of the enterprises.

Procurement of weapons and equipment represented 45 percent of the defence budget during the 1967 to 1983 period. This figure included 25 percent for aircraft, 15 percent for ground forces weapons, and about 10 percent each for naval and missile systems. China's military-industrial complex, the third largest in the world, produced a wide variety of weapons, including light arms and ammunition, armor, artillery, combat aircraft, fast-attack craft, frigates, destroyers, conventional and nuclear submarines, electronic equipment, tactical missiles, and ballistic missiles.

With the notable exception of China's indigenously produced nuclear submarines, nuclear missiles, and satellites, most Chinese weaponry was based on Soviet designs of the 1950s and 1960s. Much of this equipment was obsolete or obsolescent, and beginning in the late 1970s China made great efforts to upgrade the equipment by changing indigenous design or by incorporating Western technology. The greatest weaknesses were in conventional arms, precision-guided munitions, electronic warfare, and command, control, communications, and intelligence. China attempted to address these weaknesses by focusing military research on electronics—essential to progress in the previously mentioned areas—and by selectively importing key systems or technologies.

TRENDS OF INDIA'S DEFENCE INDUSTRY

Trends in global defence industry have impinged India in many ways. India's defence industry has witnessed significant changes since the end of the Cold War. In the 1990s, changes in both institutional and policy spheres became more prominent. The most far reaching change that has occurred in recent years in India's defence-industrial sector is related to its opening up to the market. Long protected as a closed sector, India's defence industry has now opened up for private participation. As if this was not enough, it is also showing enough willingness to become an exporter and dares to venture into the competitive global arms market. How far it will succeed in its objectives is examined elsewhere, but changes are certainly a product of and response to the contemporary changes in the global industrial defence scenario. At the same time, it is also showing willingness to diversify its range of products, which not only include modern weapons systems but also technologies for wide and popular civilian uses. The Indian defence-industrial sector targets the national, and even global, civilian market to sell its products, especially in the fields of civilian space, medical, and electronics. Thus conversion through diversification has been witnessed in many areas of defence production in India.

India's defence industry has come a long way from being at the lowest end of the production spectrum, catering to the maintenance and repair and overhaul of imported weapons, to a stage where it can boast of designing and developing a range of state-of-the-art weapons systems. Half a decade of defence-industrial experience in India shows that while it started from scratch, it has been able not only to learn and absorb various stages of production intricacies but also produce complex systems that are primarily an indigenous activities. Another important factor is that the Indian defence industry has produced various weapons systems under licenses acquired from various foreign sources.

Although the first Prime Minister of India, Jawaharlal Nehru, believed in 'self sufficiency' in arms production, which became a policy mantra for subsequent years, it had to be supplemented by what is roughly called 'self-reliance in defence'. Self-reliance does not preclude accessing external sources for technology and systems, or external help in any stage of the production cycle. It is the degree of dependency on external sources that is tested in the case of India's quest for self-reliance.

India opted to choose an incremental path, in which it was necessary to continue to meet urgent requirements through imports while striving hard on achieving indigenous capabilities in defence production. Both policies continued till the late 1980s and many of the components of both still continue till today. The 1990s witnessed a series of far-reaching initiatives in the field of national security, of which defence industry was a critical component.

The creation of six Special Task Forces to reform major aspects of national defence coordination and management, under the Chairmanship of the then Defence Minister in 1994 may effectively be considered as the first major step after a long time to initiate and implement much-desired reforms in the defence-industrial sector. This was followed by a series of intensive interactions between various organs of the armed forces, government departments and institutions like the Confederation of Indian Industries (CII). The 'Army-Industry Partnership', a partnership between CII and the Indian Army to get acquainted with each other's needs and to facilitate channels of communication between the armed forces and the private industry, was a result of this process and, in turn, led to other cooperative initiatives. Events like India's nuclear tests in mid-1998 and the Kargil conflict in mid-1999 provided grounds for an intense debate on various aspects of India's national security. Also, as a by-product of the current disinvestment programme, which is primarily aimed toward lessening or wiping out government control and responsibilities in state-owned public enterprises in India, the debate on a reform of the defence industry got a major boost as demands for a privatisation of and private participation in this hitherto closed sector grew more in tune with the changing times.

In January 2001, the Government of India initiated a series of major initiatives that, among others, included Foreign Direct Investment (FDI) up to about 26 percent and full private participation in certain sectors in the defence industry. This policy indeed marks a critical departure from the past. Followed by this, the Group of Ministers (GoM) Report on 'Reforming the

National Security System' was made public in early 2001. This laid stress on reforms in all-encompassing aspects of national security, of which changes sought in higher defence management emphasised the need to create specific institutions like the Defence Acquisitions Board to adapt and facilitate changing needs of the defence industry.

While these far-reaching institutional and policy-oriented changes have been underway for quite some time especially since the early 1990s, the demand for private participation has assumed significance in recent years. In such a scenario, analyses of India's defence-industrial sector and policies have become critically important to understand the complex web of linkages that determine national policies in the defence-industrial sector. This, in turn, needs a closer look into the past performance of the defence industry, lessons learnt and a peep into the likely future course.

Research Objectives

The objectives are primarily four-fold. First, we will examine critical aspects of defence-industrial policies adopted by India in the past and link those to performance. It will examine the factors that have influenced India's defence production and their co-relationship with policies and decision-making in this sector. Second, we will examine the main trends during the 1990s, during which major policy changes occurred. It will critically examine the impact of such policy changes. Third, we will examine the contemporary scenario. Fourth and last, it will look into future problems and prospects. The last two are essential in understanding the intricacies involved in India's defence-industrial strategies and are expected to give some clues related to the future course of action in this sector. Some of the major queries that will be examined here are: Why a quest for self-reliance in the past? Has the policy of self-reliance paid off? If not, what are the options for the future? Why the changes in defence-industrial policies during the 1990s? Are the objectives achievable? What are likely options for the future? Does it have scope for more diversion, thus leading to conversion through the increase in civilian production, in future? We will invariably try to find answers to these queries, although not necessarily in the same order.

Methods and Sources

We will follow a general descriptive-analytical approach. The scope is limited somewhat to policy analyses due to constraints in the availability of information. This is because India's defence industry has long been a 'closed' sector and thus been under exclusive government control. It is only in recent times that it has opened up, thus leading to an availability of information in a low to medium scale. We will also follow a historical method whereby it will emphasise linkages at policy- and decision-making levels to performance, and this is important in understanding the nature of development that this sector has undergone for the past half-a-century. Available data on specifics will be evaluated. Emphasis will be on an evaluation and interpretation of data from primary (especially government) sources. In brief, the overall approach will be descriptive and analytical.

Literature on the subject is scarce. At international level, the study of India's defence industry has attracted very little attention. The same is true at national level. Barring a few books, written by scholars like K. Subrahmanyam, Air Marshal Samir Sen, Major General Pratap Narain, Chris Smith, WPS Sidhu, and others, substantial work is not evident on this subject. Occasional research papers by G. Balachandran, Rahul Roy-Choudhury, Ajay Singh and others have also focused on limited themes. Secondary and tertiary sources are scarce. Primary sources, however, constitute the most important component of this study. Annual Reports (published by the Ministry of Defence, Government of India), Annual Reports of major Defence Public Sector Units (published by respective organisations), periodic reports published by the Comptroller and Auditor General of India, Parliament Secretariat and similar other reports constitute primary sources for this endeavour. Select interviews with senior government officers, analysts and industry-watchers have been taken into account.

SYSTEM CLASSES AND RELATIONS MANAGEMENT

The System and SoS context class hierarchies, together with relation management, should strengthen architecture management for the Defence capability process. It has the potential to capture the supplementary system knowledge regarding SoS architectures required to support Defence's architecture activities and concurrent engineering practice. The taxonomical structure captured in the System Package can help users to identify system types and their relations to other system objects in the context of capability and system development. The exercise of creating system objects with its context information and managing this information throughout a system's life cycle can significantly improve the awareness of its relations and impact on other components of DAIM.

The DAIM-based repository will have a rich repertoire of systems relations, including *pattern-with, component, based-on, part-of, interoperate-with,* and *used-by.* These relation often have different impacts on evolutions of SoS and require different strategies in development and management. The pattern-with relation, for example, defines a binding or collaborative relation of two systems that is not as strong as the interoperate-with relation, which requires detailed specifications and interface design. The System Class package is one of the six main class packages included in the DAIM. As a result, the relation management achieved through the DAIM is established across all these class packages. All knowledge relating to the core concepts (scenario, capability, system, architecture and project) can be integrated through relation management and form a body of knowledge on systems and capabilities throughout their life cycles. With the support of such a systematically established body of knowledge, capability planners, analysts and other stakeholders can, easily and effectively access relevant information and knowledge linking strategic scenarios, operation or exercise scenarios, capability development scenarios, to systems, capabilities or platforms involved. In the current practice, unfortunately, these relations across concepts are not defined, specified and managed. They are also missing components of SoS architecture. In traditional practices of Systems Engineering and architecture development, systems relations are addressed in the activities of design and development. In the phase of design, systems relations must be fully investigated and defined. The issues related to interfaces and composition then need to be addressed through design and represented in the form of architecture that guides the implementation and evolutions of SoS. The relation management can effectively enhance the applications of Systems Engineering and architecture practice.

BENEFITS AND APPLICATIONS

The DAIM is a foundation to generate an integrated architecture capability for planning and managing Defence capability and its information environment. Through using the well-developed mechanism for the relation management, DAIM can play a number of important roles in defence capability knowledge engineering and supporting systems and capability management.

With the established knowledge schema that can manage complicated relations among concepts such as operation scenarios, capabilities, systems, and architectures, and their real world objects, DAIM provides the basis for a solution for enterprise-wide architecture knowledge integration and management, that addresses three important issues, that is, defence scenario management, systems and capability relation management, and architecture data management, in an integrated manner. As discussed earlier, relation management requires an object store as a solution for implementation of the object context management. DAIM can then be used as a data schema for architecture repository development. Based on an object store, it would provide a facility to enable traceability, dependency analysis, synthesis, visualisation, simulation, SoS analysis and experimentation, and capability analysis and development. The repository can provide context descriptions of all DAIM objects and can help generate, understand and synthesize "big pictures" of various SoS contexts of interest from capability and systems planning and development. The dependency is a kind of relations that exists between two objects of the same class or different classes. Dependencies can be classified into the following categories:

- Function dependency;
- Structure dependency;
- Information dependency
- Effect dependency;
- Time dependency; and
- Financial dependency.

One of the great challenges in planning, managing and developing SoS is to develop an ability to handle traceability when dealing with "big pictures" of defence capability in various contexts and for different purposes.

The establishment of mechanisms for the relation definition and object context management provides a basis and support for highly desirable functions or activities in relation to analysis and visualisation of dependence and traceability. The traceability, as one of main benefits from the relation management, hopefully achieved through the DAIM and its associated object store is characterised as follows:

- Captured in an architecture repository (an object store);
- In a context of the whole defence capability and system architecture space or across concepts, projects and business areas, including:
    - o Inter-system
    - o Inter-capability
    - o Inter-project
    - o Inter-architecture
    - o Inter-process
    - o Inter-business area.

With the ability to effectively handle dependency and traceability in the whole defence information environment (DIE)

SoS context through relations defined between concepts (or classes) and specified between objects, DAIM offers an opportunity to develop a knowledge management system and process for Defence capability architecture practice.

The benefits to Defence's many business areas should be substantial, enabling knowledge to be captured, applied at the appropriate time and reused. The consequence should be that Defence should derive substantial additional benefits from its architecture investments.

Through systematic definitions of concepts and relations, in summary, DAIM becomes a conceptual model that describes the entire architecture space of capability and systems It provides:

- A method for concept management (taxonomies and an ontology for scenarios, capabilities, projects, systems and architectures).
- A method also for relation management that covers
  - o Scenarios relations;
  - o Systems relations;
  - o Capability relations;
  - o Projects relations;
  - o Architecture relations; and
  - o Relations across concepts.
- A foundation to enable important architecture activities, such as:
  - o Architecture planning;
  - o Architecture analysis and evaluation; and
  - o Architecture management.
- An environment to deal with issues concerning "big pictures" of defence capability and DIE. It will, in a SoS Context, support :
  - o Traceability;
  - o Visualisation;

- o Dependency analysis;
- o Interoperability analysis.

With the mechanism of concept and relation management in the architecture repository, capability planners, analysts, architects, developers or even war-fighters can query, search and trace various relations and dependencies. All real world objects captured in the repository are searchable with their attributes and relations and can be visualised with its full context in terms relations to other objects in the same class of different classes. If the relation definitions can be further formalised, it should be possible to explore more semantics and rules that can be used to develop automatic reasoning functions related to capability and system relation analysis, synthesis and visualisation.

Another advantage of developing the systems and capability relation management solution in the context of DAIM is that it allows the extension of the relation management coverage to include other related concepts, such as scenarios, projects, architecture and references. Consequently, it also supports the traceability of relations and dependence to be linked with associated scenarios and architecture descriptions. Theses advantages prove the improvement of integrated knowledge management for the defence systems and capability management as a whole.

5

Financial Geography and Regional Growth in China

Considerable disparity in regional incomes is a reality in every geographically large country, and the causes of the disparity are numerous and complex. The enduring character of many cases of regional backwardness is also a reality, for example, the Appalachians in the United States, Northern Shaanxi in China, Chiapas in Mexico, and Madura in Indonesia. The persistence of poverty in these locations has led many prominent social scientists to see the main causes of entrenched regional poverty to be inter-related in a self-reinforcing or self-perpetuating manner. Sociologists talk about the culture of poverty. Psychologists highlight the absence of the drive to achieve. Classical Marxists expound about the systemic need of the capitalist economy for a reserve army of unemployed. Latin American *dependenistas* see domestic regional disparity to be the inevitable reflection of the neo-imperialistic relationships in the international arena, the global metropolis-periphery arrangement reproduced within the dependent economy. Finally, neo-classical economists explicate the working of local dynamics that produce multiple equilibria, with the "low-income trap" being one of the stable outcomes.

Usual scientists too have their own discipline-based explanations for spatial inequality in economic development. The most well-known recent example of which is the book, Guns, Germs and Steel by the physiologist Jared Diamond

(1997). One of Diamond's main arguments is that many types of innovation (especially those in agriculture and construction) are not applicable across ecological zones. So, in ancient times, while new improved varieties of crops and beasts of burden can spread from northern Asia in the east to Europe in the west (and vice-versa), they cannot be transmitted from the temperate zone in north America to the temperate zone in south America because of the intervening tropics. Biological endowments also matter. Most of Asia and Europe have more naturally-pliable livestock (horses and cows) that can be harnessed to help in war and production. The African-equivalent of those animals, e.g. zebras, hippopotamuses, antelopes and wildebeests, have proved themselves, up to today, resistant to domestication efforts to turn them into beasts of burden. Even the African elephant is temperamentally uncooperative compared to its Asian cousin.

There is obviously no shortage of explanations for regional disparity and its, sometimes centuries-long, durability. This surfeit of views is suggestive of ignorance about this phenomenon, and confusion about what to do about it. What is clear however is that the successful development strategies of some countries cannot produce the same salubrious results when implemented in other national settings. When China opened some coastal pockets for foreign direct investment, these Special Economic Zones (SEZs) quickly blossomed into vibrant export platforms and created backward linkages with the immediate hinterland. Whereas, when landlocked Mongolia turned the entire country into a free trade and investment zone in the late 1990s, the inflow of foreign capital was a mere trickle compared to China's experience. The specific lesson in this case is that the time-tested effective growth policy package for a coastal economy, and minor modifications of it, are unlikely to work for an interior economy.

Public apprehension for regional income disparity in China has been increasing quickly since the early 1990s. This concern is rooted in the widening of provincial income gaps that started in the 1988-93 period, with the exact timing dependent on the method of measurement. The coefficient of variation of provincial incomes for 29 provinces fell from 0.73 in 1978 to 0.63 in 1989 and then rose to reach 0.70 in 1998. By 1995, the obvious rise in regional inequality had caused the international news media to raise the possibility of the political disintegration of China.

The "optimistic" situation for China's breakup is an amicable one. The affluent provinces could now afford to quietly ignore the authority of the central government, or to indirectly control the central government – a situation of de facto political independence for the affluent provinces. The May 11, 1995 issue of the Far Eastern Economic Review carried on its cover the heading "Fragile China: Affluent Regions Go Their Own Way", and it reported that the political scientist Susan Shirk: "knows of a half-dozen provincial functionaries who 'have declined promotions to Beijing and opted to stay at home to get rich and exercise informal political influence.' With regional fortunes so drastically on the rise, Shirk says, national politicians are tempted to play [to] the provinces and outbid each other in pandering to local interests."

The "pessimistic" scenario for the political disintegration is a civil war sparked by the resentment of the poor provinces. According to the economist Hu Angang who advocates the abolition of the special economic zones:

"If Deng Xiaoping knew the disparities were as big as they are, he would be more militant than I am in trying to eliminate them... In America, the deep differences between the North and the South more than 100 years ago led to the Civil War."

"We must cease subsidizing rich coastal cities. Preferential treatment should be reserved for the poor."

Regardless of whether it is concern for social equity or for social stability, China's top leaders have now clearly committed themselves to accelerating the economic growth of the interior provinces. The budget for infrastructure investments in the poor provinces have increased substantially every year, and a Western Region Development Office has just been established under the State Council (the Chinese cabinet) to formulate a comprehensive development strategy and to coordinate its implementation.

This paper seeks to integrate some recent advances in regional science, ecology and geography into economics to arrive at some preliminary findings on the barriers to economic growth in China's interior provinces. In particular, we present estimates on the role contributions of preferential economic polices and geographical location to the growth of China's provinces. The quantification and policy suggestions presented here are necessarily tentative and primitive because this is the first phase of our collective efforts to understand this longstanding problem of large regional inequality in China's history.

THE SIGNIFICANCE OF GEOGRAPHY

On a global scale, the wealth of nations is well characterised by two geographical divides. The first geographical divide emphasizes differences in ecological conditions, the temperate zone versus the tropical zone. The second geographical divide emphasizes differences in the ability to conduct international trade, the coast versus the interior. As we will show, both of these geographical divides are a combination of independent causes of economic wealth and of proxies for some important determinants of economic prosperity.

The empirical validity of the temperate-tropical divide is well-vouched for by the fact that over 90 percent of the world's poor lives between the Tropic of Cancer and the Tropic of Capricorn. The result is a GDP per capita (PPP-adjusted) of $3,326 in 1995 for tropical economies, and $9,027 for nontropical economies. This strong correlate between ecological zone and income level is not a new observation in economics, e.g. Lee (1957) and Kamarck (1976), but it has not been a major analytical organizing principle in development economics. The incorporation of new insights from physical geography and societal dynamics have led Jared Diamond (1997), David Landes (1997), Stanley Engerman and Kenneth Sokoloff (1997) and Gallup, Sachs and Mellinger (1998) to focus on physical geography as an over-arching explanation of economic performance. Because most of Africa lies in the tropical zone, Bloom and Sachs (1998) have identified the virulence of diseases and the limited potential for large gains in agricultural productivity in the tropics to be the key obstacles to economic development there. This biology-based analysis of Bloom and Sachs is of course not the only recent attempt to explain the upward income gradient that begins at the Equator. Hall and Jones (1997) have suggested that the distance from the Equator proxies for the relative penetration of European economic institutions, and European-style economic institutions are the ultimate engines of growth.

The coast-interior dichotomy highlights the importance of transportation cost in determining a country's participation in the international division of labor. In the industrial age, water transportation has the lowest cost for extended distance. The growth effects of trade are well-known, beginning with Adam Smith's observation that productivity improvements are enabled by the greater division of labor that, in turn, is enabled by the expansion of the market.

The clear policy lesson here is that investments in physical infrastructure and transportation technology can change the comparative advantage of a region.

The temperate-tropical dichotomy will not be a major analytical organizational principle in this paper. This is because China, unlike Brazil and Australia, does not have a substantial part of its territory within the tropical zone. The southern border of China extends only a little miles beyond the Tropic of Cancer. This feature is of interest in itself because it is more than coincidental that after centuries of steady southward expansion, the Chinese empire stopped at approximately where the tropical zone begins. While we will not dwell on the temperate-tropical divide, the general point about differences in the development potential of different ecological zones is an important one. The appropriate development package for the arid plateaus of northwestern China has to be different from the grain-growing plains of central China, and the relevant development package for the wet, warm southwestern provinces has to take disease vectors into greater account.

CHINA IN TIME AND SPACE

China covers 9.6 million four-sided figure kilometers and stretches from the temperate to sub-tropical zones. It is similar in size and climate to the United States but its topography is quite different. The most important difference being that the U.S. has coastlines running the length of its eastern and western borders, whereas western China is landlocked. China is also more mountainous and hilly, with plains at less than 500m elevation making up only 25 percent of the total land area, and mountains and plateaus accounting for 60 percent. These topographic features of China imply higher transportation costs and a greater requirement for physical infrastructure construction. The task of economic development in China is hence more challenging than in the U.S..

Physically, China resemble a three-step staircase running downward from west to east. It begins with the 4,000 meters high Qinghai-Tibet Plateau in the west, proceeds to the highlands and basins in the center which are about 1,000 to 2,000 meters above the sea level, and ends with hilly regions and plains that are less than 1,000 meters high. The combination of higher precipitation, warmer climate, and access to navigable rivers and the sea have made the central and eastern provinces more conducive for farming and trade, and, hence, the population centers of China. The Qinghai-Tibet Plateau was traditionally the poorest region.

The location of China's economic center has changed over time, moving eastwards from the Loess Plateau and the Yellow River Valley in the northwest (where Chinese civilization began in 2000 BC), which is about 1000 kilometers away from the coast. The reason for this original location is because, in ancient times, high agricultural productivity and land-based trade was much more important than sea-based trade. The bulk of China's international trade at that time was conducted through the famous Silk Route that went through the northwestern corner of China. The southeastern coastal region, where Guangdong and Fujian (two of today's most dynamic provincial economies) are located, was largely remained uncultivated and sparsely populated in early Chinese history. Although the natural conditions in the southeast were favorable for agriculture, farming was undeveloped because malaria ('zhangqi' in Chinese) and other subtropical diseases checked population growth, and the high temperature sapped human energy faster, resulting in lower labor productivity. Guangdong was considered an almost uninhabitable place in ancient times.

Over time, the pressure of expanding population and the frequent invasions by the northern tribes caused more of the population to move south and into the mid-coastal and southeastern regions. By the 12th century, the Yangtze River valley had become very developed and densely populated. The economic importance of the coastal region increased dramatically after the Opium War in 1840 when the Western powers forced China to first open several ports and then the whole country for trade. China's economy and subsequently politics were quickly (by historical standards) transformed. International trade expanded, foreign direct investments flowed in, and local industrialists made their appearances, especially in the mid-coastal and southeast regions. The Qing dynasty was overthrown in 1911, followed by a long chaotic period of protracted civil wars and Japanese colonialism, that ended with the declaration of the People's Republic of China on October 1, 1949 by the Communist Party of China (CPC) under the leadership of Mao Zedong.

Some key physical and economic characteristics of China in the six regional groupings that are useful for analyzing the post-1978 period.

The municipalities of Beijing, Tianjin and Shanghai that have province-level status (Chongqing was granted province-level status in 1997, but we have included its data under Sichuan province). These are the richest pockets of China, and have had high growth in the 1990s. These cities are highly industrialized, and over 71 percent of their population lives within 100 kilometers of the coast or navigable waters. Beijing, Shanghai and Tianjin are *the exceptionally rich (city) provinces*.

The northeastern provinces of Heilongjiang, Jilin and Liaoning, which are collectively called Manchuria, and was the industrial heartland of China in 1949 (because of the Japanese control of the economy that started in 1905). During the central planning period, their early start in industrialization was consolidated, making these provinces the part of China that most resembled the Soviet Union in industrial organization and production structure. In the national ranking of per capita GDP, omitting the three municipalities, Heilongjiang and Liaoning ranked first and second, respectively, in 1978, and ranked seventh and fifth, respectively, in 1998. Heilongjiang and Liaoning are *the traditionally rich provinces*.

The coastal provinces of Hebei, Shandong, Jiangsu, Zhejiang, Fuijian, Guangdong and Hainan (Hainan was separated out from Guangdong in 1988). These seven provinces have 82 percent of their population living with 100 kilometers of the sea or navigable rivers. They have grown the fastest of these six groupings in the 1978-1998 period, an annual average of 10.7 percent. The result is that Zhejiang and Guangdong have soared to the top of the per capita GDP ranking, omitting the municipalities, from fourth and sixth, respectively, in 1978 to first and second, respectively, in 1998. Zhejiang and Guangdong are the archetype of *the nouveau riche provinces*.

The central provinces of Shanxi, Henan, Anhui, Hubei, Hunan, and Jiangxi, through which the plain runs relatively unimpeded from the north of the Yellow River to the south of the Yangtze River. The temperature and rainfall make this region the agricultural heartland of China, which explains why its population density is almost twice that of the northeaster and southwestern regions. The two large rivers and their many tributaries endow 57 percent of the population with easy water transportation. The Yangtze between Wuhan and Shanghai has the industrial potential of the Rhone Valley multiplied several times.

The northwestern provinces of Inner Mongolia, Shaanxi, Ningxia, Gansu, Qinghai, Xinjiang and Tibet (data of Tibet omitted) are truly isolated. The center of the land mass is 1,400 kilometers from the coast. This region is more arid and steeper compared to the four previous groupings, and it is marked by desert on its western and northern borders. Furthermore, 5 percent of the land has a slope of greater than 10 percent compared to 2.5 percent for the northeastern, coastal and central provinces. The general lack of water makes the region difficult for agriculture, only 8 percent of the land is arable, which helps explain why it has the lowest population density in China in 1998, 46 persons per km^2 versus 126 persons per km^2 in the southwestern region, which has the next lowest population density. A large number of residents are of Turkic origin, and are practicing Muslims. The Han people are in the minority in Xinjiang and Tibet.

The southwestern provinces of Sichuan, Yunnan, Guizhou, and Guangxi have rainfall and temperature conditions that are ideal for crop cultivation but they suffer from being too mountainous. The average elevation is 1,400 kilometers, the average slope is 5.2 degrees, and 14 percent of the land has a slope of greater than 10 degrees. The proportion of arable land of 10 percent is barely above that of the arid northwestern provinces. Lacking the mineral resources of the northwestern provinces, the southwestern provinces have the lowest GDP per capita in 1978, and the lowest growth rates in the period of market-oriented reform.

A significant proportion of the population belongs to non-Han ethnic groups.

Local Economic Policy, 1949-1978

Industrialization was shallow in 1949, and a largely coastal phenomenon. In 1952, the secondary sector produced 8 percent of GDP and employed 7 percent of the labor force compared with the primary sector, which produced 74 percent of GDP and employed 84 percent of the work force. The coastal provinces had 72 percent of fixed assets, and accounted for 69 percent of the gross value of industrial output. Naturally, just like the Communist Party of the Soviet Union in 1917, CPC saw its most important economic task to be industrialization.

China adopted the two key sets of guiding principles behind the Soviet development strategy: (a) the Marxist principles of common ownership with the state as trustee, and of generalized egalitarianism; and (b) the Stalinist practices of central planning for resource allocation, suppression of light industries and services in favour of heavy industries, and minimizing trade and financial linkages with the capitalist economies.

Mao added a third guiding principle to China's economic policy-making, the principle of regional economic self-sufficiency, a region should be self-sufficient not only in food production but also in industrial goods as well. This third principle had unquestionably the greatest impact on regional economic outcomes. The self-reliance principle had several virtues. The first was that it overlapped with the egalitarian principle because it reduced provincial inequality, which Mao had identified to be one of the key social contradictions to be eliminated in the new China.

The second virtue was that the biggest beneficiaries of the self-reliance principle were the poorest provinces (because they were overwhelmingly agricultural), and this was in accordance with the gratitude that many veteran party leaders felt toward these provinces. Many of the poorest provinces were where CPC had retreated to and rebuilt their strength after the Kuomintang had driven it out of the urbanized areas.

The third, and most decisive, virtue of self-sufficiency was that, beginning in 1963, it coincided with the national security considerations of China. The worsening Sino-Soviet political relationship and the growing military presence of the United States in Vietnam convinced Mao that regional economic self-sufficiency was key to China being able to engage in protracted defense of the motherland. Mao and his generals envisaged three lines of defense (coastal, central and western), and they decided in 1964 on a massive construction of military-industrial complexes in western China, the third line of defense, popularly translated as the "third front." To minimize the vulnerability of the third front industries to air attacks, Lin Biao, then the Defense Minister and Mao's designated successor, instructed that these projects be located "in mountains, in dispersion, and in caves."

The first two virtues of the self-sufficiency principle helped to ensure that the First Five-Year Plan (1953-1957) allocated 56 percent of state investment to the interior provinces, and that the Second Five-Year Plan (1958-62) allocated 59 percent. As the concern for national security grew in the early 1960s, the Third Five-Year Plan (1966-1970) allocated 71 percent of state investment in the interior provinces, with the bulk of it in Sichuan, Hubei, Gansu, Shaanxi, Henan, and Guizhou. Furthermore, many companies in Shanghai and other coastal cities were relocated to the mountains in Guizhou, Sichuan, and Hubei, where highways and railroads were deficient or non-existent, water and electricity were in shortage, and the sources of raw materials were far away. A significant proportion of the relocated factories could not produce anything for many years, with the equipment rusting into junk.

Post-mortem studies of the third front industries concluded that: "only half of the factories built performed to design specifications and the rest were either only partially completed (30 percent) or not completed at all (20 percent). Fully one-third of the total investment was wasted..." One such example of wastage was the Second Automobile Company built in the mountains of Hubei. The part and assembly plants were scattered over the mountainous region, transportation among the plants was poor, and they were long way away from their input suppliers and the final consumers of their products.

Known the large amount of wastage that occurred in the industrialization of the interior provinces, it is no wonder that even though the interior share of fixed assets went from 28 percent in 1952 to 57 percent in 1983, its share of gross value of industrial products only went up from 31 percent to 41 percent. The primary cause of the higher productivity of coastal industries was that the coastal provinces had deeper pools of management and technical expertise, better linkages between the industrial enterprises and the local economies, and more developed infrastructure. It was been estimated that 100 yuan of fixed asset investment in 1978 yielded 70 yuan of output from the third front enterprises compared to 141 yuan from the coastal enterprises. The profit rate in 1978 was 9 percent for the third-front enterprises compared to 23 percent for coastal enterprises.

The pouring of investment funds into the interior provinces was a clear violation of the comparative advantage principle. The growth of the interior provinces not only occurred at the expense of the coastal provinces, it also lowered the overall growth rate of the economy. The discrimination against the coastal region was so severe that although Shanghai provided more 40 percent of the state revenue during the Cultural Revolution period, it was not even allowed to retain enough funds money to cover depreciation of its capital stock.

The wastage that occurred with this discrimination against coastal investments was further increased because of the poor planning, poor execution and poor management of the investments in the interior provinces. As we will argue later, the appropriate development strategy for the interior provinces should not be focussed on making the production structure of interior provinces identical to the production structure of the coastal provinces. For example, given the strong extractive capacity and implementation ability of the government under Mao, it would have been more efficient to have located the investments in the coastal provinces, taxed the profits, and used the tax revenue to benefit the interior benefits. What should have been important for the government was not where the investments were located but whether the dividends from the investments were used to enhance the development of the interior provinces.

It is interesting to note that by 1972, China was reducing its discrimination against investments in the coastal provinces and increasing its economic interaction with the capitalist economies. This policy shift occurred because the government realized that China's economy and technological capacity was falling further behind the rest of the world. If this negative trend were not reversed, China might not be able to defend itself. Furthermore, because the Soviet Union was fast becoming a bigger threat than the United States, an invasion by the traditional land route was therefore much more likely than a coastal landing. The national security justification for the third front industries was hence undermined. Economic modernization required the import of foreign technology, and this necessitated that China increased its export earnings.

With the improvement of Sino-US relations on course after Kissinger's secret visit in July 1971, the coastal enterprises, especially those in Guangdong, were expanded in order to increase their export capacity. Total export earnings jumped from US$2.6 billion in 1972 to US$3.4 billion in 1973, and continued soaring to reach US$9.8 billion in 1978. Just as national security considerations in the 1950s and 1960s have played a large part in justifying the bias in favour of investments in the interior provinces, national security considerations in the face of changes in international politics in the 1970s helped to reverse this bias.

Regional financial Policy, 1978-98

The process of increased economic interaction with the outside world accelerated at the end of 1978 upon the decisive political victory by the rehabilitated cadres over the remnants of the Maoist establishment at the Third Plenum of the 11th Party Congress. The emphasis on the domestic front was the decentralization of agricultural production, the decentralization of the fiscal system, and the deregulation of prices; and the emphasis on the international front was the Open Door Policy.

Fiscal decentralization took the form of tax contracting between the central government and the provinces. Each fiscal contract was individually negotiated, and it ranged from fixed lump-sum contracts for five years like in the cases of Guangdong and Fujian to highly complicated (province-specific) revenue-sharing formulae. The provincial governments in turn negotiated individual revenue contracts with the local governments. Since the marginal tax rate set by the central government varied tremendously across provinces, the incentive of the provincial and local governments to engage in local economic development in order to generate tax revenue also varied tremendously. Given the importance of Shanghai to the central coffers, its marginal tax rate was set higher than that of most coastal provinces until the early 1990s.

The fiscal decentralization might have helped economic growth, but this led to state revenue declining from 35 percent of GDP in 1978 to 14 percent in 1992, producing a near fiscal crisis for the state. The state lacked the funds to invest in infrastructure projects to remove production bottlenecks, and to undertake poverty alleviation programs. The practice of each provincial government covering more of its expenditure from local revenue necessarily meant reduced development expenditure in the poorest provinces that had been receiving fiscal subsidies from the center. The tax reform of 1994 that had the value-added tax as its center-piece has reduced the discriminatory elements of the fiscal system, and restored the fiscal capacity of the state to help the poorer provinces.

The deregulation of prices in the industrial sector mainly took the form of a dual track price system for industrial inputs. Since the central and western provinces were the main suppliers of raw industrial materials, the continuation of artificially low prices for these industrial inputs meant that the dual track pricing system was in effect transferring income from the interior producers to the coastal factories. The elimination of the dual-track price system in the 1990-91 period was an equitable move from the viewpoint of regional disparity.

The Open Door Policy was initially limited to two southern provinces (Guangdong and Fujian), then gradually extended to larger geographical units: first along the coast, then in the inland provinces. The distributional consequence of this selective opening-up process was a heavy concentration of foreign investment flows and international trade activity in the coastal provinces, particularly Guangdong. The dominance of Guangdong is a natural consequence of the fact that this province is one of those having received the greatest benefit from the open door policy, notably through the establishment of the three Special Economic Zones of Shenzhen, Zhuhai and Shantou as early as the beginning of the 1980s.

The implementation of regional preferential policies has gone through 3 broad stages during which open economic zones have been settled to provide investors with various preferential tax treatments, exemptions on duties, etc.:

1. Early 80s: limited extent to Guangdong and Fujian provinces, with the establishment of Special Economic Zones (SEZ) in 1979-80.
2. Mid to end of the 80s: coastal preference strategy enforcement, with the designation of Coastal Open Cities (COC), entitled to settle their own Economic and Technological Development Zones (ETDZ), in 1984, followed by the establishment of Coastal Open Economic Zones (COEZ) in 1985, an Open Coastal Belt (OCB) in 1988 and the Shanghai Pudong New Area in 1990.
3. Early 90s: further extension towards whole China, after Deng Xiaoping southern tour in 1992. During this year, new open economic zones were officially started in Major Cities along the Yangtze River (MC), Border Economic Cooperation Zones (BECZ), Capital Cities of inland provinces and autonomous regions (CC), ETDZ and Bonded Areas (BA).

The establishment of these various types of economic zones over time. As pointed out by Yang (1997) and Ma (1999), the acceleration in the opening-up process in 1992 led to an inflated number of so-called open economic zones set up by local official without proper authorization. Besides the official policy launched by the State Council, the 30 provinces, as well as hundreds of counties and townships indeed started to formulate their own preferential policies for foreign investment in specific "development zones". As a consequence of this "zone fever"

(Yang, 1997, p. 53), there were around 2,000 open economic zones of any kind at and above the county level by 1993 (and probably even more below the county level), offering tax exemptions and reductions of all sorts in order to attract investment. Following the implementation of the austerity program in 1993, most of these unapproved zones have been closed, and regional policies have tended to equalize over time (at least up to the end of the 90s).

The gradual geographical extension of the reforms brought about a highly unequal regional distribution of foreign capital flows throughout the period. In 1983, nearly 93 per cent of foreign direct investment went to the coastal provinces, including 69 per cent for Guangdong alone. This imbalance decreased slightly over time, but 88 per cent of foreign direct investment (FDI) flows still went to the coastal region in 1996; however, the share of Guangdong had dropped sharply (to 28 per cent) in favour of other coastal provinces such as Fujian, Jiangsu and Shanghai, which attracted approximately 30 per cent of total FDI. If we reason in terms of disparities, as above, these developments indicate a trend towards equalization within the coastal zone. In the inland provinces there are inverse trends, however, between an increase in the central region's share of FDI over time (from 1.1 percent in 1983 to 9.5 percent in 1996) and a decrease in the western region's share (from 6 percent to 2.5 percent).

The cumulative FDI flows for the 1983-96 period was 88.3 percent to the coastal provinces, 8.3 percent to the central provinces, and 3.4 percent to the western provinces. Guangdong received 30 percent of it.

Examination of international trade reveals the same inequalities between coastal provinces and inland provinces. At the national level, exports grew at an average annual rate of 17 per cent over the 1978-96 period, but once again it was Guangdong that derived the greatest benefit from this growth. In 1978, Guangdong was the third-ranking province in terms of exports, after Shanghai and Liaoning, but in 1996 it was far ahead of the other provinces and accounted for 34 per cent of

China's exports. As in the case of FDI, the coastal provinces were much more export-oriented than the inland provinces, and although the coastal region's share of total exports fell over the period (87 per cent in 1996 versus 93 per cent in 1978), it remains very high. The share of exports in GDP is also four to five times higher in the coastal region (30 per cent in 1996) than in the two other regions (around 6 per cent each).

The geographical distribution of imports has changed very little since 1978, and the figures for 1996 are very similar to those for exports: 87 per cent, 8 per cent and 5 per cent respectively for the coast, the center and the west. As was the case for exports, the structure of imports within the coastal region changed in favour of Guangdong province (whose share in total imports rose from 26 per cent in 1978 to 40 per cent in 1996) to the detriment of the municipality of Shanghai in particular.

The high level of foreign trade activity in the coastal provinces is generally linked to that of FDI, since foreign enterprises are supposed to be inherently more export-oriented than domestic firms.

Indeed, the contribution of foreign firms to China's total foreign trade has grown since the mid-1980s. Exports by firms with foreign ownership amounted to 41 per cent of total exports in 1996, as against 1 per cent in 1985. Enterprises established in the coastal region accounted for nearly all of these (98 per cent on average in 1994). Moreover, the share of foreign firms in total imports rose from 5 per cent in 1985 to 54 per cent in 1996, since such firms on the whole imported more than they exported. As in the case of exports, the import share of foreign firms is highest in the southern coastal provinces.

Provincial enlargement experience, 1952-1998

The distribution of per capita GDP growth rates is given in Tables 3 and 4. The periodisation follows the following policy episodes:

-1953-58: the normal centrally-planned economy

-1959-65: the Great Leap Forward, the economic collapse and recovery

-1966-1978: the Cultural Revolution

-1979-1984: first reform phase, emphasis on agriculture

-1985-1991: second reform phase, Oskar Lange-inspired reforms

-1992-1998: third reform phase, ultimate goal is a market economy with substantial diversification of ownership structure.

Any unconditional b-convergence across Chinese provinces, during the planned and reform periods. This is confirmed by cross-section regressions on the whole period and by sub-periods (not reported here) which all indicate that there is no significant relationship between the per capita GDP annual growth rate and its initial level, except for the last sub-period (1992-98) during which a b-divergence phenomenon emerged.

Provincial Income Disparity, 1952-1998

The movements of the coefficient of variation of provincial income summarized that:

1 China experienced much greater fluctuations in income disparity in the planned period of 1952-1978 than in the reform period after 1978. During the planned period, the coefficient moved up 0.13 in 1952-60, down 0.16 in 1960-62, and then up 0.29 in 1962-78 compared with the 0.05 decline in 1978-87, and the 0.09 rise in 1987-98.

2 Periods of extremely low inequality were economically difficult periods when much of the population were brought to subsistence level. 1952 was right after a warring period that lasted over twenty-five years, and 1962 was the depth of the famine caused by the Great Leap Forward. To put it cynically, poverty is always distributed equally because those with extremely low income will not be around to be counted.

3 The overall increase of 0.26 in inequality during the planned period greatly exceeded the 0.03 increase in

inequality during the reform period. Market economics may not have decreased inequality, but economic planning certainly increased it faster.

The ranking of provincial income in key years of China's economic history, and summarizes the changes in the relative fortune of each province in the planned period of 1952-1978, and in the reform period after 1978. They show that:

1 The chief beneficiaries of the planned period were Beijing, Qinghai and Ningxia, and the biggest losers of the reform period were Qinghai and Ningxia. The rise of Beijing's relative standing, and its maintenance of the attained income rank, reflects its paramount political status in the country. The initial large gains of Qinghai and Ningxia (up 10 and 8 places respectively), and the subsequent large reversals (15 and 10 respectively) showed the tremendous transfer of resources under the third front industrialization program.

2 There has been basically no change at the very top and the very bottom of the scale. Indeed, the three municipalities remained the richest throughout the whole period and Yunnan, Shaanxi, Gansu and Guizhou remained the poorest provinces. Mobility, both upward and downward, is a middle-class phenomenon.

3 The significant winners of the reform period were generally the coastal provinces, especially Fujian, Shangdong, and Hainan. The traditional industrial bases of northern China (Heilongjiang, Jilin, Liaoning) and western provinces experienced a decline in the relative scale of regional per capita income.

The two tails of the income distribution, the movements in the gap between the five richest provinces and the five poorest provinces. The absolute income gap has increased tremendously over both the planned and reform periods. When we examine the gap in relative terms first by normalizing the absolute gap with the average national income, and second by the ratio of the two incomes, the evidence is mixed. The relative gap decreased from 1.5 in 1978 to 1.4 in 1998, but the income ratios rose from 3.4 to 3.6. In any case, the widening of relative income in the reform period is small compared with the widening in the planned period, confirming the conclusions drawn from the movements of the coefficient of variation.

PROVINCIAL DIFFERENCE IN GROWTH: GEOGRAPHY AND POLICY

We are presenting this section in telegraphic form because we are out of time. Please accept our apologies. (Wing Woo is responsible for this situation, the other co-authors completed all their contributions in good time.)

Regional inequality in China has been extensively studied in recent years.

The reform pogrom has increased growth rates of the coastal provinces by

(a) allowing them to take advantage of their locations to participate in the international division labor, i.e. pure geography effects,

(b) giving them preferential tax policies which enable them to have more retained funds to invest more and hence grow faster, i.e. fiscal subsidies

(c) giving them preferential access to foreign capital which increased total capital formation, and hence income. i.e. foreign funds.

So coastal dummy proxies for two effects: geography and preferential policy. Jian, Sachs and Warner (1996) Unconditional convergence in 1978-93, but convergence disappears with addition of agricultural share of GDP and coastal dummy. One interpretation is that the convergence is temporary.

Since coastal provinces were initially discriminated against, and in the middle-income group, the reform program allowed them to grow faster to catch up with the traditionally rich Manchurian provinces, so provincial inequality falls. But if the coast effect is constant, the growth of the coastal provinces need not slow down once they reach income level of the Manchurian provinces. If so, then inequality will increase. If the coast effect comes from the preferential policies, then their removal will slow down the coastal provinces and maintain existing inequality.

If the coast effect represents geographical advantage, removal of preferential policy would slow increase in provincial inequality but would not reduce it.

Problem: geographical and policy effects not disentangled.

Wang and Hu (1999)

Preferential policies generated the high growth of the coastal provinces. Proof is that foreign capital has flowed most to the provinces that received preferential policies.

Conducted horse-race between economic model and policy model. Economic model says foreign funds flow to areas with best growth potential (indicated by adequacy of infrastructure, availability of educated workforce, and size of market) Policy model says foreign funds flow to areas with most preferential tax treatment. Addition of preferential policy index removes statistical significance of variables championed by economic model.

Since provincial FDI is highly correlated with provincial GDP growth, Wang and Hu regressions could be interpreted as provincial growth regressions. Coastal growth is thus more the result of preferential policies than of their more favorable economic conditions.

Wang and Hu talks about importance of physical terrain in determining economic growth. They also note that their "policy variable may also reflect a province's geographical location." Yet, their policy discussion ignores the geography factor as the main reason for the success of the coastal provinces.

Debatable assumption is that if coastal region did not have preferential policies, then more of FDI would have flowed into interior provinces. If FDI was aimed at producing for China's market, FDI might have moved to central provinces. If FDI was aimed at export-processing activities, then FDI could have gone to Southeast Asia instead. Given existence of preferential tax policies in other developing countries, absence of it in China would have reduced export-oriented FDI, and hence growth.

Problem: geographical and policy effects not disentangled.

Bao, Chang, Sachs and Woo (2001) Assumes that each province is a small economic unit (a price taker), and there is adequate labor and capital mobility within China. So individual growth not constrained by own amounts of L and K.

Finds that geographical determinism fits the data well.

Problem: Did not show that policy does not matter, especially if policy stance is collinear with geographical location.

Demurger (2000) Specification based on conventional growth model fits the data well.

Significance of FDI represents presence of externalities because total investment is already in equation, albeit not significant.

If FDI had come in for export-processing activities, was FDI geographically-induced or policy-induced?

Zhang (2000) Export (more generally, international integration) reached critical mass to become important boost to China's economy only after 1985, which explains why coastal dummy and export variable are insignificant in 1978-84 and significant in 1985-95.

Same problem: geographical and policy effects not disentangled.

Our approach in this paper We replace the black box of coastal dummy with two variables:

(a) transportation cost and pure geography effect represented by the proportion of provincial population in 1994 living within 100 kilometers of the coast or navigable rivers (excluding coastline above the winter extent of sea ice and the rivers that flow to this coastline).

(b) a preferential policy index for each province.

We also try other geographical variables like: Distance from the coast [*Distf* = 1/(1+distance in km)] Percentage of area within a province with a slope greater than 10% [*Slope10*] Average slope of a province [*Slavge*] Average elevation [*Elavge*] Note that topography indicators can be considered as measuring both agricultural feasibility (important up to the end of 70s) and market accessibility (from the 80s onward).

Two sets of regressions are run: one including all provinces, but Tibet; the other excluding municipalities (considered as potential "outliers" due to their particular size, economic structure, administrative role, etc.).

Constructing the "preferential policy" index The is based on the number of designated open economic zones in a province, and the extent of the preferential treatment The construction of this index relies on available information on designated "open economic zones" across China, gathered from different sources, as well as a subjective classification according to their importance in terms of special treatments given to investors and industrial enterprises.

Given the various degrees of preferential policies open economic zones offer, we gave to their host provinces the following weights: Weight = 3: SEZ and Shanghai Pudong New Area. Weight = 2: ETDZ and BECZ. Weight = 1: COC, COEZ, OCB, MC, BA, and CC. Weight = 0: No open zone.

First set of regressions: cross-section on 1979-98 average per capita GDP growth rate. Topographical variables not significant and hence omitted final specification. *Pop100km* and *Policy* always statistically significant. Amount of SOEs negatively related to growth, albeit not statistically significant. Municipalities don't fit into equation well, which explains why Eq 4 is better than previous three. Use of Coast (instead of Pop100km and Policy) worsens the results, suggesting that its inclusion results in misspecification. Eq 7 is preferred equation. Being a coastal province yields a higher growth rate of 1.4 percentage points.

THE LIMITS OF FINANCIAL INTERDEPENDENCE: SINO-JAPANESE RELATIONS

The principal argument of this paper is that the growing economic interdependence between China and Japan in the post Cold War period has not been matched by a corresponding improvement in relations in other spheres. On the contrary many in the foreign policy elites in both countries sense that the differences (or the 'gap') between them is widening. This suggests that unless accompanied by social, intellectual and political exchanges, economic exchanges - however extensive - cannot be relied upon to overcome the many problems that beset relations between the two great countries of East Asia.

Perhaps the most important newly emerging dimension of the relations between China and Japan is the strategic one involving the management of their bilateral relations and more broadly those of the region as a whole. Neither appears to take into account the national security interests of the other and there is no mechanism for them to meet on a regular basis to discuss the broader strategic issues. In practice both sides address these matters through the prism of their relations with the United States -hence the emphasis both sides give to the so-called triangular relationship. However, even if seen within the framework of such a triangle the Sino-Japanese side is much much thinner than either that of the US and Japan or of the US and China.

It will be argued that in the absence of closer social and intellectual exchanges the prospects for an historic reconciliation between China and Japan will be remote and in the absence of a thoroughgoing strategic dialogue the prospects for their emergence as regional partners rather than regional competitors will diminish. The result will contribute to uncertainty and instability within the region that no amount of economic interdependence will be able to redress.

Economic Interdependence

China's leaders have long claimed that the Sino-Japanese economies are highly complementary. Japan with its resource poor and high-tech advanced economy, it is argued, should find a natural partner in China with its resource rich, more backward, but developing economy. Indeed it would seem that Chinese expectations have at last begun to bear fruit as Japan has emerged as China's greatest trading partner and China as second biggest to Japan (after the US). The value of their mutual trade, according to Chinese figures, has grown from c. $12 billion in 1990 to $83 billion in 2000 when it accounted for more than 22% of China's total trade. Paralleling this has been a corresponding growth in Japanese FDI. Following their caution in the 1980s Japanese companies have rapidly increased their investment in China in the 1990s. Again according to Chinese figures, Japanese FDI in 1991 came to $579 million and in 1998 it reached $3.2 billion. By May 1999 there had been 18,140 Japanese direct investment projects in China with a total agreed investment of $33.6 billion and actual investment of £23.6 billion. By the late 1990s China ranked second only to the US as a target for Japanese investment.

As a 'civilian' power Japan has long used its economic capabilities as one of the principal instruments in the conduct of foreign policy. Ostensibly, Japanese Official Development Assistance (ODA) involves the separation of economics from politics. But as it has been used to promote Japanese business interests, it can be seen to have advanced Japan's interests as a whole, especially in the context of a country that was the first to advance the concept of 'comprehensive security'. It had its origins in the war-reparations agreed to compensate countries in Southeast Asia, when they were used to to reinvigorate Japanese corporations. Although ODA was not extended to China until 1979 and as late as 1993 Indonesia received most aid, China has become the main beneficiary of the Japanese ODA. Apart from serving Japanese commercial interests, the extent of ODA to China may also be seen as in part a means to assuage Japanese guilt and in part to serve Japanese interests in seeing China develop economically so as to encourage domestic stability and to promote China's integration into the wider world. According to Chinese figures, Japanese governmental loans (at minimal interest) to China from 1979 to 2000 came to 2.58 trillion Yen, accounting for over 40% of all the financial cooperation between China and other governments. From 1979 to 1995 Japan provided three batches of energy loans to China valued at 1.7 trillion yen. Over and beyond that Japan provided free aid from 1979 to March 2000 totaling 1.153 trillion yen.

Interestingly, this significant degree of economic interaction between the two sides, does not appear to have produced significant constituencies in either country who have been ready to promote publicly the importance of cultivating good relations with other. In 1995/6 when Japan suspended ODA to China because of its conduct of nuclear tests, there was not much evidence of opposition within Japan. Indeed the Ministry of Foreign Affairs was the recipient of considerable criticism from other ministries and LDP politicians for its eagerness to resume ODA. In so far as ODA was politicised it was to the detriment of China. Japanese also complained that the Chinese side had withheld from its own people the true extent of the Japanese contribution to China's economic development. Until 1995 the bulk of its ODA went to infrastructure projects such as roads, bridges, power plants, etc. In fact it was only after this was raised with Premier Zhu Rongji during his visit to Japan in 2000 that the Chinese authorities began to make the figures about the magnitude of the Japanese contribution more publicly available. Since 1995 Japanese ODA has reflected another dimension of the interdependence of the two countries that underscores elements of concern rather than cordiality. Japanese ODA is no longer targeted at promoting economic development as such, but it has been re-targeted to address environmental problems and poverty alleviation. The former stems from Japanese worries about acid rain and dust blown in from China and the latter reflects Japanese anxieties about potential social instability in China that could also be damaging to Japan.

To be sure the economic interdependence between China and Japan is crucially important to the relationship as a whole. The leaders are particularly conscious of its beneficial significance. It also ensures that both sides can point to underlying positive value in the relationship. Arguably, the economic interdependence acts as a constraint against allowing relations to deteriorate unduly. But so far there is little evidence of these considerations spilling over into other aspects of their relations. Thus although there are arrangements for military exchanges and security consultations, there is no sign that these have led to serious discussions about the management of security in the region. More indicative of the nature of the relationship is the complaint by a leading official of the Japan Center for International Exchange of there being a "huge lacuna" in the absence of a system of cooperation involving in particular China and Japan as well to a lesser extent China and the US.

THE POST COLD WAR CONTEXT

The end of the Cold War fundamentally changed the strategic context of Sino-Japanese relations. The demise of the Soviet Union brought to an end their shared opposition to the threat from Moscow. This necessarily cast the US-Japan alliance in a new and ambiguous light, especially as Japanese and American security interests were no longer as closely congruent as before. Indeed it was possible to argue that as far as China was concerned Japan faced the twin problems of either being 'entrapped' or 'abandoned' by its more powerful ally on whom its security depended.).

Evidence of fearing of being entrapped into a hostile policy of isolating and applying economic sanctions against China appeared soon after the Tiananmen massacre. Japan was the first of the Western allies to resume loans and it was the first to send an incumbent head of government to visit China. The fear of 'abandonment' was evident in the so-called 'Japan by-passing' practiced by President Bill Clinton in the course of his visit to China in 1998. As seen from China, the US-Japan Security Alliance was acceptable if it did indeed keep the 'cork' on the bottle of Japan's military potential, but it was quite a different matter if the alliance were to serve the purpose of co-opting Japan into becoming an active partner in American regional security objectives. This is precisely what some in

China suspect as a result of the 1996 agreement on new guidelines for US-Japan defence cooperation and of Japan's commitment to participate in research into theatre missile defence (TMD).

More broadly from a strategic perspective, the end of the Cold War brought to light fundamental problems in the place that Japan and China envisioned the other occupying in the region and in the wider world. Most Japanese saw their alliance with the US as central to their strategic security into the indefinite future. Accordingly, they accepted implicitly or explicitly a version of *Pax Americana.* That ranged in Japanese thinking from a vision of America as the provider of hegemonic stability to a vision of a more liberal order centred on free trade and the promotion of democracy. Moreover the security alliance with the US is seen as central to cultivating a durable stable relationship with China. The alliance is seen as providing China with a reassurance against the re-emergence of Japan as a military power while allowing it sufficient space to develop a more political international profile commensurate with its economic standing.

The problem with this Japanese outlook in its various formulations is that it is at variance with the vision emanating from China. In the Chinese view American hegemony (benign or otherwise) is the problem rather than the solution. Chinese leaders have made it abundantly clear their preference for a multi-polar world order in which their relations with other important countries will be conducted through partnerships of different kinds. These are to be buttressed by dialogues about security and consultations about economic exchanges as conducted in different multilateral fora. While they accept the basics of a liberal order that is confined to the promotion of free trade in the interests of 'peace and development', they reject the intrusiveness of the promotion of democracy. The bottom line for China's leaders is the preservation of Communist Party rule.

Many Japanese see the Chinese position as favouring a balance of power approach arising out of their realist thinking that is deeply embedded in the outlook of China's leaders. Whether or not the Chinese seek a new balance of power, there is no doubt that they see their power and international standing on the rise and the key question for them is whether or not the Americans will try to obstruct that rise. Hence they are concerned by what they see as the emergence of Japan as a more active partner of the United States in the pursuit of American military strategy in the region. At the same time the Chinese have expressed their displeasure at every Japanese attempt to chart an independent role for themselves. Thus even the participation of Japanese Self Defense Forces in non-combat roles in UN PKO has drawn criticism from China. However, it is not clear what Japanese role would be acceptable to China's leaders other than one it is politically and strategically quiescent until such time as presumably it would be overshadowed by China.

Against this background it is hardly surprising that the remaining legacy of the Cold War in East Asia has not brought Japan and China closer together in finding means to address them. That legacy includes the unresolved problems of Korea and Taiwan and the continued rule of China, North Korea and Vietnam by communist parties.

Even though all of these issues were transformed in the new era none of them may be said to have led to a closer understanding between China and Japan. China was closely involved in the formal negotiations affecting North-South relations through the 'Two+Two" arrangements (i.e., the two Koreas, China and the US) and it did not respond positively to Japanese (or even Russian) attempts to join. China meanwhile was active behind the scenes in both supporting the North and facilitating the American negotiations that led to the 1994 Framework agreement. Privately, Chinese diplomats made no secret of their expectation that a unified Korea would come under China's influence at the expense of Japan. The democratic transformation of Taiwan increased Japanese sympathy for the island and the Chinese attempt at intimidation by missile testing in 1996 had the effect of intensifying popular Japanese concerns about the resurgence of China. Chinese protests about the possible application of TMD to Taiwan and about the operational extension of the new US-Japan guidelines to Taiwan waters received little or no sympathy in Japan. Meanwhile although Japanese have welcomed the Chinese continued emphasis on the priorities of economic growth and development, the underlying concern about the destabilising effects of rapid economic growth and the decline of the capacity for good governance in China has, if anything, increased.

The multilateral fora established within the region since the end of the Cold War, such as APEC (Asia Pacific Economic Cooperation) and the ARF (ASEAN Regional Forum) whose formation was very much assisted by Japan may have played some role in encouraging cooperation within the region, but they have done little to promote closer interactions between Japan and China. They have not served as a vehicle for 'rehabilitating' Japan in Chinese eyes, nor can the Japanese be entirely satisfied with them as vehicles for consolidating China as a good regional citizen. Indeed when the financial storm broke in Asia in 1997, many in China blamed Japan for having earlier revalued its currency. Bilateral relations were hardly improved by China receiving much praise especially from the Americans for refraining from revaluing its currency, while Japan received opprobrium despite being the largest international donor to the rescue packages and despite having its proposal to establish an Asian Monetary Fund thwarted by the US. The lack of coordination between China and Japan became manifest when China turned down the invitation publicly offered by Japan for it to join the Group of 7 (or 8), then due to meet in Japan. A prominent member of a key think tank in Beijing told me that an important reason for the Chinese refusal was that the invitation came from Japan. It remains to be seen whether the group ASEAN + Three (the 10 Southeast Asian states, China, Japan and S. Korea) that was formed two years ago in the aftermath of an ASEAN meeting will bear fruit. A currency swap arrangement has been agreed, but it has yet to be tested.

BILATERAL DIFFERENCES: THE AGENDA EXTENDED

There have been three long-standing problems in Sino-Japanese relations: The treatment of the historical legacy of Japanese invasion of China; the Taiwan question; and the disputed sovereign claims to the Diao Yu Dao /Sengaku Islands. None has approached solution in the post Cold War period and, arguably, the intensity of the first two has increased. It is significant, however, that the agenda of the issues in dispute has increased and that the gap between the two sides has widened.

It has been argued on both sides that relations at the governmental level have improved and that whenever problems threatened to disrupt relations they were dealt with fairly rapidly. Nevertheless new issues of substance emerged in the 1990s associated with each side's strategic worries about the other. These included Japanese concerns about Chinese military activities in the Straits of Taiwan and the South China Sea and, more recently, Chinese ships surveying close to Japanese waters; Japan's freezing of aid in response to China's resumption of nuclear tests in 1995; Japan's identification of China as a potential source of external threat in the 1997 Defence White Paper; Chinese concerns about the re-invigoration of the of the US-Japan Security Treaty, particularly due to Japan's ambiguity about its application to Taiwan and Japan's participation in America's TMD programmes; and lastly, China's continuing warnings about a renewal of Japanese militarism.

It will be seen that the common thread to the problems of the 1990s is the growing uncertainties in each country about the strategic significance of the perceived growing military clout of the other. It is that which gives an edge to Chinese criticisms of the history issues, whether because of activities and statements by right wing politicians or because of ministerial approval of school textbooks that skate over the excesses of Japanese aggression, or because of disparaging remarks by ministers and visits by them to the Ysakuni Shrine to the war dead. In the Chinese view these illustrate Japan's failure to come to terms with its past history of aggression and war crimes and demonstrate that it is not legitimate for Japan to acquire force projection capabilities. That is regarded as all the more pressing in view of Japan's new commitments in relations to the US. At the same time Japanese complaints indicate concern about growing Chinese ability to project force in the adjacent seas and its readiness to engage in coercive diplomacy, especially with regard to Taiwan. Additionally, there is concern that difficulties in managing the social consequences of the rapid economic growth at home may make China more aggressive in the pursuit of its national goals abroad.

These strategic worries have acquired greater salience in view of separate social and political changes in each country that have combined to make each one less receptive to the concerns of the other. The change of generations has brought to the fore leaders in both countries who have little first hand knowledge and interest in the other. The late Zhou Enlai had actually lived in Japan and many of his generation had studied there. Indeed there was a saying in China that those who studied in Japan (1890s-1920s) returned as revolutionaries and those who returned from study in the United States were reformers. Even those like Mao and Deng who had not visited Japan, nevertheless had a high respect for their capabilities and achievements, notwithstanding the war of aggression. But the current generation of leaders in China headed by Jiang Zemin had no such experience, nor have their successors, as typified by Hu Jintao. Moreover few of the generations following them will have studied in Japan, although many would have studies in the West. On the Japanese side, the post war leaders who had intimate knowledge of Japan and/or were personally affected by a sense of war-guilt, such as those who had normalised relations with Beijing in 1972, have long since passed on. The current Japanese leadership lacks intimate experience of the war that ended more than 55 years ago and is more likely to be affected by experience of Japan's post war privations. As a result the lack of institutionalised patterns of exchanges is no longer compensated for by the kind of personal links that matter so much in East Asian political culture especially in China.

The generational divide is more evident among the young. In China the overwhelming evidence is that younger people have negative images of Japan and that much of this may be derived from the one-sided accounts of the officially inspired media. Responding to both Chinese and Japanese newspaper polls in December 1996 and June 1997 respectively, roughly 41% of the Chinese respondents either had "bad" impressions of or "disliked" Japan and between 17% and 10% had a "good" impression or "liked" Japan. While 44% in the one, and 35% in the other, had neither good nor bad feelings about the country. As far as Japan is concerned public opinion has swung decisively away from a very positive attitude towards China in the 1980s to a more negative one in the 1990s. Thus for most of the 1980s more than 70% of respondents to official polls had "friendly feelings" towards China with around 20% claiming "unfriendly feelings". By 1996 the ratio for the first time showed that more felt unfriendly feelings towards China by the margin of 51: 45%.

Perhaps more significant is the impression of leading scholars on foreign relations in each country that generally speaking there was a lack of interest by the young especially in the culture and contemporary developments of the other country. By comparison, the younger generation in each country was much more interested in developments in the United States. Although they conceded that the products of each country were being bought more extensively in the other, they nevertheless held that that did not lead to a corresponding growth in interest or curiosity about the other. They claimed that intellectual circles in their respective countries were far more familiar with intellectual and academic debates in America and Western Europe than they were with corresponding developments in the other country. Interestingly, the evidence of student interest in each other's countries as illustrated by numbers studying there would imply a growing interest. Following changes in law and the provision of funding by the Japanese government in the 1980s student numbers from China began to grow from about 2,000 in 1986 to nearly 20,000 in 1992 and to over 24,000 in 1995. They accounted for 45% of all foreign students in Japan and constituted about 60% of the number of Chinese students in the United States. Meanwhile nearly 13,000 students from Japan went to China for study or technical training in 1995, or about a third of those who went to the US. These figures clearly go against the general impression conveyed by the scholars I had interviewed. But a closer look suggests that they may not have been so wrong after all. A more telling set of figures as far as intellectual development is concerned is that about 82% of the Chinese students in America in 1995 were graduate students. Only about 35% of all foreign students in Japan were graduate students and the Chinese proportion would have been even less. Moreover there were 9,228 Chinese students carrying out research in the US as compared with only 317 in Japan. There can be little doubt as to the intellectual dominance of the United States in this regard. This not only illustrates an important dimension of American "soft power", but it also suggests that, despite the animosity felt towards the United States on nationalistic grounds in China, or indeed in Japan, there is a fundamental reserve of understanding and curiosity in both countries towards America that is lacking in either country with regard to the other.

The passing of the Cold War has also given rise to a new national assertiveness in both China and Japan as each seeks to establish a more active and independent national identity now that the biploar constraints have been removed. Japanese self-confidence may have become muted after the burst of its bubble economy in the early 1990s and its apparent incapacity to break out of the sterile impasse that gripped both its economy and its politics. Nevertheless Japan has initiated a number of important diplomatic and political moves that are indicative of a more internationally active country. These have been accompanied by debates about foreign and defence policy that not only call for more political activism, but which raise the prospect of a more fundamental change in Japan's international identity. Interestingly, Japan's key role in the launching of regional multilateral consultative organsiations, notably APEC and the ARF, was not challenged by China's leaders. The PRC was pleased to join both even though it recognised that one of the objectives of the organisers was to involve China in the hope that it would come to accept the restraining norms implicit in regional cooperation. Doubtless China's leaders saw positive benefits for them in earning goodwill by joining these essentially consultative organisations that could not commit China to do things that it did not wish to do. However, nearly all of Japan's other initiatives have elicited varying degrees of hostility or skepticism from China. The Chinese, for example, were not happy with the sending of Japanese minesweepers at the end of the gulf War, or the deployment of members of the Self Defence Force to serve with UN PKO in Cambodia even though were explicitly prohibited from assuming combat roles. Although the Chinese did not openly oppose Japan's bid to become a permanent member of the UN Security Council, it was clear that they did not support it. However, the Chinese opposed and therefore vetoed the Japanese proposal to establish a combined force against piracy in the South China Sea.

As we have seen, the new national assertiveness has separately led each side to take a harsher view of the other. In the case of China the officially inspired education in patriotism has emphasised an interpretation of modern history that places China as a victim, with the concluding and unresolved chapter focusing on Japanese aggression. As a consequence, indignation about Japan and its alleged failure to express an adequate apology is central to the new found nationalist ideology of the young, which in turn constrains the Chinese leadership. Having stoked the fires of youthful nationalism as unifying element at a time in which communist ideology has lost meaning and support, China's leaders are now fearful of allowing it full expression. Conscious of modern Chinese history when student demonstrations against alleged humiliations by foreigners end up being turned against the incumbent government for being too pusillanimous, China's leaders in the 1990s have deliberately prevented students from demonstrating against Japan. But as several of prominent Chinese scholars and advisers on foreign affairs pointed out to me in July 2000, the leadership in Beijing has been "too weak" to give a proper lead on the issue. They argue that insufficient recognition is given to Japanese accomplishments in developing its economy and its technology to extremely high levels. A few also deplored the way in which the strength of feelings about adherence to peace and to the pursuit of a role as a civilian power was ignored in the official media. At least one professed admiration for Japan as a democracy.

In Japan with the passing of the 'war generation' there is a growing impatience with Chinese criticism of Japanese failure to come to terms with its past. Chinese official complaints are seen as instrumental and manipulative as they always seem to intensify when the Chinese government is pressing with its demands either for more ODA or to prevent Japan from pursuing policies to which it objects. In particular Japanese have long objected to the way in which the Chinese seize on remarks by unrepresentative right wingers. But more recently some intellectuals representing mainstream conservatives and more central opinion have written a controversial new textbook that seeks to find pride in modern Japanese history and see virtue in the Meiji Restoration of 1868 and in the wars against China in 1895 and against Russia in 1905. Such views, of course, widen still further the gap with China and other neighbours, notably South Korea.

Some Strategic Conundrums

Currently, stable relations between China and Japan is only possible because of the role played by the United States. The American security alliance with Japan assures the Chinese that the cork remains on the bottle of Japanese "militarism". However, as realists, China's leaders may believe, like Kenneth Waltz, that it's only a question of time before Japan is driven by the logic of international anarchy to become a military power commensurate with its economic power. But China's more immediate security concern regarding Japan is not that it will emerge any time soon as an independent military power in its own right, but rather that it will play a more active security role within the region in support of the United States.

That raises several problems for Chinese strategists. While they object to what they see as "American hegemonism" that they perceive as seeking to subvert communist rule at home and contain China's rise abroad. In this perspective Japan and its new strategic guidelines agreed with the US has become its partner in establishing a ring of containment. But any attempt to weaken the alliance risks accelerating the rise of Japan as an independent military power that could project force throughout maritime East Asia long before China could do so. Meanwhile in attempting to demonstrate sufficient military strength to exercise coercive diplomacy to intimidate those who favour independence in Taiwan, the Chinese have unwittingly provoked a security dilemma with Japan. Chinese missile exercises against Taiwan in 1995 and 1996 were instrumental in changing the image of China in Japan and China's fulminations against any form of missile defence as undermining their deterrent drove home to many in Japan that they (through the American bases in Japan) were a target for China's missiles. That was intensified by the shock of North Korea's Taepodong missile test in 1998 that splashed in the sea after passing over the central island of Japan. As a result there is greater support within Japan for participating in American research towards the development of a TMD system.

Whether or not the continued presence of American military bases in Japan is sustainable, China's leaders have to think through how a regional order can be made stable. Essentially, three options present themselves: To find a way of establishing a cooperative security framework that accepts the US-Japan alliance as an enduring structure. The second involves coming to terms with the prospect of Japan as a "normal" country that will develop into a military power free of the constraints of the American alliance. The third would result in a rising China that exercises dominance in the region with the acquiescence of a quiescent Japan and a tolerant America. Each one would involve considerable adjustments and mature leadership by the Chinese. They would have to display a great sensitivity to Japanese concerns and attitudes than they have shown so far.

The first option presents in one form or another a continuation of the present pattern. This is one that has served China well, enabling it to pursue its principal goals of economic growth and development in an international environment in which China has been free of threats of invasion for the first time for at least two hundred years. But it is an option that rubs up against China's nationalist aspirations as expressed in the officially endorsed campaigns of patriotic education. It would call for a leadership that could succeed in promoting the goals and values of cooperative security as against the realism that has dominated Chinese foreign policy. It would also call for a patriotism that ceased to portray the country as a victim of modern history with an unlimited sense of entitlement from the outside world.

The second option requires even greater adjustment. The removal of American forces from Japan would automatically bring about the multi-polar order that China's leaders claim to want. But it would also usher in a balance of power system into the region in which Japan would become a fully-fledged independent military power. That would require such a transformation of Chinese views of Japan that at present it seems almost inconceivable. However, the logic of Realism requires the Chinese to think along these lines.

Lastly, the option of *Pax Sinica* as an alternative to *Pax Americana* assumes that China can overcome its massive domestic problems and carry out political reform of sufficient depth as to make it acceptable and even attractive to its neighbours. China's leaders would have to be able to offer incentives and rewards to others rather than continue to make demands on its own behalf. They would have to project their rise in terms of universal ideals and principles.

Even to lay out these alternatives is to show that for the immediate future and probably the foreseeable future, China has no alternative, but to settle for some version of the first option. It possible to characterise Chinese debates about foreign policy as between those who look forward to a China that will continue to reform economically and ultimately politically at home and integrate more closely with the international economy abroad and those of a more conservative outlook who fear the dilution of communist party rule amid growing social dislocation and favour a slower course of reform and a nationalist resistance to integration with the outside world. It is tempting to suggest that much depends on the success of the reformers. But it seems that the prospects for operating successfully within the framework of the Japanese -American alliance depend ultimately on the capacity of China to remain relatively stable while continuing with its rapid economic growth.

Most Japanese cannot envision their immediate future without being bolstered by the alliance with the United States. But they too face difficult choices. On the one hand there are those who argue that Japan should become more of a "normal" country that lends greater support to American military campaigns according to the right of collective self defence. On the other hand are those that want Japan to emerge as a global "civilian" power as a model and contributor to less developed countries that promotes human rights, participates in UN PKO and contributes to improving the environment. If the former sees the alliance with the US in security terms, the latter understands it in terms of social relations, friendship and commitment to common values. The "civilianists" also place the alliance in a balance with a range of multilateral for a such as the UN, APEC, etc. The crucial difference between the two is their attitude towards China. The "civilianists" favour the cultivation of friendly relations and the promotion of a greater social and intellectual links between the two countries. The "normalists" are more wary of the rise of China and assert the need for containing it..

6

Prevention and Regional Permanence in South Asia

INTRODUCTION

During the times of crises, Indian and Pakistani leaders have claimed that their countries eschew nuclear "war-fighting," implying that their nuclear weapons are meant only for deterrence. Hence, Pakistani and Indian policy to develop short-range ballistic missiles, the so-called tactical nuclear weapons (TNWs) or non-strategic weapons, raises the question whether it is a volte-face.

The Western retrospective thinking of the Cold War holds that short-range ballistic missiles (SRBMs) are the sinews for nuclear war fighting whereas the so-called strategic nuclear weapons have just the opposite function. Pakistan flight-tested Hatf-IX — Nasr (victory) on 19 April 2011 and some considered it provocative. Three months later, India unveiled Prahaar (strike) through a flight test on 21 July 2011 but the debate remained muted.

Consequently, several questions have come to the fore, which are either partly explained or left unanswered. What prompted Pakistan and India to develop the short-range nuclear-capable ballistic missiles? If India enjoys conventional supremacy to "draw out [a] war and eviscerate Pakistani military capabilities," why would it secretly develop Prahaar for almost two years and react to the Nasr test within three months? How would the SRBMs affect deterrence and strategic stability in South Asia? Is the South Asian situation similar to the Cold War competition involving the TNWs, which has hitherto dragged on between Russia and the US?

This paper attempts to answer these questions by offering and validating the South Asian perspective as an alternative. For instance, the notion that nuclear weapons can be 'tactical' or non-strategic would be challenged. In the first part, a detailed profile of Nasr and Prahaar weapon systems has been given. The content analysis of available information on Nasr and Prahaar offers some unique inferences about the developmental trajectories, technological limitations, technological spin-offs, and command and control issues regarding these weapons. For instance, while Pakistan may exercise assertive control over deployment and employment of Nasr, analysis indicates that India may exercise delegative control over Prahaar, thereby increasing the possibility of inadvertent or unauthorised use.

In the second part of the paper, an attempt is made to establish the impact of these SRBMs on deterrence and regional stability. The assessment is based on the causal relationship of short-range ballistic missiles with deterrence and regional stability variables, using the assumptions of deterrence and rational choice theory. Effects of South Asian politics, economic factor and military developments on deterrence and strategic stability have been debated in detail.

Deterrence, strategic stability and SRBMs

The theoretical framework regarding the effect of short-range ballistic missiles on deterrence and stability in South Asia. It begins with operationalizing and testing two vague terms – TNWs and strategic stability. Thereafter, an attempt is made to establish a correlation of deterrence and strategic stability against political, economic and military factors peculiar to South Asia. While this causal relationship is identified between these complex and intertwined factors, the impact of SRBMs — like Nasr and Prahaar — on these factors has been dovetailed into the discussion.

The analysis in this part suggests that the Western categorisation of nuclear weapons into tactical (non-strategic) and strategic realms is inadequate, especially in the South Asian environment. Secondly, the so-called TNWs can add to credibility of deterrence if the will-to-use is unequivocally communicated to the adversary. Short-range ballistic missiles affect the strategic stability once a causal relationship is established with the military factors. If history is any guideline and assuming that both India and Pakistan behave as rational actors, then it is likely that SRBMs would only be used as a last resort. By way of causal relationship of likely impacts of these missiles on deterrence, it has been re-established that an assured second-strike capability would enhance the credibility of deterrence amongst these two rational actors. As mentioned in the first part, it may take up to seven years to induct Prahaar and Nasr into the land forces due to production and technical imperatives. The South Asian SRBMs would thus start affecting deterrence and regional stability around 2018 and by that time the new war fighting doctrines of India and Pakistan would also mature. Until then the existing regional dynamics in political, economic and military domains could continue to define the security landscape.

Definitional Issue

Given that there is no standard definition of TNWs, this paper offers an argument that what constitutes tactical or non-strategic in Western terms does not hold for South Asia, for several reasons. From the Western perspective, the so-called TNWs could be defined as short-range (from as less as 2-4 kilometres to a maximum up to 500 kms), low-yield weapons (0.4 - 40 kilotons to a maximum of 150 kilotons) meant for counter-force targeting in the battlefield. These can be both surface- — ballistic and cruise — and air-launched weapons.

Available literature on the so-called TNWs shows that the differentiation of tactical and strategic nuclear weapons is blurred and primarily rooted in American endeavour aiming to target Soviet/Russian mainland and its extended deterrence commitment to the European NATO allies. Range, and not the yield, would thus be the primary factor in deciding what constitutes a tactical or strategic nuclear weapon in the Cold War parlance. This implies that any weapon that could reach and hit American mainland would have 'strategic' effects and would be classified as a strategic weapon. If a weapon remained within the European battleground it could both be tactical or strategic.

"The distinction between what is tactical and what is strategic [is becoming] increasingly vague," infers a 2010 study by The National Defence University (NDU), Washington, DC. This could be illustrated by Israel's example where one-third of the population is under the threat of tactical ballistic missiles from regional adversaries. Hence, "those tactical missiles are a strategic threat."

Translating these definitional nuances of TNWs to South Asia, the following inferences can be drawn. Unlike the East-West proxy battlegrounds in Europe, which were geographically detached from the American and Soviet/Russian mainland, Pakistan and India have contiguous borders. Several cities and towns along the border and the Line of Control (LOC) in Kashmir would be within Prahaar as well as Nasr's range. Since India cites China as one of its security concerns, it could deploy Prahaar against it. Contiguous South Asian territory implies that the Indians could easily hit Lahore by Prahaar. Hence, the range and yield distinction used for SRBMs in a classic sense, would be irrelevant if Prahaar was used against Pakistan close to the border or LoC.

Hence, if the South Asians are forced to believe that their under-development SRBMs are theatre nuclear weapons in strictly Western sense, only a Kafkaesque definition comes up: Short-range ballistic missiles in 50-150 km range, with a maximum yield of 5 KT that would primarily target armed forces and affect only small border towns in desert terrain.

It is obvious such fine distinction cannot be maintained for the SRBMs. Theoretically, all nuclear weapons in South Asian territory would be strategic because they would have strategic effect in terms of damage, number of casualties, radiation fallout as well as the administrative and logistical challenges long after the weapons have been used. This does not factor-in in the dramatic consequences of larger yield weapons, if war escalates to an all-out nuclear exchange. That might be the reason why Pakistan and India did not use the term TNW in their statements for their short-range ballistic missiles. The TNW moniker appeared in the Western analyses and was conveniently bought by experts in South Asia.

Notional Paradigms

Deterrence theory provides the overarching framework to test the impact of SRBMs on the bilateral deterrence relationship and regional stability between Pakistan and India. However, two aspects related to the deterrence theory are more applicable to South Asia. These are "credible, minimum deterrence" policy and the "stability-instability paradox." The stability-instability paradox means that the probability of a direct war between two nuclear-armed states greatly decreases due to these weapons, but the probability of minor or indirect conflicts between them increases.

Both India and Pakistan essentially profess a policy of minimum deterrence. The adjective 'credible' is used either before or after "minimum" without a comma, hence creating an impression that there is either a doubt in the 'credibility' or in the 'minimum' nature of deterrence. "Credibility", Freedman once observed, "is the 'magic ingredient' of deterrence." The emphasis on 'credibility' is unique to South Asian nuclear powers. The nuance was probably invented to communicate to each other and to the older nuclear powers the 'credibility' of their will to use weapons. As and when the South Asians enhance their nuclear weapons capability to deliver an assured second strike, the word 'credible' might eventually fade away.

Impact of Military Factors

To establish a causal relationship between the SRBMs, regional stability and the credibility of deterrence, an overview of security paradigms and drivers that dictate nuclear doctrines and the force postures in South Asia, has been taken. Their cumulative relationship with these missiles has been established to assess the effect on strategic stability and the credibility of deterrence.

Pakistan considers India as the sole external threat to its security and its security policies and the nuclear doctrine appear to be driven by this paradigm. This India-centric security approach may be myopic and can be termed "Indyopia." Post-1998 security environment of Pakistan shows that the list of its external security challenges seems to be expanding and requires taking into consideration other entities or states. While national security policy, defence and nuclear doctrines, and consequent strategies account for India, potential adversaries must also be factored in.

Pakistan maintains ambiguity about its nuclear weapons employment policy and its nuclear doctrine. However, both can be discerned from several policy statements and positions taken over the years in arms control and disarmament affairs at domestic and international forums. The decision to develop short-range nuclear-capable ballistic missiles is considered a major development relating to Pakistan's credible deterrence policy. Previously, both Pakistan and India eschewed the so-called TNWs, but the situation has now changed. While the possible Pakistani in developing the 60-km-range Nasr are documented subsequently, it is unfathomable why India has been developing Prahaar since 2009 once it is considered to have "an interest in regional stability."

Besides countering India's proactive defence strategy that seeks to punish Pakistan by fighting a limited war, remaining below Islamabad's nuclear threshold, another contributory factor behind development of Nasr would be to address the growing conventional weapons asymmetry between the two countries. Pakistan army's Azm-e-Nau III — roughly means: renewed will — and the PAF's High Mark exercises were concluded successfully in April 2010. These exercises were tests of Pakistan Army's new war-fighting concept and PAF's new air strategy that were developed in response to India's proactive defence strategy.

It is fair to question why would Pakistan develop Nasr once it claims to have developed a credible conventional strategy to deter India? Also, why Pakistan would readily accept that it is a conventionally weak state compared to India? Is Pakistan not confident about its nuclear deterrence? Development of SRBMs can be considered adding 'another layer of deterrence' providing redundancy to the new war-fighting concept. Like India's proactive defence strategy, Pakistan's new war-fighting concept would also take some time to come into effect. Like India, Pakistan's policy of minimum deterrence "is not a fixity." Considering that India was already developing Prahaar, Pakistan would have followed suit through a Nasr-like project in any case.

Some experts interpret Nasr's development as Pakistan's willingness to initiate or fight a nuclear war. Their rationale is that the nuclear weapons are supposed to deter nuclear war and SRBMs ostensibly increase that risk. Command and control issues and risk of an inadvertent nuclear war are considered inherent to these missiles. Similar concerns exist to this day about the so-called TNWs of the US and Russia in their European initiative. This fear factor is best expressed in an excerpt from a 1998 paper: [TNWs] might have to be deployed rapidly out of their storage 'igloos,' [short-circuiting] the normal PAL codes and procedures. Decisions to use such weapons might devolve to low-level military officers, highly decentralised and subjected to immediate threats of being overrun by hostile forces. Even if someone on 'our' side did not initiate the use of nuclear weapons and subsequent 'progress up the escalation ladder, the threat of such decentralised and largely inadvertent escalation might well produce a supposedly [pre-emptive] strike by the Soviet side.

Dyer dispels the fears about the command and control of short-range ballistic missiles in these words: ...that the ['fail safe'] system for TNWs, sometimes referred to as Permissive Action Link (PAL), is at least as effective as it is for strategic weapons. Thus, at the present time, it is unlikely that a field commander on his own initiative could overrule the president's decision. One further assumption underlying this discussion is that there will be a certain degree of rationality exercised by decision makers even after hostilities start.

While developing new weapon systems, states make a rational choice based on cost-benefit analyses and risk calculation. Presence of the so-called TNWs in Europe to this day and Russia's unwillingness to dispense with them vindicates this assertion. Hence, if Nasr forecloses India's dangerous option to fight a limited war under nuclear overhang, it contributes to the regional stability and makes Pakistan's deterrence more credible.

The problem of deterrence would, however, arise if India considers Pakistan's will to use Nasr incredible. In an interesting development, India has started distancing itself from this perilous proactive strategy. While this may be an expression of Indian intent, Pakistan must nevertheless base its force posture and anchor its nuclear doctrine on India's capabilities. Another reason for India re-styling its Cold Start Doctrine as Proactive Defence Strategy could have been that the former is inherently aggressive in nature, tending to tag India as an aggressor state. The latter term is a more benign formulation that can be related to the reference to India's 'inalienable right of self-defence.'

As discussed in the first part, the warhead and missile technology used in Nasr could be mutated for nuclear submarine platforms. It would, however, be a challenge to make a naval version since the missile would have to be fitted into conventional submarines, and then there is the bigger technological challenge to navigational mechanism before the missile surfaces. Once developed, it would give Pakistan a second-strike capability and hence improve deterrence against India and contribute to regional stability. An assured second-strike capability would develop if and when Pakistan has a nuclear- powered and armed submarine and has the finances to do that. Zalmay Khalilzad, the former US ambassador to Afghanistan, said in

1976, "Given the poverty of Pakistan, it will be very difficult for it to acquire a second strike capability in the foreseeable future." Khalilzad appears to be supporting the point that possession of second-strike capability would be stabilizing.

Similarly William Walker, a noted analyst — also points to the stabilizing nature of second-strike capability when he says, "Pakistan and India face each other across contested borders and zones, and neither has established a second-strike capability, thereby making Islamabad and New Delhi more fearful of pre-emptive attacks."

Such arguments indicate that Pakistan and India did not develop the SRBMs in reaction to other's similar capability; only the flight-testing of Prahaar was a reaction to the Nasr test. The development of short-range weapons systems capability hence, was a well-considered rational choice and both states seem to follow the same course that NATO and the erstwhile Warsaw Pact did in the 1960s. If strategic stability sustained with the so-called TNWs in East-West relationship, the rational actors in South Asia would also remain similarly deterred. The history of crises between Pakistan and India is a proof that de-escalation occurs below the nuclear threshold. However, as the stability-instability paradox shows, that should not be the source of overoptimism.

It is also important to evaluate the effect of Prahaar on deterrence and strategic stability. Presence of Prahaar in the same theatre as Nasr should ideally deter both states from crossing the Rubicon. If rationality is at play during a conflict, both states would go for a "tit for tat" response involving SRBMs only and the fear of horrific fallout would deter them from massive retaliation. Cold War literature indicates that the adversaries would be deterred from using the SRBMs. However, the heat of fighting can quickly erode rationality and war could spiral out of control. This "confusion argument" about short-range ballistic missiles is best understood from the following narration: The deterrent value of TNWs is the "confusion argument" which suggests that even [if] all the objections raised against TNWs are true, the weapons would still have sufficient deterrent impact precisely because of the ambiguity surrounding them. Neither the first user of the TNW nor the retaliator would be able to control the course of events.

The corollary of the "confusion argument" is that both the Soviets — now Russians — and the NATO did not fight a war even after the SRBMs were introduced; the deterrence held despite the change in doctrines, weapons system advancements and relative conventional forces balance that shifted in NATO's favour.

Since India projects China as its adversary, therefore deploying Prahaar against China, at some point, cannot be ruled out. This can lead to an arms race and the instability would not remain limited to the region. Another related factor that would destabilise the region and may force Pakistan to rely heavily on SRBMs is India's pursuit of a ballistic missile defence (BMD) shield in collaboration with the US and Israel. Even a basic BMD capability may encourage a first-strike and pre-emptory tendency in Indian thinking. This suggests that Indian pursuit of BMD would affect the minimum deterrence levels and would nudge India towards a pre-emptory policy. A recent analysis provides the following opinion:

In the final outcome, the minimum deterrence levels currently exhibited could quickly disappear as the two sides enter a tit-for-tat upgrading system...[India] could adopt a more aggressive posture...and even [contemplate] pre-emption against Pakistani nuclear assets.

William C. Potter also considers a state's no-first-use doctrine incredible and mere lip-service until it possesses short-range ballistic missiles. According to him: It is very hard to see how, under no-first-use doctrine, short-range nuclear weapons in [arsenal would] serve a useful and legitimate purpose...If a no-first-use agreement is to be more than mere lip-service to a popular objective, it should be reflected in nuclear postures. A NWS subscribing to a no-first-use will have a hard time, justifying the continued possession of TNWs.

Russia's reliance on the so-called TNWs despite conventional force advantage offers a lesson. The American-led BMD shield in Europe has forced Russia to rely more on SRBMs and it is unwilling to negotiate reductions in this genre of weapons until the US addresses Russian concerns over BMD. Russia has hinted that short-range missiles could be used to neutralize deployed US antimissile systems in Europe and threatened to deploy Iskander missiles to the Kaliningrad." Some argue that the so-called TNWs, owing to short time of flight, would render the BMD less effective. However, there are competing claims that ABM systems — like the American PAC-3 — are also effective against tactical ballistic missiles. If the former contention were true, Nasr would offer similar advantage to Pakistan through its short-range and possibility of saturating the BMD shield by firing multiple missiles at a target.

The above discussion shows that short-range ballistic missiles would have a direct impact on strategic stability and nuclear deterrence. No one can be certain if short-range ballistic missiles would ever be used. In this sense, Pakistan-India situation mirrors that of the Cold War competition between 1960s and 70s. Dyer's following comments may be equally appreciable to South Asia, "It is very difficult to see under what combat conditions, especially in Europe, these weapons would ever be employed."

Nasr was produced to deter India from pursuing its Cold Start Doctrine, which has recently been re-styled as Proactive Defence Strategy. India evolved this strategy to punish Pakistan for attacks like the one on Indian Parliament in New Delhi in December 2001 and Mumbai in November 2008. Pakistan maintains that these attacks were not State-sponsored and was forthcoming in cooperation to investigate the despicable attacks and bring the perpetrators to justice. Nasr's development is also linked to the growing conventional force asymmetry between Pakistan and India. Prahaar was not developed in reaction to Nasr but its flight test was a reaction. Since Prahaar can be deployed or used against China, it would reduce. the strategic stability of the region. The military imperatives of

Pakistan raise the question about the limits of dynamism in its policy of credible, minimum deterrence. Can Pakistan sustain an arms race in the longer run? If the answer is no, then Pakistan would have to set a limit on the size of its nuclear arsenal. The Cold War model shows that an assured second-strike capability offers credible deterrence. Hence, economy permitting, Pakistan needs developing a triad of nuclear forces with a credible submarine-based nuclear missile capability. Nasr's warhead design may be the first technological step in that direction.

ASSESSING AVOIDANCE AND STRATEGIC STABILITY

In a classic sense, deterrence is 'absence of war' and a stable condition. Over 65 years of the nuclear age shows that it would be impossible to validate that nuclear weapons prevent war. From South Asian perspective, the Kargil War of 1999 is a unique example in which two nuclear-armed states fought a limited war yet were deterred from using nuclear weapons. Hence 'absence of nuclear war' would realistically define the environment to judge stability in South Asia. However, accepting the fact that nuclear weapons only prevent a nuclear war creates the stability-instability paradox. Hence it would be difficult to quantify what constitutes deterrence and strategic stability between Pakistan and India and what role would their so-called TNWs play.

In this paper, deterrence would constitute absence of nuclear war and it is assumed that deterrence would hold if both Pakistan and India develop an assured second-strike capability. It is difficult to quantify strategic stability because the literature on this variable is vague and concerns East-West competition from the Cold War period to this day.

For South Asia, strategic stability would be a situation between South Asian nuclear powers, in which Pakistan has the confidence that India is serious in resolving the territorial disputes and that Indian strategic partnerships with the developed world are not at the cost of Pakistan's security. Likewise, India's confidence in Pakistan's willingness to resolve bilateral disputes without alleged indirect strategy. The paper attempts to test both variables in the subsequent sections.

Factors Affecting Avoidance and Stability

Dr Zafar Iqbal Cheema, in his seminal work, has addressed the nature of South Asian deterrence at length. He argues that Pakistani officials and analysts claim that an elementary form of nuclear deterrence between India and Pakistan has been operative since 1988.

He identifies six factors that contribute to instability in deterrent relationship between India and Pakistan. These are: existence of outstanding disputes, existence of low-intensity conflict, occasional outbreak of crises and conflict situations, geographic proximity and [low] early warning time and divergent perceptions about nuclear and security doctrines. The following section amplifies these findings, links these with the perceptions of other experts and seeks to establish correlation with the TNWs.

Correlation of SRBMs, Avoidance and Regional Stability

The development-time of Nasr and Prahaar would be the first factor that would affect deterrence and stability in South Asia. As analysed earlier, Prithvi-I's development and induction took almost seven years. Both India and Pakistan have not tested their weapon systems in salvo-firing role. Additionally, India has indicated that it intends reducing the weight of Prahaar. Depending on how many units ultimately get these SRBMs missiles, the numbers of weapons needed would be certainly more than the medium-range missiles in the current inventories.

During this period three other factors would continue to influence the future of deterrence and stability in South Asia. These can be broadly classified into political, economic and military factors and can be tested against the 'Three Cs' — capability, credibility, and communication — of deterrence. It is worth noting that these factors have no absolute value and impinge on and interact with each other in complex ways.

Crash of Political Factors

A segment of British strategic thinkers considers the need to change status quo and resolution of political grievances underlying conflict as significant for stability. India-Pakistan animus over territorial issues falls in that category of regional instability. Hanwee et al argue that during a crisis the leadership would face the dilemma of maintaining a balance between assertive and delegative control over nuclear weapons. An assertive control could be fatal and a delegative control irreversible, thus destabilising. To achieve political stability, they suggest steps beyond "freezing the status quo" with the following argument:

> An enduring political stability... must allow for the resolution of grievances and conflicts by changes to forms of political organisation and ultimately to the boundaries and legitimacy of current nation-states. But while states hold each other under threat with nuclear weapons, it is hard to see how such change could take place. This system of stability, in other words, may be self-defeating.

The political stability between Pakistan and India rests on three territorial disputes (future of Jammu and Kashmir, Siachen, and Sir Creek). These apparently 'territorial' issues are really about water. J&K and glaciers including Siachen are a source of water for the entire subcontinent and Sir Creek's small territorial boundary has implications on marking of exclusive economic zone. From Pakistani perspective, Indian ingress in Afghanistan and alleged involvement in fanning instability in Balochistan and elsewhere would be of particular concern. Likewise, for India the prospect of a Mumbai-II and alleged militant activities in Indian-held Kashmir (IHK) would compel it to operationalize its Proactive Defence Strategy. The prospect of limited war would, in turn, induce Pakistan to ostensibly rely on short-range ballistic missiles. India would also feel justified to continue to develop Prahaar to balance Pakistan's capability. Interestingly, India eschewed (the so-called) TNWs earlier.

Weighed against the Three Cs of deterrence and the rational behaviour of both states during the post-Kargil crisis, the credibility of nuclear deterrence would hold. The communication of willingness to use nuclear weapons would continue as well. While hiatus over these long-standing disputes may exist, the likely wild card would be a terrorist activity in Pakistan or India that the affected side would view the other to have given covert state-patronage. In that case the crisis behaviour of both states and ensuing instability would be difficult to predict.

Hence, from the political perspective, development of SRBMs would have little impact on deterrence and regional stability, at least until 2018. Once Prahaar and Nasr have been commissioned in the land forces, the risk of a nuclear exchange during a crisis would only enhance if either side considers the other's willingness to use these weapons a bluff. It can be argued that the domestic political stability indirectly contributes to regional and strategic stability.

Collision of Economic Factors

The international media's spotlight on Pakistan has three hues: domestic instability due to militancy, proliferation record and the dismal economic situation. In marked contrast, India's internal instability and its proliferation record — that is the mother of nuclear proliferation in South Asia — is overlooked by the West because India has a buoyant economy and it is a haven for investors. The Western experts consider "India has an interest in regional as well as domestic stability and space to maximise its economic growth," implying that Pakistan has marginal interest in regional stability.

The Aman ki Aasha (Hope for Peace) joint initiative by Pakistan's *Jang Group* and *Times of India* holds that economy has a *Yin-Yang* relationship with strategic stability in South Asia. In their view, if Pakistan and India develop their trade and economic relations, mutual interests could become serious incentives for peace and friendship and a point may arrive that they have a serious disincentive in starting or escalating crises. The Cold War history shows some merit in economic factor as a disincentive to escalate crises to the point of nuclear war. However, owing to South Asia's peculiarities this desire here may remain a pipedream for several reasons.

Pakistan's economy is not likely to jumpstart for domestic and external reasons. Rife corruption, poor tax regime, circular debts, inconsistent economic policies coupled with lack of political will, investor-hostile security environment and the dire energy crunch are some of the major reasons for Pakistan's poor economy. There is growing discontent with the dismal economic situation. In a departure from issuing only security- related statements, Pakistan's apex National Command Authority (NCA) expressed its concerns about economy and the strategy to resolve these problems in the following words:

As part of energy security strategy, the NCA also reviewed and approved the futuristic, self-sustaining Nuclear Power Program – 2050, to meet the existing energy shortfalls and to respond to the future requirements of a growing population and economy. The NCA emphasized the need to focus on socio-economic development of the people as a foremost priority.

Though the onus of improving its economy lies on Pakistan, there are two areas where the international community has to make its contribution. First, Pakistan needs a level playing field in international trade. For instance, Pakistan's textile industry does not get the same incentives in the American market as the Indian or Bangladeshi industry does. Second, a more serious matter is the energy sector. For instance, the US offers assistance in improving existing energy infrastructure but refuses offering civil nuclear technology to Pakistan — in open contrast to the cooperation it has with India in this field. There may be three possible reasons behind the denial. One, Pakistan is not a signatory of the Nuclear Nonproliferation Treaty (NPT), but so is India. Two, Pakistan cannot afford to invest in the nuclear energy sector and economy's uplift is nurtured over a long time. Three, Pakistan's proliferation record is not considered 'as clean as India's,' despite the fact that New Delhi diverted material from its safeguarded facility (CIRUS Reactor) to test its first nuclear device in 1974 and the Nuclear

Suppliers Group (NSG) was created the following year as a reaction. Pakistan's steps to punish the chief perpetrator in the A.Q. Khan private network and its export control measures after 2004, such as the Export Control Act 2004, are generally disregarded for political reasons.

Both lines of above reasoning have flaws. Pakistan took credible measures after 2004 and its cooperation in implementing UN Security Council Resolution 1540 (2004) is commendable as Pakistan plugged all holes that could be manipulated by non-State actors for proliferation. Also, the safeguards required by the International Atomic Energy Agency (IAEA) would cover civil nuclear energy cooperation and the mechanism is effective enough to prevent proliferation.

Incentives similar to those offered to India could be offered to Pakistan — Islamabad has been a major non-NATO ally and the key country that supports international efforts in the fight against terrorism. Actually, what prompts discrimination is Western geo-politico-economic imperatives that see India as a larger market and a possible bulwark to contain rising China. Pakistan, therefore, does not fit in the immediate or mid-term Western interests in the region.

The above trend of selectivity against Pakistan encumbers its meagre efforts to give a fillip to its economy. That in turn increases discontent in Pakistani society, thus contributing to the propensity for violence and resultant instability that affects the region. Like several other states, Pakistan gives its security concerns a higher priority thereby affecting the investment in public sector development, which consequently gets lower priority than the defence expenditure. Even with greater expenditure in the defence sector, Pakistan finds it difficult to address the growing conventional weapons asymmetry with India.

If India and Pakistan's decision to develop short-range ballistic missiles is judged purely against 'expense factor,' both would face difficulty in footing the bill for the number of weapons that would be required for deployment on the multiple fronts that India or Pakistan could open up against each other, in a future conflict in line with their new war-fighting doctrines. Economy factor would impinge upon India more if it decides to cover its Chinese front with Prahaar or other SRBMs. According to Dyer:

> TNWs [would] not play a sufficiently significant role in the deterrence of Soviet aggression against Europe to justify their expense. With each individual atomic artillery shell costing perhaps $ 400,000 this weapon system is not cheap.

Dyer posited that the [TNWs] only "complicated [Soviet] plans for overrunning Europe. The security and control of these weapons [consumed] the equivalent of over one full division of American troops who could be used more profitably in another role."

From the above discussion, it can be inferred that even India would be reluctant once it decides to make 'enough' SRBMs to deter both Pakistan and China. The lesson for Pakistan is somewhat different. While Pakistan needs bolstering its security through credible, minimum deterrence, it must offer "credible economic assurance" to the investors in the developed countries.

The West may reconsider its policy of de-hyphenating Pakistan and India and use an evenhanded approach with Islamabad, especially in the energy sector. Until progress is made in these areas, the South Asian region would continue to be strategically unstable and nuclear deterrence between the two states would continue to be fragile. Considering the state of its economy, there is also the risk that an arms race may exhaust Pakistan.

Profiling Nasr and Prahaar

This part is a collection of declared specifications and assessments made on Nasr and Prahaar ballistic missile systems. A technical and technological assessment of these systems would assist in ascertaining their effect on the stability of deterrence between Pakistan and India. Incidentally, Pakistan's Inter-Services Public Relations (ISPR) Directorate issued a prompt, short and rather ambiguous press release after the first flight test of Nasr. In obvious contrast, India flight-tested Prahaar on 21 July 2011 and a delayed, though less ambiguous, official statement appeared on the Defence Research and Development Organisation (DRDO) website in August 2011. Other details on the test were, however, instantly available in the Indian media. This degree of ambiguity about the results of missile flight-tests is understandable as the states do it to maintain technological advantage and to hide operational details that might reveal the trajectory of progress.

Experts were quick to amplify the officially released information on the Nasr flight-test to make technical and other assessments. While Nasr remains in the spotlight, there was muted response or analysis on the implications of the Prahaar test. The Western assessments on Nasr carried strains of disbelief in the technological feat of miniaturising a warhead that could fit into a missile of about 300-mm diameter. Since primary sources and academic work on Nasr and Prahaar is scant, all available information has been considered for a swift content analysis of both weapon systems.

The Nasr

Soon after the Nasr test, Rodney Jones, the noted US expert, made a comprehensive analysis about its implications. The ISPR Press release and Jones' assessment have been compared below. Rodney Jones wrote:

> Pakistan has either developed or acquired nuclear warheads small enough to fit inside [a thin 300-mm diameter missile] and possibly of relatively low-yield [warhead]... Pakistan probably produced significant quantities of weapons-grade plutonium only after the May 1998 tests and has not test-detonated any weapons systems since then. Hence, the Army would be averse to using untested weapons...Making a plutonium-based implosion device for a 300 mm diameter missile would be a real feat.

The above assessment is circumspect about Pakistan's capability to miniaturise the warheads and might imply that the weapon system could be a bluff and the army would resist its induction at the operational level. These aspects have been addressed in the following paragraphs. The ISPR's partly ambiguous press release on the Nasr test offers various points of analysis. It reads:

> Pakistan today successfully conducted the 1st flight test of the newly developed Short Range Surface to Surface Multi Tube Ballistic Missile Hatf-IX (NASR). The missile has been developed to add deterrence value to Pakistan's Strategic Weapons Development programme at shorter ranges. NASR, with a range of 60 km, carries nuclear warheads of appropriate yield with high accuracy, shoot and scoot attributes. This quick response system addresses the need to deter evolving threats.
>
> The test was witnessed by [DG SPD], Lieutenant General (Retired) Khalid Ahmed Kidwai, Chairman National Engineering and Science Commission (NESCOM) Mr Irfan Burney, senior officers from the strategic forces, scientists and engineers of strategic organisations.
>
> On this occasion, the [DG SPD], Lieutenant General (Retired) Khalid Ahmed Kidwai said that the test was a very important milestone in consolidating Pakistan's strategic deterrence capability at all levels of threat spectrum. He said in the hierarchy of military operations, the NASR weapon system now provides Pakistan with short-range missile capability in addition to the medium and long-range ballistic missiles and cruise missiles in its inventory.
>
> The successful test has also been warmly appreciated by the President and Prime Minister of Pakistan, who have congratulated the scientists and engineers on their outstanding success.

If the available information on Nasr is analysed in the backdrop of Pakistan's cold and hot tests of nuclear weapons in March 1983 and in May 1998, seven important inferences can be made.

One, the extent of missile's accuracy cannot be ascertained since the circular-error-probable has not been publicised and the statement only identifies that the missile is "highly accurate." This ambiguity looks pronounced once compared to similar information about Prahaar. There is also no information about what kind of navigation system has been used in Nasr. If Nasr can carry a nuclear warhead of "appropriate yield," accuracy becomes a secondary issue. The explosive and destructive power of nuclear weapons would compensate for accuracy. Use of the word "appropriate" in the press statement appears deliberate. The yield can also indicate the type of device tested, i.e. plutonium- or uranium-based, or a device that is a combination of the two, with added tritium. The information available immediately after Pakistan's 28 May 1998 tests gave a combined yield of devices at 40 kilotons only. Likewise, the device tested on 30 May 1998 was of 12 kilotons yield, which indicates that it would have been a boosted fission device that used a mix of uranium, plutonium and tritium.

Two, emphasis that it was the "first flight test," indicates the desirability of more tests to further improve accuracy and validate other design parameters. While Nasr's flight parameters can be improved, the yield and other technical parameters of the nuclear warhead can only be effectively validated through hot testing.

Three, out of the six tests on 28 and 30 May 1998, four were reported to be of sub-kiloton yield. This shows that Pakistan had kept its options of making all genres of nuclear weapons – including the low-yield warheads – open. That said, the desirability of hot-testing of warheads and missiles should not be ruled out. While Pakistan continues to flight-test its missiles, it remains to be seen how it would develop appropriate and reliable warheads for each delivery system without further testing. It may be recalled that even after conducting 1032 tests and having developed other means to test reliability of warheads, the US is still reluctant to ratify the Comprehensive Test-Ban Treaty (CTBT), as it may need more testing.

Four, notwithstanding the sceptical view that Pakistan could not achieve technological mastery of miniaturising the warheads to fit a short-range ballistic missile, there are indicators that it had cold-tested and then hot-tested such state-of-the-art warheads by 1998. Almost 14 years on, it might be safe to assume that Pakistan would have developed highly sophisticated plutonium-based warhead designs to suit [short-range ballistic missiles].

Five, the above arguments lead to the issue of employment, as to when, if at all, and which land forces would induct Nasr. As Rodney Jones alluded to the fact in the above-cited article, the militaries are usually cautious about inducting weapons without proven reliability. Hence, if they forego hot tests to validate the reliability of low-yield warheads for Nasr, the land forces would opt for a series of flight tests in all probability. Nasr would most likely become Pakistan Army's Strategic Force Command (ASFC) asset. As indicated in the press statement, only the senior members of the "strategic forces" were present to witness the flight test. An implication of Nasr going to ASFC could be that Pakistan would exercise assertive control over short-range ballistic missiles and would preclude the likelihood of pre-delegation. Though, assertive control would be a factor of stability, it would create the attendant 'use them or lose them' dilemma that Pakistan will have to delicately balance by further augmenting the delivery system survivability.

Six, since Nasr is mounted atop the AR1A/A100-E Multiple-Launch Rocket System (MLRS), it was presumed to be of 300-mm (11.8-inch) diameter. The MLRS is a two-round system believed to be carried atop Chinese-origin 8x8 high-mobility truck chassis. Its shoot and scoot attributes mean that the launchers can quickly fire (shoot) and change location (scoot) to avoid counter-targeting. Rodney Jones thinks:

This system is probably a four-tube adaptation of a Chinese-design [MLRS], possibly the A-100 type, on an eight-wheeler truck, capable of carrying four, ready-to-fire 20-foot ballistic missiles of about 300 mm (11.8-inch) diameter...The truck-launcher otherwise may be a Chinese knock-off of the Russian 300 mm Smerch [MLRS] sold to India. Seven, stretching the idea of miniaturising further, some analysts have contemplated that Pakistan could now forge ahead to make multiple independently targetable re-entry vehicles (MIRVs) for ballistic missiles, make submarine-launched ballistic missiles (SLBMs) or re-model these to fit the torpedo bays of existing submarines and improve the cruise missiles designs.

The Prahaar

Unlike Pakistan's prompt press statement, within hours of flight-test, Indian official and measured stance appeared on the DRDO website a month after the test. Before that, the Indian media carried excerpts of the statements made by Dr. VK Saraswat, DG, DRDO, and other unnamed scientists. By then several experts had vented all their intellectual steam against Nasr's test and were probably not inclined to critically evaluate Prahaar by reconsidering their expressed positions. A gist of the DRDO statement and other statements on Prahaar is given below:

DG Indian Artillery also witnessed the test besides others. Developed in a short span of less than two years – support from Indian industry and quality assurance agency MSQAA...will be the battlefield support system for the Indian Army: cost-effective, quick reaction, all weather, all terrain, and highly accurate battlefield support tactical system...Diameter 420 mm...length 7.3 meter...Range 150 km...apogee 35 km...time of flight 4 minutes and 10 seconds...weight 1280 kg...single-stage solid propulsion system...payload 200 kg (carries different types of warheads...terminal accuracy is <10m (high accuracy navigation, guidance, and electromechanical actuation systems, latest onboard computers) ...the road mobile system carries 6 missiles at a time...can fire a salvo in all directions covering entire azimuth plane.

Some additional information that appeared in the media coverage immediately after the flight test is also worth noting. Prahaar "has high [manoeuvrability] and [an] excellent impact accuracy." The missile has a quick reaction time of launch "within a few minutes." Dr. Saraswat, who is also scientific adviser to the Indian defence minister, said:

It is an all-weather missile that can be launched from canisters. Since it can be fired from a road mobile launcher, it can be quickly transported to different places. It can be deployed in various kinds of terrain such as snow-bound areas or jungles...after a couple of more flights; we will be ready for production.

The short-range missile would fill the gap "between unguided multi-barrel rocket system Pinaka with 40 km range and guided missiles like Prithvi, which can strike at 250 km to 350 km range."

Related news items reflected that the Prahaar system "can tackle multiple targets and allows a mix of different kinds of missiles to be used from a single launcher. "Prahaar can hit a target 50-150 [kilometres] away," read the short report in the *Economic Times.* The available information on the flight test of Prahaar leads to seven main inferences:

One, since the Director-General Indian Artillery — Lt Gen Vinod Nayanar — was specially mentioned in the statement, it indicates that Prahaar may be inducted into the Indian army's field artillery formations. That opens the inherently risky proposition of this weapon system's control falling into the hands of junior commanders, delegative command and control and associated risks of inadvertent or unauthorised use. While the concern over command and control risks regarding Nasr remained exaggerated, surprisingly, no analyst has referred to such an obvious risk relating to Prahaar.

Two, the DRDO worked in complete secrecy and in collaboration with the national industry for almost two years, which shows effective civil-military-industrial synergy and cooperation. More importantly, the development time span clearly shows that India did not develop Prahaar as a reaction to Nasr. India was already developing its short-range ballistic missile even if Pakistan's Nasr had not come to the fore. The flight test on 21 July 2011 – three months after Nasr – also suggests that development of Prahaar was not at a very successful or advanced stage. The flight test was initially planned on 18 July but was delayed till 21st, probably due to technical reasons. The video footage of the test shows that the flight test was done on an overcast day, thus precluding the option of not testing on 18 July due to weather limitation. Like Prithvi I (liquid-fuel missile), Prahaar (solid fuel) may still have technical glitches to overcome.

Three, since the missile has a maximum range of 150 kilometres and can be deployed even in snow-bound areas or jungles; it can also be deployed against China. If deployed against its 3,380-kilometres border with China, it may provoke Beijing and add to the arms race in short-range ballistic missiles too. If India decides to deploy Prahaar against China, it would require a large number of missiles. It will, nevertheless, have sufficient fissile material to make the required number of warheads — thanks to the pressure relieved on its domestic sources by several civil nuclear energy cooperation deals as well as the 'recently discovered' uranium mines in Andhra Pradesh that started production in December 2011.

Four, due to Pakistan's geographical shape, Prahaar can engage both counter-force and counter-value targets. Likewise, Prahaar's range is identical to Prithvi-I. Hence, it can be argued that Prahaar is a solid-fuel-Prithvi I.

Five, since the missile can be launched within a few minutes, it would give the Indian forces good reaction time and quick launch options. If India decides to delegate the control to junior leaders in the battlefield, it will further telescope the decision time and the senior leadership will have little time to reverse the decision.

Six, though the Prahaar weapon system allows a mix of different kinds of missiles to be used from a single launcher, only one missile was fired on 21 July. Hence, more tests would be required to check weapon systems' performance once all missiles are simultaneously fired in multiple directions. The reason that some DRDO scientists suggest attempts to reduce the missile-weight points that launcher will be more manoeuvrable once the load is reduced.

Seven, Dr. Saraswat was intentionally vague about the time Prahaar would reach the production-ready status. If the timeline of the induction of Prithvi-I missile is any guide, it may take up to seven years before Prahaar is actually handed over to the ground forces. Given the complexities involved in developing multi-barrel capability, Prahaar would take even longer than Prithvi-I.

Seven, specifying minimum range as 50 kilometres is significant in the sense that a vertically fired missile can fall back at the launch site too.

This becomes more important as some Indian missiles have failed at launch in the past. The 50-km minimum limit could be interpreted that the system would be deployed in a way that it is 80-100 kilometres away from the target. Besides, the 50-km limit also indicates the safety distance that would be kept between the Indian troops and the ground zero of the very low-yield explosion.

This argument can be extended to ascertain the yield of warhead and device type. The warhead for Prahaar-type SRBMs can be an enhanced radiation (neutron) bomb. This can be understood from the excerpt of an online source, which offers the following information on the yield and destruction capacity of a 0.01-kiloton bomb:

The smallest warhead at present capable of providing significant tactical effort is.01 KT (10 tons). Deriving its effect from neutron and gamma radiation it produces loss of co-ordination in 1 minute (death in 36 hours) against troops in the open up to a distance of approximately of 70 yards. It can be fired with safety at a distance of 600 yards from our own troops.

At 1 KT (1000 tons) the same effect as above can be sustained up to a radius of nearly 400 yards while the safety distance increases to 1,500 yards.

If the information on minimum range is juxtaposed to Prahaar, it can be inferred that India may be using neutron bombs atop Prahaar missile – which would leave the structures intact and kill only the humans within 36 hours and keep the effects localised. It may be recalled that the US reversed its development of neutron bombs because there were protests over their employment in Europe — these would kill humans and retain the structures. A high-energy neutron warhead (atop) Prahaar would theoretically allow India to use it against mechanised forces in an area the Indian forces would want to use for further ingress into Pakistani territory. A fission bomb, due to its blast effect, would render the territory impassable.

7

The Russian and Northeast Asia Security Cooperation and Regional Integration

Geoeconomics, the ascendancy of trade, investment, and finance as factors in shaping the calculus of national strategy and regional and global priorities, is a key element in the larger notion of "comprehensive security." This concept defines security expansively to include issues beyond traditional politico-military factors that are part of the gestalt of stability. It addresses a number of cross-cutting issues where economic and traditional security concerns intersect such as maritime safety, nuclear cooperation, and arms sales. Apart from such double-edged issues, patterns of cooperative security behavior may also have a synergistic effect on economic issues by helping to improve overall bilateral relationships, improve the sub-regional security environment, and/or reduce perceived risks which will stimulate direct foreign investment.

This analysis is based on the assumption that Russia will continue in the direction of economic privatization with a pluralist, rule-of-law political system and on the continuity of the U.S.-Japan security alliance.

There appears to be a broad range of issues, including cooperative action in regard to traditional security concerns on the principal security challenge to the region in general and the sub-region in particular - the North Korean nuclear threat and the process of reunification of the Korean Peninsula - which hold varying degrees of promise for a new Russian engagement in Northeast Asia. The Russian proposal last March for an international conference on the Korean nuclear problem was but a thinly veiled advertisement for recognition of the fact that Russia is a great power with important interests in the region.

Throughout the Cold War, as a Eurasian power, the Soviet Union was a defining factor in the security equation in Northeast Asia, though it was marginal in the economic realm beyond the security guarantees and subsidies it provided to allied Asian communist regimes and decidedly possessed a Eurocentric mindset. Like its predecessor, Russia is also a significant factor in the subregional security equation, albeit of a lesser magnitude in military terms. But while the USSR's relationship to the dynamic Asia-Pacific economies was defined primarily as a threat, Russia is pursuing a course of positive engagement and is increasingly viewed as a real or potential partner. This is a trend that began in the late 1980s with the new policy towards East Asia pursued by Gorbachev whose thrust, albeit with a lower profile, has continued with the same goal of enhancing Moscow's economic and political engagement in the region.

A NORTHEAST ASIAN AGENDA

In spite of lingering security concerns in Northeast Asia, no formal cooperative political framework or multilateral process has been initiated. This reflects in part, the weight of the sub-region's checkered history, and in part the solidity of the U.S.-Japan and U.S.-ROK bilateral alliances which remain the keystone of stability in the region. But there is an urgency to the current political environment which suggests that the situation may be ripe for developing a new Northeast Asian political framework, which along with APEC and the ASEAN Regional Forum could evolve into a component of an emerging Asia-Pacific architecture comprised of overlapping or multi-layered mechanisms. Over the past several years there have been several official proposals to create some type of Northeast Asian political, security dialogue or framework.

As the crisis over the nuclear issue has unfolded, the momentum towards such a sub-regional framework has gradually begun to evolve. In a speech by former President Roh Tae Woo's at the UN in September 1992 and in Han Sung Joo's October 1993 speech to the Asia Society in Hong Kong, and his proposal tabled at the 1994 initial ASEAN Regional Forum (ARF) meeting. South Korea has formally proposed a forum among the two Koreas and the four major powers. All parties with the possible exception of North Korea have some measure of interest in the idea. Former Secretary of State James A. Baker HI raised the idea in a Foreign Affairs essay. Such a Northeast Asian initiative is also a logical follow-on to Seoul's 'Nordpolitik' which has fulfilled its objectives. Moreover, the prospect of a smaller power taking the lead would give it a special credibility.

The experience of the United States and Russia could facilitate CFE-type negotiations in such a forum for Northeast Asia. As discussed above, the interests of the four major powers (U.S., Japan, China, Russia) overlap: all support a denuclearized Korean Peninsula, all prefer a 'soft landing' for North Korea, all have an interest in minimizing turmoil resulting from Korean reunification, and all support expanding economic growth in the region. Korea has a strong interest in harmony among the major powers to whom its security has historically been hostage. Thus, it is possible to build on a "form follows function" basis. South Korean, U.S, Russian, and Japanese officials all have expressed an interest in some form of a Northeast Asian political forum.

Beyond Korea, there are a host of issues particular to the sub-region around which Northeast Asian interests converge. In this regard a sub-regional political framework should adopt the notion of "comprehensive security" including a range of issues beyond traditional military concerns: marine resources, environment, piracy, nuclear safety, narcotics trafficking, refugee flows, and peacekeeping.

Equally important is carefully structuring an agenda to keep contentious bilateral issues, particularly territorial disputes such as the Northern Territories or Senkaku Islands, outside the scope of any such forum, and to set dear parameters so none of me participants ~ particularly China or Japan - will fear that the forum would be used to " gang up" on them over issues in dispute. Moreover, the magnitude and immediacy of me Korea crisis instructs that limiting the participation to essential players would increase the chances of success. For this reason, a separate Northeast Asia forum - alone or as a subset of the ARF is needed.

Informally, the diplomacy surrounding the North Korean nuclear issue over the past three years has begun to build a sense of security, and of associative interests which are prerequisites for any such mechanism to be effective. U.S.-led efforts to end North Korea's nuclear weapons program and achieve a denuclearized Peninsula have involved intense consultation and coordination with South Korea and also with Japan at the Assistant Secretary level. Over the past three years this has evolved into a trilateral diplomacy coordinating efforts towards North Korea. The U.S. has also worked closely with Russia, and has increasingly engaged China on this issue. This pattern is a key building block to new multilateral efforts in the region.

Beyond the nuclear issue, however, there is an important agenda of managing the transition on the Korean Peninsula. That three of the four major powers concerned are Permanent Members of the UN Security Coundl give any sub-regional consensus reached by a consultative mechanism a potentially global impact. The Korean question will ultimately be resolved prindpally by the Koreans through the North-South dialogue, which has already produced on paper, a framework for reconciliation and arms control signed in December 1991.

While Korea is not analogous to Germany and the " 2+4" process in legal/political terms, there is an important role for the outside powers in managing the external aspects of North-South reconciliation. If the Koreas turn the armistice into a peace treaty, achieve a denuclearized peninsula, and if they reach arms reduction agreements, there is a role for the outside powers in endorsing, respecting, and/or guaranteeing the outcomes of such developments. With the United States and China as signatories to the armistice, at the very least, they should have some notary role to play in realizing a peace treaty between North and South Korea. Currently, Russia remains a treaty ally of North Korea. In regard to security issues, if the agreement for a denuclearized peninsula is implemented, with three of the four regional powers as members of the nuclear dub, they could provide more specific security assurances or a no first-use pledge.

If North Korea collapses, managing the fallout would be primarily a Northeast Asia problem. In terms of crisis management, there is a logic to multilateral consultations to coordinate efforts among the four powers and Seoul to manage the resulting crisis should Pyongyang collapse, which could produce refugee flows to China, Japan, and Russia as well as South Korea. If the current nuclear crisis is not resolved and North Korea continues on what is likely to be a suicidal trajectory, such a five power forum - or perhaps five plus an empty chair to leave open the option should North Korea change course - makes sense as a preventive diplomacy mechanism.

Beyond Korea, there is an equally important sub-regional agenda which could serve to mitigate concerns about China and Japan, to help integrate Russia into the region (Moscow should also be invited to join APEC) and regional concerns about a reunified Korea. A Northeast Asia political, security consultative mechanism would embed both China and Japan in a multilateral framework mat could help foster an atmosphere to overcome traditional fears, build trust and confidence, and provide a larger stage for addressing both Russo-Japanese issues as well as Sino-Japanese relations which will be a major determinant of stability in the Pacific in the 21st century. Over the longer term, in the event of the withdrawal of U.S. forward deployed troops in Korea, such a political framework could help anchor the U.S. in the region.

The Korean Catalyst

The strategic fulcrum of the Pacific is Northeast Asia, where the interests of the four major powers - the U.S., Japan, China, and Russia - and the two Koreas are joined. It is relations amongst these states (which include three of the five declared nuclear powers and the world's three largest economies) particularly, U.S.-Japan, Sino-Japanese, and Sino-American relations, that are key determinants of Asia-Pacific security and stability - and of the possibilities of cooperative approaches to it.

While examining the dynamics of bilateral relations among these major powers is outside the mandate of this paper, the interests of the four major powers overlap on the Korean Peninsula. The recently negotiated U.S.-North Korea nuclear agreement and the new set of issues resulting from an acceleration of the North-South reconciliation process are likely to occur if the accord is fully implemented may catalyze new possibilities for sub-regional cooperation.

Managing the external aspects of the Korean question strongly suggests a role for the surrounding major powers in the process, as well as giving impetus to economic prospects such as schemes to develop the Tumen River basin and the Sea of Japan development. It is the range of possibilities that may be opened up by the consequences of a resolution of the nuclear problem in particular that is worth examining.

Even upon resolution of the nuclear issue, the principal and immediate source of tension most likely to result in instability and/or conflict remains with the heavily-armed stand off on the Korean Peninsula. The most urgent issue is the North Korean nuclear weapons program, though the U.S.-North Korea October 1994 accord provides a framework and the promise of that program being terminated. Their are rumors of North Korea 'preparing war plans' and inflating the extent of the food shortage in order to use aid for its troops.

In regional terms, the nuclear issue is inextricably bound to the question of Korean reunification, the scenarios for which run the spectrum from implosion and a Rumania-type collapse to explosion and a second Korean war. How reunification occurs is likely to have major implications for the regional balance, particularly on the future of the U.S. forward deployed military presence in the region. All four major powers (and South Korea) hope to achieve a denuclearized Korean Peninsula and to avoid a second Korean war, while also avoiding the devastating collapse of North Korea.

In pondering Korean scenarios, the starting point is the best case scenario, a "soft landing" for North Korea, the preferred choice of both North and South Korea as well as the four major powers. Such a scenario rests on the realization of a negotiated termination of North Korea's nuclear weapons program. That in turn rests on the willingness of the new leadership in Pyongyang to pursue Chinese-style economic reforms and to trade its nuclear program for economic and political engagement with the international community in a step-by-step redprocal confidence-building process. The theory behind the 'soft landing' is that foreign trade, aid, and investment would cushion and begin to refurbish the failing North Korean economy, so that a gradual, peaceful reunification process could result with help from a magnanimous ROK. While not inconceivable, the fears of the Pyongyang leadership that even a controlled opening of the most hermetically sealed state on earth would lead to an undermining of their political control, suggesting that such an outcome is rather problematic.

An implosion scenario could involve large flows of refugees from North Korea across me demilitarized zone (DMZ) to South Korea, to various ethnic-Korean areas of China, to Japan, and even perhaps to Russia. While it may be peaceful, a collapse of the regime or a struggle between factions in North Korea could also involve military force, and become destabilizing for Northeast Asia, as well as to South Korea which would bear primary responsibility for a reunification by force majeure. A possible explosion would be a worst-case scenario in which a desperate North Korea would launch a suicidal assault on the South hoping to seize Seoul and then sue for peace.

In the case of either implosion or explosion the result would be rapid unification by absorption. Such an outcome would resolve the nuclear issue (though in the worst case scenario it could lead to a Ukraine-type problem of an inherited nuclear capability). It could have a palliative effect on a prospective sub-regional Northeast Asia nuclear arms race, the specter of which has been greatly exaggerated by many analysts. Korean nuclear proliferation has not been a factor in Chinese nuclear modernization plans, and Japan, which has lived with hundreds of Chinese bombs will not abandon its Constitution or pacifist political culture, certainly not in the short-term, just because Pyongyang proliferates. But North Korea provides a convenient political rationale for Japanese development of Hitech dual-use capabilities (from accumulating plutonium to the H-2 rocket) and defensive systems designed in no small measure, with China in mind. Russia has become a secondary factor in the equation as it muddles towards a democratic transformation. However sizeable its military and technological ties to China and the fact that it shares borders with each, as well as its coastline on the Sea of Japan, continues to make Moscow a player in regard to the Korean Peninsula.

Maritime Cooperation

There is also a Northeast Asian dimension to environmental concerns. Add rain from China is already showing up in South Korea and Japan. Moreover, management of marine resources in and around the Sea of Japan lends itself to cooperative action. These problems require sub-regional solutions, such as the pooling resources to monitor pollution as part of a larger maritime cooperation agenda which should be pursued in a Northeast Asian framework. Issues such as piracy, refugee flows, illegal narcotics trafficking, unlicensed fishing, the monitoring of marine pollution, and creating a database and information to share on shipping and sea lane safety offer a beginning agenda for a modest initiative.

Perhaps the easiest part of the initiative would be search and rescue, maritime safety cooperation. This would entail multilateral planning and mechanisms to share real time information to respond to emergencies. Recent dashes between the Russian military and Japanese fishing boats, or the reports of piracy in the East China Sea are vivid examples where maritime cooperation might play a preventive role. Building on such endeavors, such cooperation could expand to sharing surveillance intelligence or responsibilities for monitoring various areas. Russia and Japan already have an incidents-at-sea agreement which could be multilateralized.

One issue that may lend itself best to trilateral cooperation is the Cold War legacy in the Sea of Okhost. While the START I and START II agreements will reduce Russian deployments of SSBNs in the Sea of Okhost, continued deployments of Russian strategic weapons and the continued U.S. response of aggressive submarine patrolling practices reflect bureaucratic inertia on both sides. A trialogue or a U.S.-Russian initiative to curb these outmoded realities in dose consultation with Japan should be considered.

Nuclear Cooperation

There is also one vital non-military security issue which bridges the Korea issue and the broader Northeast Asia agenda: the nuclear safety of Japanese plutonium reprocessing. Japan's reprocessing program, its transporting and stockpiling of plutonium, has set off alarm bells across Asia. It is of questionable economic rationale. Most estimates suggest the glut of enriched uranium and plutonium and general economics of energy render commercial breeder reactors not viable before the next century. Plans drafted in the late 1970s by Japan, Germany, France, and Britain have been overtaken by economic reality. Thus far, only Germany has begun to retreat from its nuclear agenda. Burning MOX fuel in power reactors might be six to ten times more expensive than uranium according to some estimates, though some studies suggest it may not be quite that costly. The start-up date for Japan's large breeder reactor has already been pushed back several times, the current date being 2030. Its estimated cost is now in the $12 billion range, with Japanese utility companies increasingly reluctant to participate. Needless to say, the Japanese public is not particularly anxious to have 70-80 tons of plutonium stored in their country.

South Korea is already more dependent on nuclear power than Japan, and a reunified Korea might have an interest in reprocessing, in part due to its fears of Japan. Some in the South Korean scientific, technical and political elites already favour reprocessing. If reprocessing is necessary, although market forces suggest the contrary, it could be done on a regional basis with facilities and all plutonium under IAEA custodianship as originally envisioned in the agency's charter with equal access for all in Northeast Asia. Given the Clinton Administration's new proliferation initiative to focus on excess plutonium stockpiles and the placement of such stockpiles from dismantled weapons under IAEA safeguards, a Northeast Asian forum could also explore a ban on enriched uranium and plutonium production. It would be a major confidence-building measure, removing latent suspicions about Japan, bolstering the global non-proliferation regime, and preempting a post-Korean reunification arms race. This issue could become part of a sub-regional energy development agenda. The consortium, the Korea Energy Development Organization, which planned to supply light water reactors to North Korea could be the initial phase of such an agenda.

A wide range of issues under the rubric of nuclear cooperation could be the agenda for a Pacific counterpart to EURATOM as an element of regional institution building to manage sub-regional nuclear cooperation, perhaps an ASIATOM. Such a mechanism might pursue cooperation not only on reprocessing, but also on safeguards, management of spent fuel (which generated tension between Russia and Japan), and cooperative efforts to enhance nuclear safety. As civil use of nuclear power is only in its infancy outside of Northeast Asia (and Taiwan), it might begin as a sub-regional enterprise and expand if and when countries in Southeast Asia moved toward nuclear energy. Certainly Russia, or at least the Russian Far East would be an important participant in such a venture. Since 1991, Japanese nuclear officials have raised the possibility of helping Russia build MOX fuel reactors which could not only supply energy for the Russian Far East, but also enhance security by burning surplus plutonium from dismantled Russian nuclear weapons.

Such a nuclear, if non-military, CBM could in turn foster a political climate amenable to military transparency (defense spending, doctrinal talks, maritime safety) discussions which also should be prominent features of a Northeast Asia agenda. Such discussions could be held on a military-to-military basis in tandem with political talks. Expanding an inter-military dialogue can be an important tool in reducing the risk of miscalculation but also for building mutual confidence and trust. Already, Japan is initiating bilateral military talks with China, providing a precedent to build on. Russian military deployments and activity would be an important item for discussion. In addition, arms sales and missile proliferation should also be part of this varied agenda.

Sea of Japan Concept

The cumulative effect of confidence-building measures along the lines of those outlined above would most likely create a synergy with economic initiatives under discussion in Northeast Asia, most prominently with the Sea of Japan concept. The logic of the Sea of Japan concept is that there are mutual linkages among Russian natural resources, Mongolian resources, Chinese and North Korean labor and light industry, and Japanese and South Korean capital and technology capable of producing a growth duster in the area. China and Mongolia are interested in an outlet to the Sea of Japan. There is some interest among localities in Western Japan; Niigata Prefecture has allocated 3 billion Yen to set up a Japan Sea Economic Region Research Center.

In the Russian Far East, the beginnings of sub-regional cooperation in the form of joint ventures and joint infrastructure development is unfolding. In Khabarovsk, there are some 250 joint ventures operating, from manufacturing to restaurants, 39 of these are South Korean. China and Russia have begun construction on a railway between Hunchun and Kraskino, and have agreed on the lease of Zarbino port. Japan's MTTI is funding preliminary studies on the development of Primorsky Krai. And there is growing interest in a proliferation of free trade zones from Vladivostok to the Rajin-Sonbong free trade zone in North Korea's Tumen River area where the borders of China, Russia, and North Korea converge.

While grandiose plans for a $30 billion Tumen River development plan of the UNDP are unlikely to be pursued, some initial infrastructure development on a smaller scale is underway. This region would be comprise of the Russian Far East, Northeast China (Heilongjiang, Liaoning and Jilin provinces), both North Korea and South Korea, Mongolia, and Japan. In early 1995, these governments signed a formal cooperation agreement to develop the Tumen River area.

The Tumen River scheme is likely to remain largely a pipe dream for at least the rest of this decade. Some modest infrastructure improvements, such as Chinese development of Chonggjin port will occur. But not until Japan, and perhaps South Korea are prepared to finance such a large-scale scheme will it have any chance of being realized. However, North Korea's behavior in regard to this project may offer a useful window into Pyongyang's thinking. The country's only designated " zone of free trade and economy" thus far is the 600 square km. encompassing Rajin and Sonbong, a coastal area in the Tumen region in the isolated northeast comer of the country.

Northern Territories

What, if any relation would either of these economic developments or confidence-building measures have on the enduring legacy of a century of enmity between Russia and Japan over the Northern Territories dispute? Devising solutions to the Russo-Japanese territorial dispute has become a veritable cottage industry. The missing ingredient has not been a failure to devise the right formula, but rather the lack of political will on both sides in the face of aggressive nationalism in both

Russia and Japan. Only when both Moscow and Tokyo arrive at the conclusion that their mutual interests are best served by resolving the Northern Territories will one or more of the proposed options be adopted.

The economic and political-military initiatives I have suggested arguably fit into Japan's policy of "expanded equilibrium." As Russia's investment climate improves, the Japanese private sector is likely to respond positively given the proximity of the Russian Far Easfs enormous natural resources, regardless of new patterns of security cooperation. With a "building block" course of enlarging areas of cooperation based on common interests, a sense of partnership in Northeast Asia may be forged. This could alter the pathology of Russo-Japanese relations over time which in turn may facilitate a final resolution of me problem. In retrospect, the solution proposed by the then Soviet People's Deputy Boris Yeltsin during a January 1990 visit to Japan appears in retrospect less far-fetched than it was judged at the time. Yeltsin declared that, "It should be a step-by-step policy which, on the one hand, would create a sense of confidence among the Japanese people that the territorial issue is not standing still and on the other hand, would put our people in a position to form an opinion in favour of compromise." Yeltsin suggested a multiphased process beginning with Russia acknowledging the problem; then by turning all four islands into a free enterprise zone for Japan, demilitarizing the islands, signing a peace treaty to formally end World War n, and finally allowing me next generation of politicians to choose a final denouement in a 15-20 year timeframe from options including a joint protectorate, free international status, or the transfer of the islands to Japan. Another variation would be an Okinawa-type reversion, acknowledging sovereignty, and agreeing on a timetable to implement it. In any case, a negotiated resolution of the issue is more likely to be a reflection of a new sense of normality in Russo-Japanese relations than a catalyst for it.

8

Bilateral Financial Interdependence on U.S.-China Relations

From the perspective of international relations theory, liberalists argue that there are three reasons to explain why economic interdependence among countries will facilitate stability and peace among countries. First, states' primary goals are to promote economic prosperity and maintain international peace, which can be achieved through economic exchange and interdependence. Second, the costs of wars will increase due to bilateral economic interdependence. Third, with greater interdependence of global financial, trade, and other economic relations, most states will be harmed by any major international conflicts, and thus, will oppose this kind of conflicts.

The liberalist argument provides a very important foundation for the U.S. in developing economic strategies toward China. The United States seeks to fully integrate China into the global economic and trading system. The U.S. argues that China's participation in the global economy will increase China's stake in the stability and prosperity of East Asia. As a result, Chinese foreign policy will become more moderate and cooperative. To evaluate the hypothesis of the U.S. strategy toward China, this paper analyzes to what degree economic interdependence between China and the U.S. increases China's stake in the stability and prosperity of East Asia, and thus moderates China's U.S. policy during bilateral conflicts. In particular, this paper examines two serious conflicts between China and the United States: The U.S. bombing of the Chinese embassy in Belgrade in May, 1999, and the reconnaissance plane incident in April, 2001. These two U.S.-China conflicts involved issues of sovereignty, and stirred severe initial reaction from the Chinese government. Therefore, they are very good incidents to explore how bilateral economic interdependence influences China's U.S. policy in the situation of severe bilateral conflicts.

U.S.-CHINA FINANCIAL INTERDEPENDENCE

According to U.S. customs statistics, in 2002, China exported $125.2 billion, or 38.5 percent of total Chinese exports, to the United States (including those transshipped through Hong Kong), making the United States China's largest export market. The two-way trade between China and the U.S. has grown from $33 billion in 1992 to $147.3 billion in 2002. The U.S. trade deficit with China was $103.1 billion in 2002, representing the largest U.S. bilateral trade deficit.

In addition, the United States is an important source of foreign direct investment (FDI) for China. American direct investment in China covers a wide range of manufacturing sectors, several large hotel projects, restaurant chains, and petrochemicals. According to Chinese figures, in 2001, the U.S. cumulatively supplied $4.4 billion, or 9.5 percent of total realized FDI in China. That year, the United States was the third largest investor in China, next to Hong Kong and Macau, and the Virgin Islands. By June 2002, the cumulative realized American FDI totaled $36.9 billion, divided among 35,374 projects.

Furthermore, the Chinese government (through sovereign bond offerings) and Chinese state-owned and other enterprises have raised significant funds in overseas capital markets in recent years. According to Morgan Stanley Dean Witter and the Wall Street Journal, Chinese firms raised approximately $41 billion through initial public offerings (IPOs) and placements in international equity markets from 1993 through 2000, $21 billion in 2000 alone. According to the estimate of the U.S.-China Security Review Commission, Chinese entities have raised more than $14 billion through IPOs in the U.S. capital markets from 1999-2001. Chinese issuers have raised an estimated $20 billion from 1992-2001 from international bond offerings denominated in U.S. dollars.

Chinese leaders are fully aware of bilateral (asymmetrical) economic interdependence with the United States. According to Hong Kong's *Ching Pao*, Chinese President Jiang Zemin warned in an internal meeting in early 2000 that the Chinese government should closely watch changes in the world situation and initiate responsive measures, noting that China has integrated itself into the world economic system. In particular, he pointed out three significant factors of uncertainty, which would significantly influence the Chinese economy: U.S. economic development, fluctuations of international oil prices, and potential risks in the international capital market.

President Jiang's concerns have been echoed by other Chinese senior officials, as well as by the media. For instance, a commentary article in the *Renmin Ribao* (People's Daily), on February 22, 2001, discussed the impact of a recession in the United States on the Asian economies. It concluded that "a U.S. economic slowdown indeed has a certain impact on Asia, and cannot be taken lightly." Two months later, Shi Guangsheng, minister of Foreign Trade and Economic Cooperation, explicitly said that Beijing was "deeply concerned about the possible impact on China's economy resulting from the slowdown of the U.S. economy."

China's concerns have been realized. In 2001, according to the U.S. customs statistics, China's exports to the U.S. increased by only 2.3 percent. Consequently, China's total exports increased by only 6.8 percent during that year, and China's economic growth rate in 2001 was 0.7 percent lower than that in 2000. In comparison, in 2002, China's exports to the U.S. sharply increased by 22.4 percent, and thus, China's total exports increased by 21.8 percent. This contributed to China's outstanding economic performance of a growth rate of 8 percent in 2002.

The following two case studies will examplify to what extent China moderates its stance with the United States, during situations of conflict, in order to preserve its economic interests of U.S.-China economic interdependence.

The U.S. Violence of the Chinese Embassy in Belgrade in 1999

The North Atlantic Treaty Organization (NATO) began bombing targets in the Federal Republic of Yugoslavia, without UN authorization on March 24, 1999. Beijing feared that a resurgent United States, placing humanitarian intervention above the traditional concept of state sovereignty, planned to use a non-UN mechanism as its preferred tool. Furthermore, facing domestic opposition, Chinese Premier Zhu Rongji traveled to Washington to secure China's accession to the World Trade Organization (WTO) in early April. However, the United States rejected the offer, and thus, gravely undermined the position of Chinese leaders who wanted to compromise with the United States. These two events together provoked strong anti-American sentiments among China's elites and the Chinese public, at large.

On May 8 (Beijing time), five bombs from an American plane slammed into the Chinese embassy in Belgrade, killing three and wounding more than twenty others. Immediately, NATO explained that the military command mistakenly believed that the Chinese embassy was a headquarters for a Yugoslav arms agency. Nevertheless, the Chinese government issued a statement, expressing its utmost indignation and strong condemnation, and lodged its strongest protest against the United States.

On May 8, both the American Ambassador to China, James Sasser, and U.S. Secretary of State Madeleine Albright apologized to the Chinese government for the incident and conveyed sincere regret about the loss of life in the bombing. On May 9, U.S. President Bill Clinton sent a letter to Chinese

President Jiang Zemin, saying, "I express my apologies and sincere condolences for the pain and casualties." However, Chinese media did not report the repeated apologies made by the U.S until May 10. On May 10, President Clinton apologized again to the Chinese leaders and to the people. On the same day, Secretary Albright again expressed her profound sorrow over NATO's bombing, stating that NATO would provide China with a full explanation.

Despite NATO's previous explanation of mistaken bombing, on May 9, up to 100,000 demonstrators besieged the U.S. embassy in the biggest protests seen in Beijing since the 1989 pro-democracy movement. Tens of thousands of protestors marched past the U.S. and British embassies, throwing stones, burning the U.S. flag and effigies of President Clinton, and shouting slogans, like "Down with U.S. imperialism." In addition, according to China's official media, more than 100,000 people protested in other major Chinese cities, including Xian, Hangzhou, Guangzhou, Shanghai, Chengdu, Shenyang, and Guilin. Demonstrators set fire to the U.S. consulate in Chengdu and all consulate personnel were evacuated.

During the demonstrations, the Chinese government not only helped transport demonstrators, but the police seemed indifferent to the damage that was being inflicted upon U.S. property. The Chinese explanation was that by allowing a "controlled" reaction, a bigger explosion was averted. Beijing understood full well, as Joseph Fewsmith and Stanley Rosen argue, that "students are going to take to the streets in any event and that if they did not throw stones at the American embassy they would throw them at Zhongnanhai (the leadership compound)." If students and others had not been permitted to vent their feelings against the United States, they no doubt would have found release through criticism of the Chinese government.

On May 10, Chinese Foreign Minister Tang Jiaxuan raised four formal demands regarding NATO's bombing of the Chinese embassy in Belgrade: First, to make an open and official apology to the Chinese government, the Chinese people and relatives of the Chinese victims; second, to carry out a complete and thorough investigation of the incident; third, to promptly make public the detailed results of the investigation; and fourth, to severely punish those who were responsible for the attack. Furthermore, the Chinese government decided to postpone the high-level military contact between China and the United States; postpone its consultations with the U.S. in the fields of proliferation prevention, arms control and international security; and suspend its dialogue with the U.S. in the sphere of human rights.

However, two-days of serious anti-American protests in China brought a severe backlash on the Chinese economy. On May 10, the A share index of the Shanghai Stock Exchange declined by 4.5 percent and the B share index by 7.3 percent; the A share index of the Shenzhen Stock Exchange declined by 5.6 percent and the B share index by 6.8 percent. Most investors worried that the situation might deteriorate and seriously jeopardize U.S.-China relations. After allowing the Chinese people to vent their frustration with the United States and presenting China's official position, the Chinese government tried to control the damage and maintain its focus on economic development.

First, Beijing emphasized the importance of social stability and reassured foreign investors that China would protect foreigners and their assets. In his televised speech (Chinese first high-level official reaction) on May 9, Chinese Vice President Hu Jintao said, "The Chinese government firmly supports and protects all the protests that tally with the law.... [However,] we must guard against any overreactions, watch out for people who may take advantage of the opportunity to disrupt the normal social order, and take firm actions to safeguard social stability.... To fully demonstrate the fine, civilized traditions of the Chinese nation, we will...protect foreign diplomatic establishments and their personnel in China, foreign nationals in China, and foreign personnel who are in China for economic, trade, educational and cultural activities." Within three or four days, Chinese officials secretly instructed campuses to discourage students from staging further protests. In May 2000, Beijing, again, issued a ban on protests to mark the anniversary of the Belgrade bombing.

In addition, Chinese officials sought to reassure U.S. businesspeople in China that their operations were safe and that economic reform policies would continue. For instance, Shanghai Mayor Xu Kuangdi traveled to General Motors's $1.5 billion plant, while a vice mayor met with several representatives of leading American banks. "Shanghai will continue to welcome foreigners to make investment in this city," said Xia Zhongguan, a senior official at the Shanghai Foreign Investment Commission. "Politics should be separated from business and trade. The bombing is one thing; foreign investment is another."

Second, Beijing tried to divert the people's focus back to economic development. On May 11, President Jiang Zemin said, "[The demonstrations against the United States have] demonstrated the enthusiasm, will, and power of the great patriotism of the Chinese people. The whole country is now determined to study and work harder, so as to develop the national economy continuously, enhance national strength, and fight back with concrete deeds against the barbaric act of U.S.-led NATO." On May 13, he emphasized again, "China will unswervingly take economic construction as its central task." In addition, he asserted that China "will continue to unswervingly adhere to the policy of reform and opening up, which is the only way to invigorate the country." On June 9, addressing to the National Party School Work Conference, he asked party cadres "must unswervingly focus our energies on continuing with economic construction," despite the U.S. bombing of the Chinese embassy.

On May 18, the *Renmin Ribao* urged the Chinese people to put aside the NATO bombing of the Chinese embassy in Yugoslavia and make efforts to improve the investment environment. On May 25, a *Renmin Ribao* editorial repeated President Jiang Zemin's call to the whole country to focus on economic development. The paper said that taking economic development as the central task all the time was the key to the resolution of all problems China faced. The editorial went on to say, "We must focus on economic development, while handling both domestic and international issues."

In less than two weeks, the Chinese government essentially put aside the NATO bombing incident and moderated its stance toward the United States, despite its rhetorical excesses. Thereafter, China gradually normalized bilateral contacts with the United States and repeatedly emphasized the importance of the U.S.-China relationship. Nevertheless, the Chinese government tried to avoid criticism of being too weak on the sovereign issues and U.S.-China relations. Therefore, the Chinese government continued to express its strong dissatisfaction about the U.S. position on the bombing incident. However, the later complaints did not become a meaningful obstacle of the normalization of U.S.-China relations.

On May 14, a week after the NATO bombing of the Chinese embassy in Belgrade, President Clinton expressed his sincere regrets and condolences directly to President Jiang in a telephone call concerning the tragic accident. One month later, U.S. Undersecretary of State Thomas R. Pickering met with Chinese officials in Beijing to offer the U.S. government's official explanation of how it mistakenly bombed the Chinese embassy in Belgrade.

Nevertheless, Minister Tang Jiaxuan criticized that the U.S. explanation of the NATO bombing on the Chinese embassy in Belgrade was "unconvincing" and therefore the Chinese government and its people could not accept the conclusion that the "bombing was a mistake." A commentary of the *Renmin Ribao* asked the U.S. side to "provide a convincing explanation of causes leading to the incident, make sufficient and effective compensation for all losses, and punish those responsible." Despite its criticism, the commentary pointed out, "China attaches importance to the development of Sino-U.S. ties, which is in line with fundamental interests of the peoples of the two countries and beneficial to the world peace, stability and development."

On July 30, China and the United States reached an agreement on the compensation for the casualties. The United States paid $4.5 million to the Chinese government. On September 11, President Jiang met President Clinton on the margins of the Asia-Pacific Economic Cooperation summit in Auckland, New Zealand, and mentioned the Kosovo bombing only once. On November 18, U.S. Deputy Assistant Defense Secretary Kurt Campbell visited Beijing in an effort to resume high-level exchanges between the two militaries. On December 16, the U.S. and China agreed to a compensation deal for NATO's bombing. The U.S. agreed to pay China $28 million for the destruction of the embassy in Belgrade, while China would pay $2.87 million to U.S. missions during the ensuing Chinese protests.

The resumption of WTO negotiations between the U.S. and China is another example of Chinese pragmatism. After the bombing incident, the Chinese government implicitly suspended the bilateral negotiation with the United States on China's entry into the WTO. On May 28, President Jiang Zemin explained that China remained "consistent in its attitude toward WTO, but the present atmosphere is inappropriate for the issue." On June 15, Minister Shi Guangsheng further explained that a proper atmosphere for negotiations with the U.S. was that the United States gave a satisfactory explanation of its bombing of the Chinese embassy in Belgrade.

Despite China's persistent dissatisfaction with the U.S. explanation of the bombing incident, the U.S. and China resumed bilateral talks on the WTO on September 9. On November 15, about half a year from the incident, the U.S. and China signed a milestone agreement, allowing China entry into the WTO. Ironically, even after signing the WTO agreement, the Chinese government continued its demand that the U.S. offer an "acceptable explanation" to the Chinese government and its people for the bombing.

Throughout the second half of 1999, Beijing never accepted the U.S. explanation, continuing to demand that the U.S. conduct a "thorough and comprehensive" investigation, provide an "acceptable explanation" to the Chinese government and the people for the bombing, and "severely punish the perpetrators." In early April 2000, the U.S. Central Intelligence Agency (CIA) dismissed one officer and punished six others for their roles in identifying and approving the target in Belgrade. Chinese spokesman criticized the CIA's dismissal of a midlevel officer blamed for the attack as inadequate, reiterating China's demands that the Clinton administration "punish those responsible." In response, the U.S. explicitly declared the matter closed.

On January 19, 2001, the U.S. government paid a sum of $28 million to the Chinese government for the property loss caused by the U.S. bombing. From the U.S. perspective, the incident has completely come to an end; in contrast, from the Chinese point of view, the incident was never finished. A Chinese spokesman said, "We call on the U.S. side to conduct a comprehensive and thorough investigation into the bombing, severely punish the perpetrators, and give a satisfactory account of the incident to the Chinese people."

Regardless of these different views on the incident, it was only a symbolic issue for China, and would hardly impede the normalization of the U.S.-China relations. Obviously, the Chinese government moderated its stance on this issue, in order to preserve the U.S.-China relations. However, another incident involving a sovereignty dispute followed two months later and again spurred a standoff between these two countries.

The investigation Plane Incident in 2001

On April 1, 2001, China held captive 24 U.S. military personnel and a U.S. Navy reconnaissance plane EP-3, which made an emergency landing on Hainan Island after an airborne collision with a Chinese fighter jet. This triggered a severe standoff between the United States and China. On the next day, U.S. President George W. Bush demanded "the prompt and safe return of the crew and the return of the aircraft without further damaging or tampering." He warned that China's continued silence about when the fliers would be returned could harm relations between the two countries. However, on April 3, the Chinese government directly rejected the U.S. demand. Instead, the Chinese government made solemn representations to the U.S. government. It strongly demanded that the U.S. government explain to the Chinese government and its people on the U.S. aircraft's actions of ramming into the Chinese plane and violating China's sovereignty and territorial airspace, and take earnest and effective measures to prevent similar incidents from occurring. Concretely speaking, the Chinese government demanded the U.S. government apologize to China, bear all the responsibility, and stop reconnaissance flights in airspace off China's coastal areas.

In explanation of Chinese policy on this accident on April 4, Minister Tang Jiaxuan emphasized that the Chinese side had, all along, taken a calm, restrained, and responsible attitude in handling the incident. He stated that Beijing attached importance to Sino-U.S. relations and hoped to see a proper solution to the incident as soon as possible. In addition, he criticized that the U.S. had adopted an opposite attitude, without considering the overall situation of Sino-U.S. relations. Throughout the incident, Beijing repeatedly emphasized that China had consistently attached importance to developing Sino-U.S. relations.

On April 4, U.S. Secretary of State Colin L. Powell struck a conciliatory note toward China. "We regret that the Chinese plane did not get down safely, and we regret the loss of life of that Chinese pilot," Secretary Powell said. "But now we need to move on." In his letter for Chinese Vice Premier Qian Qichen, Secretary Powell stressed the importance of the crew's release, repeated the expression of regret, and suggested some ways to resolved the dispute through a series of discussions.

However, Chinese Ambassador to the United States Yang Jiechi said on CNN, "Our side has said very clearly, that the U.S. side should shoulder all the responsibility and should apologize to the Chinese side." President Jiang Zemin also reiterated a demand that the U.S. apologize. Meanwhile, Minister Tang Jiaxuan berated U.S. Ambassador to China

Joseph W. Prueher for what he called American arrogance by making groundless accusations against China. Nevertheless, he stated that China wanted to resolve the dispute "appropriately as soon as possible," while protecting its "sovereignty and dignity."

China might want to resolve the dispute because many congressional critics of China said the continued detention of the plane's crew could endanger the renewal of normal trade status for China. In addition, some of ranking U.S. officials threatened China to link the incident with other issues involving China-U.S. relations. The president of the United States Chamber of Commerce issued a warning to China, "We want the Chinese government to understand that failure to resolve this matter in the immediate future could and would likely damage the current and potential economic exchange between the companies in our two nations."

On April 5, President Bush repeated an expression of U.S. regret, urging China to free the U.S. crew without further delay. "I regret that a Chinese pilot is missing, and I regret one of their airplanes is lost," he said. "Our message to the Chinese is we should not let this incident destabilize relations. Our relationship with China is very important. But they need to realize that it's time for our people to be home."

Despite the U.S. regret, the majority of the Chinese people wanted a U.S. apology. According to a poll, conducted by the Social Survey Institute of China on the collision of Chinese and U.S. warplane, 98 percent of respondents believed that the incident was deliberately created by the United States, and was a blatant act of provocation against China's sovereignty; while 89 percent of them believed that the U.S. side should and must apologize to China and indemnify Chinese losses.

On April 7, a letter from Vice Premier Qian Qichen to Secretary Powell stated that U.S. expressions of regret were not enough to end the stalemate. However, on the next day, U.S. Vice President Richard B. Cheney and Secretary Powell again rejected China's demands that the U.S. apologize for the collision, warning that Beijing's delays in returning the Navy plane's 24 crew members risked long-term damage to relations between the two nations.

In turn, on April 10, Beijing bluntly rejected U.S. statements of regret. "We are extremely unsatisfied by statements made thus far by the United States," Chinese Foreign Ministry Spokesman Zhu Bangzao said. "The United States should apologize," he added. "If not, it is going to make it more difficult to find a solution to this very serious incident."

On the same day, President Bush began to take a tougher tone, demanding the speedy release of the spy plane's crew. "Every day that goes by increases the potential that our relations with China could be damaged," President Bush warned. White House Spokesman Ari Fleischer further implied that Washington might end support for Beijing's long-sought membership of the World Trade Organization.

On April 11, after ten days of demanding the United States offer an official apology and admit full responsibility for the incident, China accepted a letter written by Ambassador Prueher to Minister Tang Jiaxuan, negotiated in English only, and agreed to release the 24 American crew members. In that letter, the United States told the Chinese people and the family of the lost Chinese pilot that it was "very sorry," and also said that it was "very sorry" that the crippled American aircraft had landed in China without permission. Notwithstanding, the United States did not accept responsibility that China had demanded.

Hoping to head off a possible backlash from the Chinese public, Chinese officials presented the deal as a victory for Chinese dignity. The Xinhua She (New China News Agency) translated "very sorry" to "shen biao qianyi" in Chinese. This literally meant to deeply express regrets or an apology, which can imply some culpability, as well as regret. However, a Chinese translation that was released by the U.S. embassy used the Chinese words "feichang wanxi," which linguists described as an expression of great sympathy, but not an apology.

Furthermore, the Xinhua She reported that, in a letter of expressing regrets (zhi qian xin) to the Chinese government, the U.S. government formally expressed regrets (zhi qian) to the Chinese government and the people. As a result, it claimed that the initial results had been achieved in the Chinese government's struggle against U.S. hegemonism.

Moreover, China twisted the language of a U.S. letter of regret into a fully-fledged apology. "The United States finally apologizes," screamed a front page headline in the popular *Beijing Morning Post*. The *People's Liberation Army Daily* added, "The U.S. apology to the Chinese people is only right." An editorial in the *Renmin Ribao* on April 12 said, "Our government and people have.... compelled the United States to change its rude and unreasonable hard line attitute and apologize to the Chinese people." In meeting with Communist Party organizations and media editors, Chinese leaders said that the United States had agreed to "a form of apology," without providing the exact language. Beijing clearly hoped to emphasize how much the United States had backed down.

Over the previous eleven days, China had insisted that the United States apologize for the collision, for the EP-3's "violation of Chinese airspace" as it made an emergency landing on Hainan Island without formal approval from the Chinese authorities, and for the loss of the Chinese pilot. While interpreting U.S. expressions of sorrow over the landing and the pilot's loss as an apology, the Chinese government chose not to notice that Washington did not accept responsibility or apologize for the collision itself. Shen Dingli, an expert on U.S.-China relations at Fudan University in Shanghai elaborated, "So if Chinese can't read the English text, they'll think it's great."

On April 13, two days after the crew's release, U.S. Defense Secretary Donald H. Rumsfeld accused the Chinese government of providing a misleading account of the collision and vowed to continue surveillance flights off the coast of China. Regarding this comment, Chinese Foreign Ministry Spokeswoman Zhang Qiyue responded, "This is not conducive to the development of Sino-U.S. relations, nor to the coming negotiations." Zhang stressed that the Chinese side has been handling the issue with calmness and restraint, taking the overall situation of Sino-U.S. relations into consideration.

Lu Shumin, a senior official of the Chinese Foreign Ministry, pointed out that after the incident, the Chinese side, taking into consideration the general interests of the China-U.S. relations, has handled the incident in a sober manner and with restraint. He added that China has always dedicated itself to developing healthy and stable relations between the two countries. Furthermore, he said, the Chinese side did not want to see any further harm to Sino-U.S. relations due to the suspension of the issue.

President Jiang Zemin elaborated, "We have always attached importance to Sino-U.S. relations and have been stressing the need to regard and handle bilateral relations from a strategic height. We do not want confrontations. However, on issues involving national sovereignty, territorial integrity, and national dignity, we absolutely will not make any compromise either." Nevertheless, he continued to say, "The people of all ethnic groups throughout the country must convert patriotic passion into an enormous strength for building a strong country, strive to push forward reform, opening up, and modernization undertakings...." A commentary article on April 12 in the *Renmin Ribao* also stated, "We must...gather up our strong patriotic fervor into all the work of promoting reform, opening up, and socialist modernization." That is, in spite of no compromise on sovereignty issues, Beijing considered promoting economic development, with maintaining stable U.S.-China relations, as the most important task.

Despite arousing rhetoric in official media, the Chinese government strictly prohibited protests against the United States on the streets and campuses of China. The Chinese government worried that demonstrations might go out of control and jeopardize social stability and economic development. To prevent the public's intense reaction from their dissatisfaction over the authorities' handling of the matter, the Chinese Communists have issued an order to strictly prohibit anyone from holding demonstrations against the release of the U.S. crew.

For the first time since the collision on April 1, on May 7, 2001, the United States resumed reconnaissance flights off the coast of China. Despite China's initial demand that the U.S. stop reconnaissance flights in this area, an U.S. official said, "There was no reaction from the Chinese." On the next day, President Jiang Zemin clearly explained the Chinese position, "A peaceful environment is indispensable for national, regional and even global development. Without peace or political stability, there would be no economic progress to speak of." Three weeks later, a commentary written by Gu Ping on the *Renmin Ribao* further elucidated that despite bilateral conflicts over the issues of the bombing, Taiwan, and Tibet, China and the United States had common interests in economic development and should cooperate with each other instead of creating a confrontation.

Obviously, the Chinese government attached significant importance to U.S.-China relations. During the incident, the Chinese government repeatedly stressed the importance of U.S.-China relations and thus "handled the incident in a sober manner and with restraint." This is not just propaganda! The Chinese government repeatedly demanded that the U.S. government apologize to China, bear all the responsibility, and stop reconnaissance flights in airspace off China's coastal areas. Furthermore, the Chinese said they "absolutely will not make any compromise" on issues involving national sovereignty, territorial integrity, and national dignity.

However, in the end, the Chinese government released the American crew by accepting a letter in which the U.S. only went as far as saying "very sorry" twice, not an official apology by Chinese standards. Moreover, the U.S. never accepted responsibility that China had demanded and even resumed reconnaissance flights off the coast of China in less than one month after the crew's release in mid-April 2001. Notwithstanding, Beijing did not adopt more assertive measures against Washington.

Appraisal and Conclusion

U.S.-China economic interdependence has significantly changed Beijing's perception of national interests, and thus, has shaped U.S.-China relations. A commentary in the *Renmin Ribao* in May 2001 pointed out, "The fast-developing Sino-U.S. economic cooperation and trade has become the main stabilizing factor and driving force in bilateral relations." An international relations scholar in Beijing expounded, "Some criticized Beijing was too weak in dealing with the U.S. and Japan. But those critics did not see a historical change. China is heavily interdependent with the U.S. and West. The interdependence has significantly constrained Chinese foreign relations. China can not comprehensively antagonize the West."

At a joint meeting with members of the Chinese People's Political Consultative Conference on March 6, 2001, Vice Premier Qian Qichen said that it was impossible to change the U.S. basic standpoint on the Taiwan and human rights issues, but China and the United States had common economic interests. He emphasized that China should bring the contradictions between China and the United States "under control and not have an outburst. We should reason things out and, if we fail, we should put aside minor differences so as to seek common ground [economic interests]."

An international relations senior scholar in Beijing stressed, "Sino-U.S. relations reflect the importance of economic development to China. China makes every effort to maintain stable Sino-U.S. relations. It is impossible for China to face off with the United States. The Sino-U.S. relationship is not an issue of face, but of economic development." An American studies senior scholar in Beijing elaborated, "The Sino-U.S. economic relationship is very important for China. Trade accounts for 40 percent of China's GDP, and 40 percent of China's trade goes to the United States. As a result, China must maintain a good relationship with the United States. The importance of the U.S. to China is much greater than China's importance to the United States. If Sino-U.S. relations worsen, it will bring severe damage to China."

In the two case studies, Beijing tried to minimize the impact of surging nationalism and public overreaction on its overall economic development and U.S.-China relations. In the case of the embassy bombing, Beijing only allowed "controlled" demonstrations and protests for two days, and then strictly prohibited any follow-up demonstrations. Afterward, Beijing tried to control the damage by reassuring the foreign investors and diverting the people's focus back to economic development. Moreover, Beijing pragmatically and gradually normalized relations with the United States, despite its tough gesture of rejecting U.S. explanation of the bombing incident and demanding the U.S. severely punish the perpetrators.

In the case of the reconnaissance plane incident, the U.S. government obviously did not meet China's three demands: apologizing, taking responsibility, and stopping reconnaissance flights in airspace off China's coastal areas. However, China strictly prohibited protests against the United States for fear of damaging its economic development. Furthermore, China frequently publicly expressed that China took a calm, restrained, and responsible attitude in handling the incident. In order to minimize a possible backlash from the Chinese public, Beijing twisted the language of a U.S. letter of regret into a fully-fledged apology, and thus, declared it a victory for Chinese dignity.

Regarding the sharp contrast between Beijing's rhetoric assertiveness and actual prudence, a Taiwan studies senior scholar in Beijing frankly stated, "The most important priority for China is economics. This is a prevailing consensus among the public and elite. Beijing should have acted stronger against the United States, Japan, and Taiwan, but Beijing had economic interests in mind." Since Beijing was not willing to sternly respond to Washington because of economic interest concerns, Beijing had to at least rhetorically assure the Chinese people of its firm position, and then prudently minimize the impact of the incidents on U.S.-China relations. In the reconnaissance plane incident, because Washington did not meet any of three initial demands Beijing raised, Beijing finally twisted the language and declared a moral victory in order to bolster its domestic position, as well as to normalize U.S.-China relations.

Many other Chinese scholars had the same perspective. For instance, an American studies senior scholar in Beijing emphasized, "Regarding the issue of the U.S. bombing of the Chinese embassy and the airplane collision, China does not want conflict. All China wants is to develop its economy!" Four international relations senior scholars in Beijing and an international relations senior scholar in Shanghai all agreed that economic interest is the essential consideration for China to deal with the issues of the U.S. bombing of both the Chinese embassy and the airplane collision.

An U.S. senior official explained, "Since the mid-1990s, Taiwanese President Lee Teng-hui's visit to the States, the U.S. mistaken bombing incident of Chinese embassy in Belgrade, and the collision incident between an U.S. reconnaissance plane and a Chinese fighter jet, all stirred strong reaction from Chinese officials and scholars. Nevertheless, with the prerequisite of maintaining U.S.-China economic interests, President Jiang Zemin finally intervened and emphasized that China had to do its best to maintain friendly relations with the United States. Beijing clearly recognized that Chinese economy heavily depended on U.S. economy. Sometimes, Washington reminded Beijing of this fact."

Looking into the future, Chinese U.S. policy would continue to be moderate and cooperative, in order to preserve the interests of bilateral economic interdependence. In the 16th National Congress of the Chinese Communist Party held in November 2002, Chinese leaders announced that, for the next twenty years, China would continue to focus on economic development. Beijing believes that a peaceful and stable international environment, particularly a stable U.S.-China relationship, is essential to China's economic development. As a result, it is a consensus within China that Beijing will continue adopting cooperative attitudes and policies toward the United States in the future.

9

Defence Economics and the Manufacturing Foundation

Disarmament since the end of the Cold War has led to major changes in the size and structure of defence industries. Change has been characterised by 'downsizing,' mergers and exits associated with job losses, plant closures and the search for new markets, including arms export markets. Technical change has also impacted on defence industries through creating requirements for new weapons (eg. unmanned combat air vehicles and the revolution in military affairs) and new forms of industrial organisation (eg. E-commerce and globalisation). Defence economics focuses on the need for difficult choices in a world of uncertainty.

The defence economics problem arises from two pressures. First, declining defence budgets; and second, rising equipment costs. Both pressures mean that defence policy-makers cannot avoid the need for some difficult choices. Economists can contribute to the policy debate by identifying the range of choices and the implications of various policy options. For example, with further reductions in defence budgets, a nation might have to abandon a world-wide role for its Armed Forces; or it might have to choose between a modern air force and a smaller navy and army; or it might have to rely more on reserve forces; or it might have to abandon support for its national defence industrial base. This article examines the economics of defence industries. It shows the importance of government, the economics of defence industries, the case for state support, the range of alternative industrial policies and possible future market developments. A starting point is a description of the major defence industries.

THE MAJOR DEFENCE INDUSTRIES

The world's major defence industries over the period since the end of the Cold War in 1990. Employment has fallen at the world level and especially in the industrialized nations (eg Europe; former Soviet Union).

Nonetheless, total world employment in arms industries was 8.7 million in 1997 with 55% of this employment in industrialized countries and 45% in developing nations. China, the USA and Russia accounted for some 70% of world arms industry employment.

Table. World's Defence Industries

Country	Index number 1990 (1997 = 100)	Number employed, 1997 (000s)
World	185	8,700
Industrialized	232	4,780
Developing	128	3,930
Europe	307	2,570
EU	162	770
NATO	150	2,850
China	129	3,100
USA	146	2,050
Russia	296	1,000
Ukraine	na	400
UK	147	300
India	100	250
France	136	220

Source: BICC (1999).

Countries have differed in the magnitude of the decline in their defence industry employment. Europe and Russia experienced major employment reductions over the period 1990 to 1997. Within Europe, employment reductions were especially severe in central and eastern Europe (eg in 1990, Hungary with an index of 600 and Bulgaria with an index of 400). In contrast, compared with the world average, employment reductions were below average in the USA, the UK, France and China. Even so, output reductions in nations such as the United States have been substantial. For example, the annual output of military aircraft for US Armed Forces declined from 3,085 units in 1970 to 664 units in 1990 and 150 units in 1998 (AIA, 2000).

The Significance of Government

Governments are central to understanding defence industries. Governments are major buyers and sometimes, the only buyers of defence equipment (monopsony). A government can use its buying power to determine the size and ownership of its national defence industry, its structure, entry and exit, prices, efficiency and profitability (structure, conduct and performance). Governments can support their defence industries by preferential purchasing and/or through direct subsidy payments.

They can also regulate the industry by controlling profits on government contracts (eg. preventing excessive profits and excessive losses); they can determine prices and profits on non-competitive contracts; they can affect the conduct of firms (eg. favouring non-price competition such as R&D); and they can control arms exports (eg. via licences).

Procurement of defence equipment involves government in a set of complex choices in a world of uncertainty. Typically, procurement decisions involve the following choices:

What to buy? Choices are required about the type of equipment to be purchased and its performance characteristics which, in turn, determines technical progress and the possibilities of technical spin-offs for the defence industry (eg. civil aircraft) and the rest of the economy.

Who to buy from? A contractor has to be chosen either by competition or by direct negotiation with a preferred supplier, with the market either restricted to domestic firms or open to foreign suppliers.

When to buy? Choices have to be made as to which point in a project's life cycle selection will occur.

Broadly, projects can be chosen at the drawing board stage, or during development, or at the prototype stage, or when the project is in full production. Risks are reduced the more project selection is delayed to the point at which production takes place and the equipment has entered operational service with a foreign air force. Similarly, competition can take place at various stages in the life cycle - ie. at initial development, or there could be competing prototypes, or competition for production work and/or for mid-life up-dates.

How to buy? Choices have to be made between alternative industrial policies ranging between the two extremes of independent development or imports, or the intermediate options of collaboration involving both development and production, or licensed or co-production, or an offset programme (each option involving different work sharing arrangements for a national defence industry).

Contracting. A contract has to be selected between the extremes of cost-plus and firm or fixed price or some form of target cost-incentive contract.

Choice criteria. Policy objectives: military v wider policy objectives. In making procurement choices, governments have to decide whether to focus on narrow defence criteria or to embrace wider economic and industrial objectives (eg. employment; technology, etc).

THE FFINANCES OF DEFENCE INDUSTRIES

In addition to the role of government, defence industries have a number of economic characteristics which are essential to understanding their performance and problems:

Cost levels and trends. Defence equipment is costly and the trend is towards rising costs. For example, the UK is purchasing three Astute Class nuclear-powered submarines at an estimated total cost of £2.01 billion, whilst the 4-nation Eurofighter combat aircraft is estimated to cost £13.8 billion for development and a unit production cost of £41.7 million per copy (1999-00 prices: HCP 613, 2000). And the trend is towards rising costs. Since 1945, the real unit costs of combat aircraft designed for the RAF (excluding strategic bombers and adjusting for different production runs) has risen at a compound annual growth rate of 11.5% (Kirkpatrick, 1995). As a result, the real unit cost of tactical combat aircraft has increased by a factor of 2.5 per decade. These cost trends reflect the technical arms race (technical leapfrogging) leading to higher development costs and higher unit production costs so resulting in fewer aircraft being purchased from a limited defence budget; but with each new generation of aircraft being "more productive" (ie. effective).

Technical progress. Technical progress has affected markets and the structure of defence industries. Technical advance has resulted in new products such as the jet engine, missiles, electronics, radar, helicopters and space systems with a greater emphasis on R&D. Since 1945, the long run structural trend has been towards a smaller number of larger firms, reflected in mergers and exits from the industry and this trend has been especially evident since the end of the Cold War in 1990.

Entry is costly. Entry requires technology and R&D expenditures, with the associated requirements for qualified scientists, engineers and other skilled labour. R&D costs will vary with the type of equipment being developed (eg. simple trainer to advanced combat aircraft). Learning costs are also significant in aerospace industries.

Learning economies and costs. Quantity is a major determinant of unit costs and hence of competitiveness. Long production runs enable fixed R&D costs to be spread over a larger volume; and in addition, there are learning economies in production. Learning reflects the fact that productivity improves with experience and through learning - by- doing. An

80% learning curve - which is often used in aircraft manufacture - suggests that man hours and labour costs will decline by about 20% for each doubling in the cumulative output of a given aircraft type (Sandler and Hartley, 1995, p124). Learning economies mean that the US aircraft industry benefits from its much larger scale of output compared with the Europeans. The US industry also benefits from steeper learning curves with typical slopes of 75% in the USA compared with 80% in Europe. Also, US learning curves show continuous learning with European learning curves tending to "flatten out" after 100+ units.

The incentives to collaborate. Ideally, collaboration between two or more nations can lead to the sharing of high R&D costs and to scale and learning economies from longer production runs as nations combine their orders. On this basis, collaboration results in cost savings to each nation (Hartley, 1983; 1991).

Industrial restructuring: adjusting to disarmament. Disarmament following the end of the Cold War has resulted in some cancellations, fewer new projects, smaller orders, shorter production runs, delays in ordering and the stretching- out of programmes. The result has been job losses, plant closures, mergers and exits from the defence business. Some firms have moved from prime contractor to sub-contractor status, whilst others have merged either with other aerospace firms or with other defence companies.

Some of the largest mergers have occurred in the US aerospace industry enabling American aerospace companies to obtain the economies of both scale and scope, although the price of efficient scale has been reduced competition. In aerospace, the US examples have included the creation of the Boeing Group (Rockwell-McDonnell Douglas) and Lockheed Martin (General Dynamics (combat aircraft business) and Loral), whilst in the UK British Aerospace acquired much of Royal Ordnance (land systems) and GKN (armoured fighting vehicles) acquired Westland (helicopters). In late 1999, there was further restructuring and mergers in Europe (BAE Systems, EADS; Thomson-Racal).

The complexity of supply chains. Typically, studies of defence industries focus on the major prime contractors to the neglect of their suppliers at the first, second and third tier. Little is known about supply chains: for example the technical capabilities of sub-contractors, their location, their dependence on defence business and their importance in local labour markets.

Change Strategies and Subsidies

Throughout their history, defence industries have been the focal point of technical change and external shocks, all of which have required appropriate adjustment strategies. For example, revolutionary technical change resulted from the shift from piston engines to jet engines, from manned aircraft to missiles and manned space flight. External shocks resulted from wars, with major increases in the demand for defence equipment, which also led to further technical change (eg. radar). Some of these "military-induced" technical changes were subsequently applied to the civil economy (eg civil aircraft). Inevitably, wartime industrial expansion was followed by contraction associated with a return to peacetime conditions.

To survive, defence industries have had to adjust to the uncertainties resulting from technical change and external shocks. Firms required R&D resources to be innovative in military and civil markets. Some firms diversified to "insulate" themselves from the uncertainties of the defence business; others merged or were taken-over to become part of a larger group; whilst others exited the industry for alternative activities which appeared to be potentially more profitable. Of course, adjustment strategies differed between state-owned and privately-owned enterprises. Privately-owned aerospace firms had to earn at least normal profits to induce them to remain in the defence business (and to satisfy their shareholders). Not surprisingly, both private and state-owned defence firms often survived through receiving government subsidies. Inevitably, following the end of the Cold War, national defence industries have been lobbying their governments for support (eg. to maintain the national defence industrial base and/or to assist the industry to adjust from defence to civil markets).

Some of the typical arguments used for state support of the defence industries are as follows:-

- Defence benefits in the form of independence, security of supply during a conflict, and the ability to design equipment for the needs of national forces.
- The infant industry argument whereby government support is needed to meet the high costs of entry into this industry. The belief is that eventually the new industry will be able to compete with established suppliers.
- Strategic trade policy where international trade is characterised by strategic rivalry between a small number of giant firms or 'national champions' of different countries (or indirectly between governments acting on their behalf). In such markets, an established firm might try to create strategic entry barriers to maintain and enhance its market power. The market for large civil aircraft is an example. Without Airbus, Boeing would be a monopolist; and it may be worth using subsidies (eg. launch aid) to prevent such an outcome. Subsidies by European governments for Airbus might also have induced other US civil aircraft firms to exit, so increasing Airbus market share; and furthermore, such European government support might send a clear signal to Boeing not to attempt a price war to try to force Airbus out of the market. Economically strategic industries are characterised by imperfect competition, decreasing costs, high technology and spin-offs. Governments might subsidise entry into such industries to obtain a share of monopoly profits. But, here, care is needed since subsidies do not guarantee market success (cf Concorde).
- Market failure in R&D as a result of which private firms might undertake less R&D than society regards as desirable: hence the need for government intervention to 'correct' this market failure.

- Externalities: external economic benefits in the form of jobs, technology, spin-offs, and the balance of payments (ie. exports and import-saving) contributions of defence industries: this is a further aspect of market failure.
- Foreign governments are subsidising their defence industries.
- The Exchequer contribution in the form of tax receipts from home and overseas sales (eg. income taxes; corporation taxes) as well as avoiding unemployment pay when projects are cancelled. Such arguments need to be assessed far more critically.

The arguments for state support of a national defence industry (as outlined above) are often dominated by myths, emotion and special pleading from groups with an (income) interest in continued state support and in avoiding the costs of change (which would make them worse-off). Such arguments need to be specified carefully and subjected to both empirical testing and critical evaluation. In particular, questions need to be asked about the alternative-use value of scarce resources. For example, consider the "foreign rivals are subsidising" argument. The obvious reply is that if foreigners wish to offer free gifts, a nation could respond by willingly accepting them and specialising elsewhere (doing something else)!

Economic theory suggests that subsidies are required to correct for certain types of 'market failure' (ie marginal cost pricing in decreasing cost activities; and where there are substantial social benefits such that private markets provide 'too little' of a socially-desirable output). However, the markets which are failing have to be identified (eg. R&D; capital market; labour market), and it has to be shown that subsidies are the appropriate solution. Moreover, it is by no means a simple matter to operationalise the broad guidelines for subsidy policy. "It is all too easy to think up plausible arguments based on externalities, merit wants and the like for subsidisation of this, that and every industry. Thus, an infant industry can be said to need a subsidy because it is growing; and an elderly industry can be said to need a subsidy because it is declining" (Prest,

1976, p71). And once introduced, subsidies attract interest groups of producers, consumers and administrators opposed to their abolition and hostile to any attempts to evaluate the results of subsidy policy! In such circumstances, subsidies are likely to depart from the economists market efficiency model and to be based on *ad hoc* interventionism reflecting various interest groups in the economy.

Globalisation and E-Commerce

Defence markets and defence industries are changing. They have been adjusting to disarmament, to 'revolutions' in both military and financial affairs and to further technical change affecting defence industries. New forms of industrial organisation have emerged as defence companies have developed their prime contracting and systems integration capabilities and have changed from national to international (global) companies. The major defence companies have both military and civil businesses, whilst some are specialist defence companies (eg. embracing air, land and sea systems).

Globalisation has already affected civil industries such as computers, electronics, information technology, jet airliners, motor cars, pharmaceuticals, telecommunications, drinks, food products and restaurants (eg Airbus; Boeing; Coca Cola; McDonald's; Microsoft). To be competitive, defence companies are following the example of the civil global corporations, seeking markets throughout the world and suppliers from overseas countries able to provide skills and components at least-cost. Global companies can achieve economies of scale and scope from supplying world markets rather than a small national market and they locate their various research and production activities in nations where costs are lowest. Defence industries have the economic characteristics of global industries, but traditionally, they have relied on their home market and sales to their national armed forces. The major civil aircraft companies have developed into global companies (eg. Airbus; Boeing); but globalisation is now affecting the major military aerospace and defence companies.

The US Spirited Threat

A long-run trend towards higher unit costs of equipment and smaller numbers creates pressures to reduce unit costs through importing and collaborative purchasing rather than buying small numbers from a national defence industry. Faced with falling defence budgets, governments will be more willing to 'shop around' to provide their armed forces with modern equipment at affordable prices: they will no longer be willing to pay the price of supporting a small-scale national defence industry. Here, US aerospace and defence companies form a major competitive threat to small-scale arms industries throughout the world. They offer proven high technology equipment at competitive prices and delivery dates, all of which are attractive to Armed Forces demanding modern equipment from falling defence budgets. Work-sharing arrangements (offsets) provide 'compensation' to the national defence industry likely to 'lose' from importing US equipment. The US competitive threat will be seen in the national markets of European countries and in overseas markets throughout the world. Mergers in the USA have created large arms companies able to obtain economies from the scale of their output and the scope of their activities. In 1997, four companies, namely, Lockheed Martin, Boeing, Northrop Grumman and Raytheon accounted for about 30% of all US Department of Defense purchases. Of course, large size does not guarantee success and mergers incur transaction and adjustment cost and take time to create a new competitive and profitable enterprise. Conflicts also arise since the price of efficient scale from mergers is the loss of domestic competition and the question of whether the benefits from mergers will be reflected in lower prices to the armed forces or higher profits for shareholders. The US competitive threat also provides a challenge to European aerospace and defence firms.

The European Defence Industry

European defence companies have responded to the US competitive threat by mergers and re-structuring to create a smaller number of larger groups able to compete with the big

American arms corporations (the US model). Two major European groups have been created, namely, BAE Systems and EADS, the European Aeronautic, Defense and Space Company. The acquisition of GEC-Marconi Electronics Systems by British Aerospace (both privately-owned) created BAE Systems which is vertically-integrated and specialised in defence, with capabilities in air, land and sea systems, as well as in defence avionics and electronics. EADS is a merger of Aerospatiale-Matra (France), Daimler-Chrysler Aerospace (Dasa: Germany) and CASA (Spain) and a joint venture with Finmeccanica (Alenia Aeronautics: Italy). Compared with BAE Systems, the EADS group is horizontally-integrated with substantial civil aerospace interests and includes state-owned organisations. There has been further European industrial consolidation in defence electronics and missiles involving a new group comprising the missile businesses of BAE, EADS and Finmeccanica.

There is also a challenge for European governments. The US model of large arms companies is based on a large home market. The re-structuring of Europe's arms companies requires that the European governments combine their various national demands to create a Single European Defence Market. Such a Single Market would provide the economic basis for European global defence companies. Currently, the four governments of France, Germany, Italy and the UK have created a quadrilateral armaments agency (known as OCCAR) and in the longer-term this could be the basis for a European Union armaments agency. However, there is a danger that a Single European Defence Market could lead to protectionism and political work-sharing (Fortress Europe and *juste retour*).

Technical Change

Technical change is also affecting defence industries in the form of the 'revolution in military affairs' and the E-commerce revolution. The result of changing technology could be new entrants and new forms of industrial organisation. A possible revolution in military affairs (RMA) will result in new technologies which will have impacts on both Armed Forces and defence industries. This 'revolution' involves the application of information technology to military command and control, the use of long-range precision weapons, unmanned combat air vehicles, automated battlefields and space weapons. There is likely to be a greater emphasis on electronics and information technology with companies from this sector emerging as new entrants and the next generation of prime contractors and systems integrators. There are likely to be further changes in the aerospace industry with a shift to "smarter" precision weapons, unmanned combat air vehicles and space systems (eg. space communications; offensive and defensive space systems). Computer-simulated training will mean computers and software replacing live firing and flight training, with a reduced requirement for equipment and spares. Elsewhere, not all defence companies will survive and adjust to the new technologies. Possible examples include the traditional main battle tank companies and firms which are specialist "metal bashers." New forms of industrial organisation will emerge. Here, the interesting question is whether, in the future, the most efficient defence company will be a specialist in the defence market with a complete range of air, land and sea capabilities or a diversified firm with both defence and civil business (including civil IT business which offers "spin-offs" to the Armed Forces).

The Impact of E-commerce and Dual-use

E-commerce is presented as a further revolutionary change for both the Armed Forces and defence industries. Economists can contribute to the debate by analysing the likely benefits and costs of E-commerce for the military-industrial complex. For the Armed Forces, Defence Ministries and Procurement Agencies, E-commerce is expected to result in more and better information leading to better decisions. For defence industries, the benefits of E-commerce will affect prime contractors and supply chains by creating global markets, by identifying new suppliers at the world level and new opportunities for "out-sourcing" work normally undertaken "in-house" (hence economising on transaction costs). There are possibilities of new entrants with knowledge companies entering as prime contractors as well as new forms of industrial organisation. For example, E-commerce might allow firms to out-source (buy-in) specialist design capabilities rather than retaining such capacity "in-house", so enabling firms to remain in the defence industry during gaps in R&D work. Overall, E-commerce is expected to lead to lower costs for industry.

Increasingly, competition will force defence firms to use new manufacturing and management techniques from civil industries (eg to apply techniques used in civil aircraft manufacture to the manufacture of military aircraft). The Boeing Joint Strike Fighter (JSF) combat aircraft is a good example of the application of Boeing's civil aircraft expertise to the military aircraft market.

The Boeing JSF design uses technology, materials and manufacturing processes from its commercial experience on the Boeing 777 and new 737 airliners, both of which were designed to achieve low weight and low cost. As a result, Boeing's success in civil aircraft markets allows it to apply similar management and manufacturing techniques to military projects, so giving it a competitive advantage in military markets (ie. compared with specialist defence firms which lack such commercial expertise).

PROJECT CHOICES AND INDUSTRIAL POLICY

Any procurement agency, whether national, collaborative or European, has to make difficult project choices. Cost-benefit analysis provides a framework for economic evaluation and for choosing between alternative defence projects and their associated industrial policies. For example, nations usually have to choose between different types of combat aircraft (eg Eurofighter; Rafale; Gripen; F-16; F-18; F-22; Joint Strike Fighter) each with different implications for meeting the national military requirement and contributing to the support and development of a national aerospace industry. Choices are further complicated by the availability of alternative industrial policies which embrace:

- Purchasing from a national aerospace industry (or supporting the creation of such an industrial capability);
- Collaboration where two or more nations share both development (R&D) and production work (eg. 4-nation Eurofighter).
- Licensed or co-production of an existing aircraft (eg. European co-production of American F-16);
- Importing a foreign aircraft off-the-shelf, where imports could be with or without some form of offset arrangement.

Using a cost-benefit framework for project evaluation requires the government to know the costs of each project and associated procurement option and the benefits in relation to military-strategic objectives and any wider economic and industrial objectives. Such an evaluation would:

- Start by identifying the government's policy objectives (ie. what is it trying to achieve?).
- Identify the range of items to be included in the cost-benefit analysis. For example, will the analysis be restricted to narrow defence criteria and hence military benefits and costs; or will it include wider economic and industrial objectives?
- Evaluate alternative ways of achieving policy objectives and their costs and benefits. For example, a national aerospace industrial capability can be retained by supporting the development of civil aircraft or by focusing on sub-contractor business or by undertaking the repair and maintenance of civil and military aircraft.

An information framework for the economic evaluation of defence equipment projects and industrial policies. It identifies some of the elements which might be included in a broad cost-benefit analysis of alternative procurement options. Usually, the options are reflected in specific equipment choices such as whether to build a combat aircraft independently, or collaboratively or under licensed production or by importing with or without an offset. For each option, information is required on acquisition and life-cycle costs, its military and strategic features in relation to the operational requirement (and the reliability of the various estimates), and its wider economic and industrial benefits. The Table is illustrative: more information can be added on specific costs and benefits; not all benefits can be easily expressed as monetary values (eg delivery) and, in some cases, policy-makers might choose to ignore some apparent benefits. Nevertheless, a cost-benefit approach is broader and more extensive than a simple investment appraisal exercise. The type of information needed to make sensible and informed choices on procurement and defence industrial policy.

The cost-benefit framework appears attractive; but project evaluation is often the focus of special pleading, myths and emotion. Reference will be made to the benefits of buying European and to the "vital importance" of the defence industry as a leading industrial sector. Such claims need to be subject to careful and critical appraisal of the following type:

- Government needs to be clear about its policy objectives: what is it trying to achieve? Is the focus on narrow defence objectives, or is there a concern for wider economic and industrial objectives; and are these wider economic objectives the proper concern of the Defence Ministry or of other Government Departments?
- The uncertainties attached to the various benefits and costs need to be indicated.
- The alternative use of resources needs to be considered. Would the resources used in the national defence industry make a greater contribution to employment, technology, balance of payments and other policy objectives (and ultimately to society's welfare) if they were used elsewhere in the economy? For example, alternative public expenditure on roads, schools and hospitals might create more jobs and contribute to other policy objectives compared with expenditure on the national defence industry.

- The willingness to pay. Government has to decide how much it is willing to pay for the benefits of buying domestically. For instance, is it willing to pay an extra 10%, 20% or more for equipment produced by its national defence industrial base?

A European Armaments Agency

Europe's defence industries have been re-structured so that the supply side of the market has been re-organised before similar re-structuring has occurred on the demand side of the European defence equipment market. European governments cannot ignore their role in determining appropriate procurement arrangements which would allow European defence firms to achieve the scale, learning and scope economies which characterise US defence firms. The alternative procurement arrangements range from liberalising or opening-up national defence equipment markets in the EU to the creation of an EU Armaments Agency. A possible basis for the future formation of a European Armaments Agency already exists in the form of OCCAR (OCCAR is the French acronym for Organization Conjointe de Cooperation pour l'Armement). Formed in 1996, OCCAR is a quadrilateral armaments agency comprising France, Germany, Italy and the UK which aims to improve the efficiency and effectiveness of collaborative ventures.

Currently, OCCAR nations account for over 80% of the EU's spending on defence equipment, which indicates the potential for efficiency savings if its scope were extended. However, OCCAR is restricted to collaborative ventures which are only part of total defence equipment spending (eg. in the UK collaborative programmes account for 10% of equipment expenditure). In principle, OCCAR could be the basis for the future development of a European Armaments Agency. However, the creation of such an Agency would complicate the organisation by adding more members, most of whom have relatively small defence budgets. More members might also increase the pressure for *juste retour* and a Fortress Europe policy of protecting European defence industries.

THE ECONOMICS OF INTERNATIONAL COLLABORATION

International collaboration involving two or more nations in the development and production of defence equipment provides opportunities for cost savings in both R&D and production. In the ideal case, costly development programmes are shared between two or more partner nations and a pooling of production orders enables economies of scale and learning to result in lower unit production costs and output levels which are more competitive with the USA.

Problems of International Collaboration

International collaboration is not without its problems, all of which lead to departures from the 'ideal model'. The governments, military staffs, scientists and industrialists in each partner nation form interest groups which will pursue their own self interest concerned with leadership, design requirements, technology and work shares. Compromise is inevitable and nations will join the collaborative club and remain members so long as membership is expected to be worthwhile (compared with the alternatives of a national programme or imports). Within the collaborative club, nations will reach agreement about the project's military specifications, the delivery dates for each partner's armed forces, work shares and the arrangements for project management. Reaching agreement on such a complex international contract involves substantial transaction costs in specifying, negotiating, agreeing and monitoring where there are information asymmetries and opportunities for strategic behaviour.

Nations might be expected to learn from previous experience with collaboration, but such learning benefits might be reduced if new partners are added to the club. Nonetheless, one rule has dominated European collaboration, namely, *juste retour*, where the emphasis is on a 'fair share' of the work between partner nations, which usually means work allocated on the basis of each nation's planned production orders (where planned production can change between the development and production phases of the programme). For example, on collaborative aircraft development work, *juste retour* means that each nation will demand its fair share of high technology work on the airframe, engine and avionics as well as demanding its own flight testing centre. Similarly, with collaborative production work, each nation demands a final assembly line. Thus, work is allocated on the basis of equity and political bargaining rather than on the basis of efficiency criteria (competition and comparative advantage).

Partner governments are not models of efficient decision-making. Governments and their officials create elaborate and complex committee structures which seek consensus at every level and require unanimity for key decisions: some decisions can only be made by the most senior committees or by ministers. For example, on the Eurofighter project there is a four level hierarchy of committees (originally 39 committees were established), with a steering committee providing overall guidance and meetings attended by national officials and other interested parties (eg. up to 60 people can be present at a meeting). Programme management is further complicated by the need for extensive monitoring arrangements as partner nations seek to 'police' costs and progress on incomplete contracts for costly and complex projects. An international agency is usually created for the day to day management of a collaborative programme (eg. NEFMA is the NATO Eurofighter Management Agency). However, such agencies often lack a clear mandate; they might duplicate the work of national project management offices; and staff posts are filled by each nation in line with the cost sharing arrangements on the programme. The result of the government programme arrangements is excessive bureaucracy and slow decision-making which can be a further source of delays and inefficiency in collaboration. Of course, politicians and officials might enjoy international travel, the glamour of meeting in foreign locations and the prestige of inter-governmental conferences. Experience also suggests that international collaboration involving a large number of countries is more difficult because of the problems of reaching agreement on defining a common concept.

Lessons of European Collaboration

There are at least two lessons from European collaborative defence programmes. First, care is needed in identifying the criteria to be used in evaluating collaborative programmes. Perfect problem-free projects do not exist. Most high technology defence projects whether they be national or collaborative are characterised by problems reflecting 'poor' procurement management and ambitious technical requirements leading to cost overruns, delays and sometimes cancellation. Interestingly, though, whilst Eurofighter is a third generation collaboration (after Jaguar and Tornado), it is characterised by the traditional problems of work sharing and government decision-making. Of course, it might be claimed that these problems and inefficiencies would be even greater without the benefits of previous collaborative experience. Second, there remain considerable opportunities for improving the efficiency of collaborative programmes. Efficiency could be improved by:

a. Allocating work on the basis of each nation's comparative advantage using competition to determine work shares;
b. Selecting a single prime contractor for the programme and ensuring that the prime contractor is subject to contractual incentives placing it at risk (via competitively-determined fixed price or target price incentive contracts);
c. Applying the principle of compensation. Adequate arrangements are needed to compensate the losers from policies designed to improve efficiency in collaborative programmes. Compensation need not be organised within the programme but could involve offsets on other defence projects or more general regional aid and manpower policies (eg. training; mobility).

THE EUROPEAN DEFENCE PROCUREMENT PROBLEM

Europe's defence procurement problem is reflected in:

a. Inefficiency in the defence equipment markets in the EU resulting from support for national defence industries, so that the EU comprises a set of separate (fragmented) national defence markets. Compared with the USA, nations in the EU have too many rival projects and short production runs resulting in the duplication of costly R&D and a failure to obtain economies of scale, learning and scope;

b. The defence economics problem resulting from rising equipment costs and falling defence budgets. Inefficiencies in EU defence equipment markets will accentuate the defence economics problem and the associated need to make difficult choices in defence policy, including procurement policy.

c. Competition from the US aerospace and defence industries offering high technology equipment at competitive prices, reflecting their large scale output. Faced with falling defence budgets, the Armed Forces and Governments of EU nations will have to choose between buying modern and cheaper equipment from the USA (with offset agreements), or improving the efficiency of European procurement policy and Europe's defence industries.

SCENARIOS FOR A SINGLE EUROPEAN MARKET FOR DEFENCE EQUIPMENT

Various scenarios have been proposed for the creation of a Single European Market for the procurement of defence equipment. These are designed to eliminate the major inefficiencies in the current fragmented national arrangements whereby independence through supporting a domestic defence industrial base is costly (the costs of non-Europe). Three broad scenarios have been proposed by the European Commission for creating a Single European Market for defence equipment (each could be the basis for an eventual European Armaments Agency). Each scenario involves different sets of benefits and costs and for each one, it is possible to envisage a liberalised competitive market either restricted to firms in member states of the EU or open to firms from the rest of the world. The scenarios are:

A competitive market which would simply extend the EU's rules for public procurement in the civil sector to defence procurement. National defence ministries would remain responsible for national procurement, and in principle, contracts would be subject to competitive tendering with open and transparent procedures based on objective selection and award criteria (this is an obvious source of controversy). Estimates suggest that this scenario might result in lower-bound cost savings of 8.5% to 11% of EU defence procurement budgets, depending on whether the European market is restricted to EU firms or opened-up to firms from the rest of the world (Hartley and Cox, 1992).

A centralised purchasing agency which would replace national Defence Ministries and would achieve substantial cost savings through purchasing common standardised equipment for all EU nations (ie. effectively for a single EU army, navy and air force thereby replicating the US model). A European Armaments Agency could act as such a centralised procurement agency. Lower-bound cost savings for this scenario have been estimated at 14.5% to 17% of EU defence equipment budgets with the higher figure applying where the market is opened to firms from the rest of the world (Hartley and Cox, 1992). Of course, this scenario is economically attractive but, politically, is the most difficult to achieve.

A twin track approach which is a mixture of competition and collaboration. Competition would apply to small and medium-size equipment (eg. small arms; light combat aircraft-trainers; small warships and small missiles) whilst large-scale air, land and sea systems would be undertaken on an international collaborative basis. In this scenario, a European Armaments Agency might act as both a competition authority and as an agency for promoting and managing collaborative programmes (cf. OCCAR). For EU defence equipment budgets, minimum cost savings for this scenario have been estimated at 11% to 14% depending on whether competition is restricted to EU firms or open to the world. In addition to offering substantial cost savings, this scenario is attractive politically in that it offers EU nations possible involvement in collaborative projects in return for opening-up their defence markets to competition (Hartley and Cox 1992).

Costs of a Single Market

Whilst the three Single Market scenarios offer efficiency improvements and cost savings, the resulting benefits are not costless. It will take time to create a Single European Defence Market and there will be adjustment costs, with some firms and regions being 'losers' in a competitive market (and these costs will be additional to those resulting from disarmament since the end of the Cold War). Article 223 of the EC Treaty (now Article 296 of the Treaty of the EU) is also a barrier to creating a Single European Market for defence procurement since it allows exemptions from the Treaty for "the production of or trade in arms, munitions and war material". Similar barriers to change arise where nations differ in their mix of public and private ownership of defence industries, where cross-border restructuring of defence industries requires government approval, and where nations differ in their arms export policies.

Creating a competitive Single European Defence Market also requires a 'level playing field' and non-discriminatory procurement. In addition to anti-competitive behaviour on the demand-side of the Market (ie. government), there is potential for similar behaviour on the supply-side. If the Market is restricted to EU firms, it is likely to be characterised by monopolies, cartels and collusive tendering with adverse impacts on prices and innovation but higher profits for contractors. A solution to the monopoly problem would be to abolish entry barriers and open-up the EU Market to firms from the rest of the world. There would, though, be a 'trade-off' as foreign competition, especially from the USA, would have implications for maintaining an EU defence industrial base.

Defence firms and national defence industries continue to face an uncertain future. No one can predict accurately the future: it is unknown and unknowable. As always, firms which have the entrepreneurship to anticipate the future correctly will survive; others will fail. Governments are faced with difficult choices about their national defence industries. Falling defence budgets, reflecting a preference for increased social welfare spending and a peace dividend, mean that supporting national defence industries can be costly. The alternative would be for governments to act like a competitive buyer, "opening-up" their national defence markets to foreign firms and buying defence equipment from the lowest-cost suppliers in the world market. Such a policy would benefit taxpayers and the Armed Forces but the losers would be the national defence industrial base.

DEFENCE MANUFACTURING AND MARKETS TASK FORCE

The end of the Cold War has changed the *nature* of the security threats that Member States face rather than doing away with them. New and complex security challenges have emerged which can only be addressed by professional forces which are well equipped with state-of-the-art technology. The Libya crisis showed (again) that Europe is still lacking military capabilities in some critical sectors, although the European Defence Technological and Industrial Base (EDTIB) could deliver most of the technologies and materiel we would need.

These capability gaps are clearly a direct consequence of budget constraints. These constraints are unlikely to disappear anytime soon. Public debt and the consolidation of state finances are the most important challenges in Europe now - and will certainly remain as such for the near future. It is therefore hardly surprising that almost all national defence budgets are under pressure and subject to significant cuts.

A major casualty in defence budgets has been spending on Research & Technology which is crucial for the development of the next generation of equipment. Cuts in current military programmes and the apparent lack of new ones are also contributing to the erosion of the EDTIB which was already suffering from structural underinvestment. For the time being, many European defence companies are still doing well, with exports to third countries (at least partly) compensating for shrinking home markets. Faced with the sharp decline in public defence spending, Europe's industry is concentrating its efforts on new emerging defence markets with a strong growth potential such as India and Brazil. Europe's industry is also strengthening its presence in highly dynamic related business segments such as electronics, security, space, and civil aviation. This indicates that European defence industries are, in many areas, still at the cutting edge of technology and globally competitive.

However, these strengths are the result of investments made many years ago and as such Europe is now reaping the benefits of that forward thinking.

Drive to Increase Exports

The drive to increase exports will be undermined as the lack of major new programmes is gradually reducing the range of high-end technology products that are still fairly competitive. Furthermore, as the US defence budget also faces significant cutbacks, competition from US companies looking for new business opportunities outside their home market is set to grow (and be boosted by US reform of export controls making it easier to do so). With European defence markets declining or at best stagnant, however, incentives to invest in European mergers and acquisitions are likely to diminish with the lack of new orders and the attractiveness of investing in buoyant third markets. Lacking new programmes, the defence industry is likely to reduce its investment in Europe or to pull out of certain sectors altogether.

Investing in emerging third countries may prove to be a more sustainable way of maintaining turnover but it may also generate a loss of technology and IPRs due to heavy offset requirements that often include local establishment and content requirements. Moving production and transferring technology is becoming a minimum requirement for many major export orders – all of which may lead to cutbacks in factories and employment in Europe and threaten the long-term competitiveness of the EDTIB. In the long run, competitiveness on world markets can only be maintained on the basis of a truly

European home market in which EU companies can operate freely in all Member States and benefit from a demand side which is consolidated at the European level. For the time being, however, the European defence market remains fragmented and lacks efficiency. Member States continue to allocate the bulk of their defence spending to manpower rather than procurement of new equipment and forward-oriented research. Furthermore, there is a lack of harmonisation of military requirements and most procurement remains national. As a result, production volumes remain small and economies of scale rare.

Under these conditions, Europe risks losing the industrial and technological capabilities that are necessary to develop and produce what it needs for its security. At stake is as such, not only Europe's competitiveness in a globalised world but also its long-term security of supply, which is in turn crucial to its strategic autonomy and ability to act at international level. Increasing or even maintaining key strategic defence assets in times of scarce financial resources will therefore be a major - if not the main - challenge in this policy domain.

The Commission's Payment

If spending *more* is difficult, spending *better* becomes even more important. In the context of the on-going structural reforms of armed forces and military organisations as is happening in other sectors of Europe's economy and society; there should be more consolidation of demand and better cooperation via pooling, sharing and role specialisation; better exploitation of civil-military synergies; and more efficient market structures.

Most of these issues lie within the responsibility of Member States and intergovernmental institutions and bodies, starting with the European Defence Agency (EDA).

However, the Commission, for its part, can use its legislative, financial and administrative tools to encourage, support and push forward the necessary transformation process. The most prominent examples of this are the two Directives on defence procurement and defence transfers adopted in 2009, which form today the regulatory backbone of a European Defence Equipment Market. And President Barroso, in his State of the Union speech of September 2011, committed the Commission within its competences to do all it could to develop the single market and industrial base in the European defence sector.

In order to look into these issues, the Commission set up a Defence Task Force with the mandate of exploring ways to move beyond the current state of play and energise the EU-wide debate over the future of the European defence sector. The Task Force is still in its early stages, but three priority areas have emerged: (a) Internal Market; (b) Industrial Policy; and

Research & Innovation

III.a. Internal Market In the area of the internal market the Commission's focus is on ensuring the effective and timely transposition as well as implementation of legislation.

With respect to the defence transfer Directive, the Commission will promote in particular the use of General Licences, which is particularly important for the sake of industrial competitiveness and security of supply among Member States. The Commission will analyse and compare the scope of general licences published by Member States to assess convergences in the Member States' approach.

With respect to the defence procurement Directive, the Commission will work to ensure that certain exclusions, such as government-to-government sales, are applied in a way that is consistent with the objectives of the directive and does not impinge on its effectiveness. It will also continue to work towards the phasing out of offsets, following the revision of national offset regulations and Member States' procurement practice in particular in the area of subcontracting. The Commission will also establish an effective market monitoring mechanism (in order to ensure the correct application of the Directive) and gather the data required to report to Parliament in 2017 on the impact the Directive has had.

Finally, the Commission will explore whether and to what extent it can contribute, through its regulatory power, to the Union's long-term security of supply. This may lead to an initiative on the control of defence industrial capabilities.

INDUSTRIAL POLICY

It is widely accepted that the present evolution of defence markets is leading to overcapacity and acceleration of restructuring processes in the European industry. No EU Member State can afford to maintain a full-spectrum defence industrial base. Perhaps more importantly, no one has a strategic need to do so, given that most military operations are undertaken by coalitions either within NATO or the Common Security and Defence Policy (CSDP).

Industrial restructuring in Europe is not only unavoidable: it is already under way. It is essential that national approaches in this policy area be developed, as much as possible, within a European framework by taking full account of its social impact (including the possible use of EU Structural Funds and the European Globalisation Adjustment Fund within the limits of the rules governing them). Such an approach should be based on the principle of inter-dependence and the concept of European centres of excellence and tailored to the three main industrial sectors (naval, land and aviation). Cooperation and specialisation are the only ways to maintain and strengthen essential capabilities and technologies and to secure supply in the medium and long term. The Commission will work, together with the EDA and all relevant stakeholders, towards the development of such a common European approach to the restructuring of the defence industry.

Another critical dimension is the impact of defence cuts on SMEs, as SMEs are an important source of employment and innovation in all sectors: defence is no exception. However, with the existing fragmentation of defence markets, SMEs find it particularly difficult to access markets in other Member States. The Commission plans to explore – once again in cooperation with the EDA - what more could be done to support

SMEs in this sector, such as: improving access to information on potential business opportunities; identifying and promoting best practice in Member States; and developing networks of clusters at European level and to support SMEs in expanding their businesses outside the European Union where appropriate.

Research & Innovation

It is worth exploring what can be done to limit the impact of the cuts in funding for defence R&D, which is a crucial element of industrial competiveness. The main objective is to develop greater synergies between dual technologies funded through the different Commission's research programmes and the defence research agenda of the EDA.

The cooperation between the Commission and the EDA is already close in this area and recently made easier by the European Framework Cooperation (EFC). The EFC is designed to maximise complementarity and synergy between the Commission's civil security research programme, the EDA co-ordinated defence-related research, and the space research of the European Space Agency. The first concrete results of the EFC came in September 2011 when a letter of coordination was signed on Chemical, biological, radiological, and nuclear (CBRN) protection.

The Commission and the EDA are building on this promising start by looking at what other areas could be brought within the EFC. Perhaps the most obvious area is cyber security as one of the few where Member States have kept, or even increased, their budgets. Other areas could include Unmanned Aircraft Systems (UAS), advanced materials, future and emerging technologies and critical space technologies. The Commission would also like to explore how best to make use of the specific Intellectual Property Rights (IPRs) and exchange of information articulated in its 'Horizon 2020' proposal. These should make it easier to exchange research results with the EDA and the Member States.

Finally, the Commission is exploring the possibility of mandating the European standardisation organisations to develop standards that could be used in both civil and defence technologies in areas where the technology is the same and the application quite similar (i.e. hybrid standards).

Looking Ahead

For most of the above-mentioned issues immediate action is possible – and arguably desirable - and targeted initiatives can be launched in the short term.

Other issues may need further reflection and deserve a broader strategic debate. The Task Force also intends to look into these issues.

The Defence Task Force would like to inquire for example whether truly European solutions can be a more efficient alternative for consolidating the demand side of the European defence market than the current purely intergovernmental pooling and sharing initiatives.

10

Military Industrialization in India

The Indian state inherited much from its former colonial master, including several ordnance factories and an aircraft factory. During the period immediately after independence, domestic production was limited primarily to small arms and ordnance. Britain was also the source of most of India's weapons imports during that time. British weaponry was generally familiar to the Indian armed forces, and the new state was in no hurry to become entangled in the cold war by acquiring American or Soviet equipment. By the mid-1950s, after Pakistan signed a military aid agreement with the United States and subsequently joined both the Southeast Asian Treaty Organization and the Baghdad Pact, India had a new set of security incentives for both increased weapons imports and the development of an indigenous defense industry. These would be reinforced by the frequently high levels of tension on the subcontinent, including a war with China and two more with Pakistan, and the continuing flow of advanced weaponry to the region.

Why India Builds

Observers of military industrialization in the third world typically highlight the "rational" or "instrumental" ends toward which indigenous arms production is directed. States acquire arms in order to improve their immediate security vis-à-vis rival states. Domestically produced arms have the added benefit of guarding against the manipulation of weapons supplies, including spare parts, which might otherwise be undertaken by foreign suppliers with their own policy objectives. Domestic arms production has also been given an explicitly economic rationale. States obviously need not purchase from abroad what they build themselves, so arms production is viewed as means of conserving foreign exchange. Military industrialization may be pursued for purposes of technological development and spin-off to the civilian sector of the economy. In addition to these commonly cited motivations for military industrialization, we argue that there are also more "symbolic" motivations.

The most obvious impetus behind Indian weapons production is provided by the country's immediate security environment, especially its strategic relationships with Pakistan and China. Territorial disputes over the Kashmir with Pakistan and along the Himalayan border with China are complicated further by religious and ideological differences. Throughout the period of Indian independence these have generated high levels of hostility and several overt military conflicts. Even when relations with Pakistan and China are relatively quiescent, India has remained attentive to these states' arms acquisitions: what they import, what they produce, what they try to produce. Levels of regional hostility and levels of regional armament explain, in large part, why India has acquired advanced weaponry for its armed forces.

While India's immediate security needs have been interpreted as requiring a well-armed defense forces, on strictly military grounds there should be no reason to prefer domestically produced weaponry over imports, assuming comparable performance characteristics. But there are reasons both to prefer and not to prefer domestic production on economic grounds. In his extensive and balanced study of Indian security policy, Thomas has noted that a policy of indigenous weapons production "would mean a substantial increase in the scientific and technological knowledge of the country with attendant benefits for the civilian sector as well." To be sure, the pursuit of "military-led industrialization" is recognized far more explicitly in the academic literature than it is acknowledged by Indian statesmen. Production of killing machines would seem to demand something other than an economic rationale, especially in a democracy like India. Still, many analysts do agree that part of what drives military industrialization in

India and elsewhere in the third world is the belief that arms production will promote development in adjacent sectors of the national economy. Of course, state leaders may be wrong — and much of the literature endeavors to show them the errors of their ways — but "[t]he skepticism of academics in industrialized countries notwithstanding, the belief remains widespread that such programs can provide tangible economic and technological benefits as well as enhanced military security."

Indigenous weapons production in India has also sometimes been justified as a means of conserving foreign exchange that would otherwise go to foreign purchases, but in almost all cases the policy of import substitution has failed to measure up to expectations. The problem is not unique to India. Scarce resources and the inability of third world armed forces to absorb large quantities of domestically produced weapons makes for very high unit costs, in which case importing weapons of even superior quality can be the cheaper alternative. Thomas has found that licensed production has been increasingly favored in India, especially by economic planners. They recognize "the need to strike an optimum balance between the cost and quality of weaponry; this is best obtained in the long run through both external technological transfers and domestic production." Here too there are costs, since licensing involves both the importation of parts and machinery as well as the payment of royalties. Still, the hope is that this paves a way for indigenization, one in the end less costly than attempts to indigenize cold turkey.

There are other reasons why India builds weapons, not unrelated to its security environment or industrial development. According to Katz, "[t]he most important factor driving LDCs to produce arms can be summarized quite easily: autonomy, that is, freedom of action in the domestic and international spheres." Actual or potential threats to national security are exacerbated when states find themselves dependent on others for defense. India, having experienced arms embargoes (e.g., those imposed by the United States during the 1965 and 1971 conflicts with Pakistan), bristles at the thought of lasting arms dependence. As Indira Gandhi put it, "We want India to be self-reliant and to strengthen its independence so that it cannot be pressurized by anybody...." Indian independence in defense policy is enhanced by an indigenous arms production capacity, particularly the capacity to initiate or expand production in a pinch, as well as the capacity to maintain existing systems.

According to the Ministry of Defence, "Modernization of arms and equipment and a maximum degree of self-reliance and self-sufficiency in the shortest possible time have been the major objectives in our defence production effort.... No *free* nation... can afford to ignore the imperative need to

maintain constant preparedness to defend [against] any threat to its borders." Self- sufficiency in weapons procurement has taken on a degree of significance beyond diminishing the impact of arms embargoes during wartime; it has become an integral feature of India's stated policy of nonalignment. Principles of nonalignment have been adhered to more rigidly at some times and not others — Indira Gandhi's foreign policy vis-à-vis the Soviet Union falling into the latter category. But the desire to remain aloof from the cold war competition which entangled so many other third world states was the closest thing to an Indian strategic doctrine. With the cold war over, the policy of nonalignment has less resonance, but self-sufficiency in arms production, and independence more generally, still have claims on the Indian imagination.

Beyond immediate security imperatives and industrial development, the possession of indigenous weapons production capacity has taken on symbolic importance for India. Foreign policy under Indira Gandhi has received much attention on this score, and the Pokhran nuclear test epitomized India's quest for international recognition. In the opinion of one of Gandhi's biographers, Pokhran "was no more than a gesture of independence and a bid for inexpensive prestige." William

Barnds, long-time observer of India's role in world affairs, detected the symbolic motivations behind India's nuclear program well before the nuclear explosion occurred: "With each of the first Chinese test explosions there was a new demand by some Indians that their country produce similar weapons. The demands often seemed as much concerned with Indian prestige as with security." He adds that "The call for an Indian nuclear force also reflected a mood that the country should depend more on itself and less on outsiders." Sisir Gupta, an Indian diplomat and academic, in 1965 referred to India as the "sixth Power in a world where only five are recognized to be great" and suggested that India could "either enter the club by defying the world and making a bomb or see to it that the bomb as a status symbol loses its significance because of effective progress towards disarmament." He was skeptical regarding the latter option because "military capability remains the most important source of a country's status, prestige and power...."

In addition to enhancing India in the eyes of the international community, domestic weapons production seems to have been partly motivated by the desire to enhance India in the eyes of Indians themselves. Again, this is a recurrent theme in defence policy under Indira Gandhi. One concern has been with the scientific and industrial community. In a 1968 interview, Gandhi lamented that "our intellectuals, our industrialists and businessmen do not yet feel proud of being Indians." She would later justify the Pokhran test by the need "for our scientists to know what they are capable of." In 1992, Prime Minister Rao referred to the successful launch of the augmented SLV (after several failures) as "a morale booster for the scientific community." The preoccupation with self-image has been extended to the whole of India as a nation. Without mentioning any specific weapons programs, Gandhi once commented that "while we must have arms to defend our country from any aggression, these arms, this military strength must be backed by conviction in our ideals and confidence in ourselves." Commensurate with India's policy of nonalignment, she also wished for an Indian identity unmolested by cold war politics: "we wanted [India] to be able to grow in its own way

— to choose its own direction, to choose its own personality." There are nations, like India, that are "sensitive, assertive and proud of their individual personalities.... What is important is that we stand for ourselves."

All of this suggests that there are multiple factors driving domestic weapons production in India, including the weapons-related nuclear and space programs. India's immediate security environment, especially its enduring rivalry with Pakistan and its often hostile relations with China, is perhaps only the most obvious. India's defense programs are also motivated by the hope that they will contribute to industrial development generally. And, most importantly for our purposes, military industrialization has symbolic meaning. It is perceived by Indian elites, and presumably by some nonelites, to enhance India's autonomy in foreign affairs, and ultimately its status and prestige in the international community. It is also seen to enhance the self-confidence of scientific and technical community directly involved in weapons development and production, and the self-image of the entire Indian nation as well. These themes resurface in our analysis of *India Today*. But first we turn to IR theory.

What India Build

Hindustan Aircraft Ltd. began licensed production of the British Gnat fighter in 1961. It later developed and produced an advanced version, the Ajeet, but with only limited success. When HAL signed the licensing agreement to produce the Gnat in 1956, it also commenced development of its own supersonic fighter, the HF-24 Marut. The first planes entered service in 1964, but the project ultimately foundered on the inability to either produce or import an appropriate jet engine. Production ceased in 1975. Prior to the Sino-Indian war, India had been looking to the Soviet Union as a source of advanced weaponry. In 1962, after the United States agreed to sell Pakistan F-104 Starfighters, to be the most advanced in the region at the time, India signed an agreement with the Soviets for the delivery and then production of MiG-21 fighters. HAL began producing the aircraft in the aftermath of the 1965 war with Pakistan and increasingly indigenized versions were manufactured throughout the 1980s.

A deal to purchase Soviet MiG-29 Fulcrums was announced in 1984 and, after some haggling over the precise version to be delivered, the planes began arriving in 1987. The deal apparently also included a contract for licensed production, but HAL-produced Fulcrums have not yet materialized. Considerable effort is being devoted to India's own Light Combat Aircraft project, a collaborative effort by HAL and the government's Defense Research and Development Organization to design and produce an indigenous fighter catered to the needs of the Indian Air Force. Although the project has captured the imagination of those extolling the virtues of Indian self-sufficiency in military production, HAL has had to resort to foreign technical assistance and imported components for LCA prototypes. General Electric, for instance, has supplied engines to buy time for the development of the indigenous GTX-35 engine. The LCA will probably make its appearance around 2000, with performance characteristics comparable to the American F-16.

Vickers of Britain licensed the production of its Mk.3 main battle tank in 1961, and Avadi Tank Works began production of the tank, renamed Vijayanta, in 1965. Dissatisfaction with the Vijayanta prompted planning for the development of an indigenous MBT, ultimately dubbed the Arjun, to be overseen by DRDO's Combat Vehicle Development Establishment. Revised design specifications have led to delays, the most serious of which relate to engine development. German engines will power initial versions, which may also rely on German transmissions, tracks, and fire control systems. Since 1983, the Indian Army has been supplied with Soviet T-72 tanks while awaiting the Arjun. Avadi was granted a production license for the T-72 in 1980, but the Indian version did not enter service until 1988. Still, this project has drawn much praise, with some even suggesting that the local content of the Indian T-72 exceeds that of the Arjun. India's regional aspirations have also prompted defense industrial activities in support of a significant naval presence in the Indian Ocean. The expense involved in shipbuilding prevented domestic production of anything other than minor vessels until the mid-1960s. At that time, after the Indian government acquired Mazagon Docks Ltd. and the Garden Reach Workshop Ltd., Britain licensed production of the Leander Class frigate. This experience facilitated the development of an improved Indian version, the Godavari Class, the first of which was completed at Mazagon in 1983. It too integrated a number of imported components, including Soviet weaponry and Western electronics. In 1987, the Type 15 Destroyer Program was announced, and the first vessel, the *Delhi*, was launched in 1991. The ship does rely on some foreign components, but also features Indian electronics, sonar, and missile systems. India is producing the Russian Tarantul I Class corvette under license as well as another corvette, the Khukri Class, which is the first Indian designed and built warship. Submarine production began as part of a 1981 deal with Germany for the purchase and then assembly of Type-209 diesel-powered attack submarines. The first Indian built boat was commissioned in 1991 and a second in 1994. The project encountered time delays, cost overruns, and technical problems. New construction was terminated in 1988. The Indian Navy leased a nuclear submarine, a Charlie I Class, from the Soviets in 1988. The deal probably reflected some ambition to eventually produce an Indian nuclear submarine. There have been reports of explorations into the viability of such an endeavor, but the immensity of such a project and the Navy's rather sour experience with the Soviet vessel suggests that nuclear submarine production is probably not high on the list of priorities. Production of an aircraft carrier has also been explored, but set aside for similar reasons.

Development and production of missile systems is a direct outgrowth of the closely watched Indian space program. India's first satellite, the Aryabhata, was launched by a Soviet rocket in 1975, with subsequent launches in 1979 (Bhaskara I) and 1981 (Bhaskara II). The indigenous Space Launch Vehicle program achieved its crowning success in 1980 with the launch of the four-stage SLV-3 rocket which orbited a 35-kg Rohini satellite. India thus became the seventh nation to place a satellite in space with an indigenous rocket. The Indian Space Research Organization and DRDO teamed up in the early 1980s to establish the Integrated Guided Missile Development program to promote indigenous development and design missile systems. By the mid-1980s, the Trishul surface-to-air missile was tested. This was followed, in 1988, by the test launch of the high-profile Prithvi surface-to-surface missile with an indigenous inertial guidance system and the capability of delivering a nuclear payload up to 150 miles. The Agni intermediate-range ballistic missile was tested in 1989 and again in 1992. Its range is said to be over 1500 miles and its payload of up to 2.5 tons is sufficient to carry conventional, chemical, or nuclear warheads.

The space program, and especially the IGMD program, take on added significance in light of India's demonstrated nuclear capability. The nuclear program began shortly after independence with the establishment of the Atomic Energy Commission (subsequently, the Department of Atomic Energy). India's first research reactor became operational in 1956, and that same year a deal was signed with Canada for assistance in the construction of the Rajasthan Atomic Power Plant around two Canadian designed heavy water reactors (RAPP-I and RAPP-II). This plant ultimately provided the plutonium used for the 1974 Pokhran nuclear test. Now India operates several nuclear reactors, including a few fast breeder reactors. The nuclear program has often encountered snags, as when Canada terminated technical assistance in the aftermath of the nuclear explosion, but the government remains committed to the program. India has always asserted that its nuclear program targets peaceful uses of nuclear energy; but on matters of principle, it has refused to sign the 1968 nuclear Non-Proliferation Treaty (and, of course, the 1995 NPT extension). Given the concerted effort devoted to missile development, particularly the Agni IRBM, it is clear that India is seriously exploring the possibility of deploying its own nuclear missile force.

SYMBOLS AND GLOBAL RELATIONS THEORY

We highlight the role that symbols and symbolism play in three theoretical frameworks: realism, social constructivism, and the literature on strategic culture. We do this not in order to formulate competing hypotheses anchored to each tradition, but rather to illustrate that the empirical examination of symbols is relevant to a variety of approaches to international relations and thus deserves a more concentrated effort. With such an effort, including some serious attention to issues of measurement, it should be possible to eventually conduct empirical research designed to shed light on disputes between these literatures regarding symbols, their relative importance in motivating state behavior, and their cultural sources.

Social Constructivism

Symbolic motivations for indigenous weapons production, or for any other form of state behavior, *may* be taken more seriously by social constructivists than by realists. But at its current stage of theoretical evolution, constructivism seems noncommital on questions of relative explanatory importance, which would include questions regarding the relative impact of symbolic versus material forces driving military industrialization. Constructivists, borrowing heavily from the "institutional" approach in sociology, do place special emphasis on the nonmaterial, arguing that "security environments in which states are embedded are in important part cultural and institutional." These environments "affect not only the incentives for different kinds of state behavior but also the basic character of states" — i.e., state identity. This latter claim sets constructivism apart not only from realism, but also liberalism which, while directing our attention to norms and institutions in international relations, has little to say about the construction of state identity. More important than taking a stand on the neoliberal-neorealist debate about the impact of institutions on state behavior is the constructivist claim that social life, including international life, is "ideas all the way down." That is, whether power matters or whether institutions matter, the effects of both operate through their impact on understandings, expectations, and knowledge shared by states. States not only behave (exert power, join institutions) in accordance with cues received from the structure of shared knowledge (or "global culture") of which they are part, they are also defined or constituted by that structure. Demonstrating the social construction of state identity, as opposed to simply state behavior, represents a major challenge for empirically inclined scholars working within this tradition. It requires distinguishing between, on the one hand, states *behaving* in ways international society tells them to and, on the other hand, states just *being*.

These sorts of issues, while important, are not of central concern to us here. The relevance of constructivist theory generally is the prominence given to symbolic motivations for state behavior — or the symbols of state identity. If state preferences are to be problematized and not taken as given, then constructivism seems more inclined than realism to entertain the possibility that symbolic motivations, and not just material interests, are significant forces behind military industrialization. Suchman and Eyre draw our attention to symbolic motivations in their examination of arms import patterns in the third world. In explaining these patterns, especially very high-end equipment acquisitions which is not obviously the most appropriate from a strictly military (material) viewpoint, they suggest we look to the "metonymical iconography of the global cultural order," which teaches states to covet advanced weaponry not necessarily for its destructive efficiency, but for its "*symbolic* throw weight." State preferences are shaped by "an essentially 'ritualistic'... belief in militaries and modern weaponry as distinguishing emblems of the modern nation-state." Military procurement and force structuring exhibit "technologism," or the "symbolic valuation of advanced over alternative technology," which may be less than optimal in the third world context. The acquisition and, ultimately, the production of advanced weaponry becomes an important feature of state identity. According to Sagan, "military organizations and their weapons can therefore be envisioned as serving fucntions similar to those of flags, airlines, and Olympic teams: they are part of what modern states believe they have to possess to be legitimate, modern states." This position has been advanced for some time by those working within the "European political economy" tradition. Kaldor, for instance, maintains that "the possession of weapons systems allows for an ordering of international military relations, conferring political influence, merely through perceptions about military power." Participation in this weapons *system* thus provides "a form of international legitimacy for Third World governments."

The agents of socialization (or acculturation) can be found in the training of third world military elites, first by their colonial authorities and then by both sides in the East-West competition. The process also operates through the international arms trade itself, since "[t]he joint possession of weapons systems and appropriate organisation creates agreement about what constitutes military power." More generally, according to this perspective, states like India adopt preferences for advanced weapons — and, we might add, the capacity to manufacture them — by virtue of being embedded in a particular global culture or "world military order," through which "symbols and meanings prevalent in advanced capitalist societies are imposed on other societies." Empirical researchers have sought to link the movement toward isomorphism in military procurement patterns to the extent of immersion in this global culture. Thus, Eyre and Suchman observe a correlation between the possession of symbolically significant weaponry like supersonic aircraft and the state's membership in international governmental organizations.

Rarely, perhaps never, have analysts adopting a sociological perspective taken the position that the forces driving third world arms acquisitions or military industrialization are solely symbolic to the exclusion of more material or functional concerns. (Here is the distinction between weaponry and other more thoroughly symbolic objects like national flags.) The empirical task for social constructivism is therefore rather difficult in this context. It requires not only demonstrating that symbolic concerns do in fact motivate state behavior (and inhere in state identity), but also overcoming a realist bias in security analysis which favours explanations resting upon the material interests of states. If symbolic and material motivations predicted fundamentally different forms of behavior, the task would not be so hard. But both in fact predict advanced weapons acquisition and higher levels of military industrialization. Deriving from the claim that all interests, material ones included, are socially constructed, the position of those doing empirical work within this tradition is that "[t]he symbolic and the functional values of social objects cannot be simply separated or assessed." We should therefore "begin the study of weapons proliferation with a question, rather than an assumption that one of these two tightly intertwined aspects necessarily dominates."

Strategic Culture

Both neorealism and constructivism would seem to predict convergence among states in regard to their preferences and behavior, as well as their institutions (e.g., militaries). In realism, state preferences are assumed to be similar at the outset and convergence in state behavior is said to occur through a process of social Darwinism whereby states mimic the successful practices others. In constructivism, the socialization process is more opaque and the analytical emphasis is on formation of state identity and the convergence of institutional forms. State preferences and behavior are affected in the process; they are not exogenous as in realism. Contrary to both realism and constructivism, the literature on "strategic culture" highlights not convergence, but divergence among states: e.g., in their strategic preferences and doctrines, their military organizational forms, or their very capacity to generate military power. The basic argument here is that domestic society and culture condition the way states perceive and respond to their international environment. States with different social structures and cultures may employ different strategies — by choice or by domestic necessity — to deal with essentially similar international situations and circumstances. One analyst has concluded that external security consideration are secondary in explaining strategic behavior: "Much more important are the non-rational cultural and ideological orientations that shape each nation's level of military preparations."

Johnston has usefully characterized the strategic culture literature as consisting of three generations. The first tended to focus on Soviet and American nuclear doctrine. Explanations for their different approaches to nuclear strategy were fairly deterministic and based on rather time-invariant conceptions of the superpowers' strategic cultures. The second generation, some contributors to which Johnston locates among the postmodern school of international relations, treats strategic culture as symbolic discourse. The dominant strategic discourse shapes the state's strategic behavior by privileging certain policy options and marginalizing others. But strategic discourse and behavior are also delinked in the sense that, for example, "declaratory strategy" differs from "operational strategy." Since analytical emphasis has been placed on the evolution of strategic discourse, it is not always clear what the implications are for comparative strategic behavior. Tracing the evolution of discourse alongside historical experience suggests, with the rest of the strategic culture literature, that strategic culture varies across states. Still, given the delinkage between declaratory and operational strategy, strategic behavior may not. The third generation, like the second generation, is more nuanced than the first in its conceptions of strategic culture. But unlike postmodern approaches, there is a commitment to assessing whether culture offers a useful explanation for strategic behavior, especially in cases where models based on material interests fall short.

Given the emphasis on symbolic forces, the literature on strategic culture is relevant to our analysis. Borrowing from Clifford Geertz, Johnston has defined strategic cultures as a "system of symbols (e.g., argumentation structures, languages, analogies, metaphors) which acts to establish pervasive and long-standing strategic preferences by formulating concepts of the role and efficacy of military force in interstate political affairs, and by clothing these conceptions with such an aura of factuality that the strategic preferences seem uniquely realistic and efficacious." Symbols are, of course, central in postmodern accounts which, following Jean Baudrillard, contend that "the defense-industrial network produces strategic weapons objects as signs more than real engines of death" and further that "a vital industrial capacity, strong R&D centers, growing technological capabilities, increasing defense budgets, and constant improvements in the defense-industrial network are a sign-set that must appear in the display of superpower sign-exchange values." Such observations apply to aspiring powers like India as well. Indeed, the advanced weaponry produced by third world states — in effect, copies of the signs themselves — would seem to be a good example of Baudrillard's "simulacra."

Contributions to the literature on strategic culture are truly an eclectic set. Most examine in a fairly thorough way the evolution and current forms of particular states' strategic cultures, and thus tend to highlight cross-national differences and the implications for strategic behavior. Positivists among them opt for the standard hypothesis-testing approach, while post-positivists operate in a more interpretive mode or perhaps, more rigorously, trace genealogies. Either approach to strategic culture involves relatively thorough examination of the culture of one or, at the most, a few states: "the writings, debates, thoughts and words of 'culture-bearing units', such as strategists, military leaders and national security elites; weapons designs and deployments; images of war and peace portrayed in various media; military ceremonies; even war literature." While there is some recognition that there may be essential ingredients of strategic culture which can be located in many or all nation-states, that concern is secondary, as is any effort to identify the source of any such commonalities. The latter, of course, is the purview of social contructivism, which otherwise shares a great deal both theoretically and substantively with the strategic culture literature.

Realism

Indigenous arms production is a symbol of Indian power, and thereby enhances its international status and prestige.

Such considerations figure prominently in realist theory. E.H. Carr wrote: "Any symptom of military inefficiency or unpreparedness in a Great Power is promptly reflected in its political status"; and "Military power, being an essential element in the life of the state, becomes not only an instrument, but an end in itself." Hans Morgenthau described the symbolism involved in diplomatic ceremonials and displays of military force. "The policy of prestige," he claimed, "is as intrinsic an element of the relations between nations as the desire for prestige is of the relations between individuals." Neorealists too recognize the importance of prestige on world politics. For Gilpin, one element in the disequilibrium which threatens to lead to hegemonic war is a disjuncture between the international distribution of power and the "hierarchy of prestige." On the issue of nuclear weapons in particular, he is troubled by the fact that they "confer an enhanced status and have become status symbols coveted by more and more states." Krasner's "modified realism," which includes the proposition that third world states are interested in the exercise of "meta-power" via the transformation of international regimes, as opposed to increased wealth, also seems to allow for such things as status and prestige as motivations for state behavior.

Although there is little explicit in the realist literature regarding symbolic motivations behind the pursuit of indigenous arms production capacity, nuclear or non-nuclear, there is nothing in realist theory that is inconsistent with such a characterization of Indian defence industrial policy. But a more serious lapse, something for which realism has been rightly criticized, is the failure to fully examine the source of those motivations (in a sense, preferences) and, more especially, the dynamic relationship between states as actors and the environment within which states interact. The question neglected by realists is not so much why states pursue the symbols of power in the form of, among other things, military industrialization. Waltz, in fact, has a perfectly good generic answer to that question: "The close juxtaposition of states promotes their sameness through the disadvantages that arise from a failure to conform to successful practices.... The socialization of nonconformist states proceeds at a pace that is set by the extent of their involvement in the system." That is, states, at minimum, want to survive, and a process of social Darwinism tells them that possession of symbols of power will help them to do that. Rather, the more fundamental question neglected by realism is: beyond the utility of symbols for state behavior, what do they say about meaning of statehood itself?

There is in realism a presumption (both analytical and normative) in favour of instrumental state action — variously referred to as "rational," "functional", "outcome oriented," or driven by "material interests." Morgenthau, for example, while recognizing the importance of diplomatic ceremony and military display, was less inclined than Carr to characterize a "policy of prestige" as anything other than an "instrumentality" for the acquisition and maintenance of power: "While in national societies prestige is frequently sought for its own sake, it is rarely the primary objective of foreign policy. Prestige is at most the pleasant by-product of foreign policies whose ultimate objectives are not the reputation for power but the substance of power." In realism, behavior driven purely by symbolic concerns is considered rare. Where behavior is driven by both material interests and symbolic concerns, it is the former that dominate. In contemplating the general notion of rationality, and not necessarily state behavior, Elster has written: "Even though, say, the feeling of gratification or self-realization is essentially a by-product and hence could not be the motivation for action, it could reinforce the motivation to undertake activities of which they are the by-products." This essentially represents a realist take on arms production in India. International status and prestige, as well as Indian self-confidence, is enhanced by the development of an indigenous arms production capacity. But the central motivation for the development of such capacity is the maximization of India's "material" power (realism) or, at minimum, the survival of the Indian state (neorealism). That status, prestige, and self-confidence also emerge from India's possession of an arms production capacity simply reinforces the more instrumental motivations behind India's policy of military industrialization.

WEAPONS PRODUCTION AND PUBLIC DISCOURSE IN INDIA

We have suggested that there are a number of factors motivating military industrialization in India. Although realist thought does not deny the existence of symbolic motivations like international status and prestige, or even such things as the state's quest for "self-realization" and "self-confidence," proponents generally downplay the importance of these sorts of motivations relative to material interests. Social constructivists do not at the outset take a stand on the relative importance of material versus nonmaterial interests, or rational versus nonrational behavior. Rather, these are questions for empirical analysis. More importantly, so are questions concerning the (cultural) sources of state interests, material or nonmaterial, and the (social) context of state behavior, rational or nonrational. Postmodern contributions to the literature on strategic culture assert the primacy of symbols and signs, both as cause and consequence of strategic behavior. Other contributions to this literature document these alongside more material elements contributing to a state's strategic culture and, ultimately, to its strategic behavior.

Neither realists nor constructivists have devoted much attention to documenting evidence for the symbolic motivations driving state behavior, especially patterns of weapons acquisition. Realists might be expected to forego the empirical analysis of symbols since they are assumed to play a minor role in the utility functions of states. Postmodern interpretations of strategic culture are often rich with references and examples, but rigorous empirical analysis is not typically of utmost concern given their rejection of positivist epistemology. Social constructivists, while in principle receptive to the documentation of symbolic motivations, have anticipated a bias in the empirical evidence. Suchman and Eyre worry that "locating empirical evidence of nonrational decision making poses a significant methodological problem, particularly for investigators employing case-study techniques." Since there is a "rational myth" associated with military strategy and planning itself, an analysis of public justifications for weapons purchases and, by extension, indigenous weapons production "is far more likely to find evidence of strategic, factional, or geopolitical logic than it is to uncover affirmations of ritual conformity." While we acknowledge this potential bias, we are not quite so pessimistic about observing symbolic, nonrational motivations in the public discourse about weapons production. In our review of biographies and memoirs of Indian elites, especially those of Indira Gandhi, we have in fact encountered statements which suggest that military industrialization in India has been driven in part by symbolic as well as material concerns. Still, a more systematic review of the public discourse in India is necessary in order to demonstrate the viability of this avenue of research.

Methodology

We assume that *India Today*, a weekly news magazine comparable to *Time* or *Newsweek* in the United States or the *Economist* in the United Kingdom, is representative of popular discourse on defense policy and foreign affairs. We reviewed all issues of *India Today* from 31 May 1977 to 31 December 1996 and identified 126 articles devoted in whole or in part to the issue of indigenous weapons production. Of these, 74 contained one or more statements regarding the motivations for India's domestic arms production programs, including its space and nuclear programs. Such statements in *India Today* do not necessarily convey official positions or policies of the Indian government.

Some are made by government officials, some by military leaders, and some by leading figures in the defense industry. Others represent statements of fact or opinion made by *India Today* reporters, and these presumably reflect in many instances the views of the magazine's editors. In any event, we are not terribly concerned with examining the official pronouncements justifying Indian military industrialization. In fact, we concur with Suchman and Eyre that *official* discourse is most likely to be biased by a rationalist myth. What we want to examine is the *popular* discourse. Popular discourse, it seems to us, subsumes (non-secret) official discourse, and therefore paints a more complete and a less biased picture of the forces motivating the development of arms production capacity. Reporting in *India Today* both shapes and is shaped by popular discourse, and is thus an appropriate medium to analyze for our purposes.

Before proceeding to the empirical evidence, we want to be clear about what sort of exercise we are engaging in. First and foremost, this is a descriptive study. We are not analyzing causal mechanisms here. We believe that the motivations behind India's military industrialization, especially symbolic motivations, can be explained in large part by the degree to which India was integrated into the competitive cold war system. This is consistent with both neorealism and social constructivism, but we do not demonstrate the causal relationship empirically. We also believe that symbolic forces play a larger part in motivating domestic arms production in the third world, including India, than realist theory seems to imply. But, again, we do not examine empirically the relative importance of symbolic versus material motivating forces. What we do show is that the symbolic motivations behind Indian weapons programs find expression in the public discourse, and that they appear regularly enough to suggest that they are significant factors driving these programs. And we suspect that they are more than mere by-products of the pursuit of material interests. We want to suggest that statements regarding the symbolic importance of an Indian arms production capacity reflect regular and consistent motivating forces — that they do not reflect mere idiosyncracies of time or space. In other words, they are not "outliers." This is the primary "descriptive inference" we draw from our systematic review of *India Today*.

Empirical Evidence

Although we were able to document several types of motivations for Indian arms production, our aim in this paper is to present a variety of statements which represent symbolic motivations. We can, however, give some indication of the relative frequency with which the various types of motivations, material and symbolic, appear in the public discourse. Of the 74 articles in which justifications for indigenous weapons programs are mentioned, 56 mention India's enduring conflicts with Pakistan and/or China, or regional security somewhat more generally. Of the 74, eighteen mention India's dependence on foreign suppliers of complete weapons systems or spare parts, with negative implications for India's warfighting capabilities. Twenty-six address economic issues such as promoting the development of civilian industries, saving foreign exchange, or obtaining technology transfers. Lastly, 24 articles make reference to what we consider to be more symbolic concerns. These in turn fall into three categories: India's autonomy in foreign affairs, India's international status and prestige, and India's self-image.

On India's International Status and Prestige

The purposes behind India's quest for autonomy in military production are both functional and symbolic, and we have tried to identify statements which reflect on the latter dimension. The reference above to Agni's potential for placing India in a "totally different league" (excerpt [8]) is echoed in other statements which reflect more explicitly India's international aspirations:

[11] "The success of the SLV-3-(E)-02, a completely indigenous four-stage rocket... *put India into an exclusive club* with only five other members.... 'This is a great day for India and Indian science,' proclaimed Mrs Gandhi echoing the popular view...."

[12] "Whether in the corridors of the Defence R&D department in Delhi, or in the Bangalore offices of the Aeronautical Development Agency (ADA), the apex body which overseas the design and development of the LCA, there is an infectious enthusiasm that the LCA prototype will fly by 1989 and that *it will catapult India into the technological superleague of nations* who produce their own frontline fighter planes."

[13] "At exactly 7:17 a.m. on May 22, Agni blossomed into a chariot of fire that *propelled India into an exclusive club* dominated by the world's technological and military giants."

[14] On the unsuccessful test of the Polar Satellite Launch Vehicle: "...PSLV's success *would have made India a major player* in the commercial space arena. As Professor Rao [chairman of the Space Research Organisation] says: 'It is a quantum leap in space technology for us and it would have given us the muscle power to put anything into space.' What was left unstated was that if PSLV succeeded, *India could have also muscled into the exclusive club of countries* having Inter-Continental Ballistic Missile (ICBM) capability."

[15] "Recently, a series of developments *have powered the nation into the rarefied strata* of strategic missile competence. Topping the list is the successful third launch of Agni, India Intermediate range Ballistic Missile (IRBM), on February 19."

All of these excerpts contain references to an elite group of nations that possess the capacity to produce one or another category of military hardware — the "superleague of nations" producing fighters (excerpt [12]), the "exclusive club" or "rarefied strata" producing longer-range missiles (excerpts [11], [13-15]) — as well as India's acquisition or impending acquisition of elite status. Other statements recognize that certain capabilities are necessary symbols of international status and prestige:

[16] Interview with Air Chief Marshal Denis A. La Fontaine: "If we do not indigenise, *how will we become a first class nation?*"

[17] "While the haggling goes on, the desperate need for the jet trainers is a grim reminder of the reality that the Indian policy makers seem to ignore in their heady *rush for 'mini-power status'*: that *no nation has ever become a real power* with its army firing mostly imported guns, its air force flying foreign aircraft and its navy riding submarines leased from another superpower."

[18] A.P.J. Abdul Kalam, head of the defence research program: "... India can now be *rated as a missile power* that can deliver a range of missiles any time, anywhere that we want. Agni *symbolises our technological capabilities*. Prithvi is a world class surface-to-surface missile. In the anti-tank class

we want to be number one with Nag. Akash is heading for a unique second in its surface-to-air class."

[19] "Says Muchkund Dubey [former foreign secretary]: '*The bomb option is a currency of power* that is critical to our survival as a strong nation.'"

Here is the assertion that if India wants to become a "first class nation," or even if India aspires to "mini-power status," it cannot rely on imported weaponry because "real power" requires something more (excerpts [16] and [17]). Again, it is indigenous arms production, especially production of "world class" missiles like Agni and Prithvi, which will "symbolise" India's technological capabilities (excerpt [18]). The option to use nuclear weapons, now that India has developed its own missile capacity, can be used as a "currency of power" (excerpt [19]). Such are the elements of international status and prestige identified in Indian discourse.

Bibliography

Ajey Lele: *Strategic Technologies for the Military : Breaking New Frontiers*, Sage, Delhi, 2009.

Arend, A.: *International Law and the Use of Military*, London, Routledge, 1993.

Atar Singh Jadoan: *Military Geography of South East Asia*, Anmol, Delhi, 2001.

Bhaskara Rao: *Military Conversion : Impact on Science and Technology*, Discovery, Delhi, 2003.

Burch, William R. Jr.: *Human Ecology: An Environmental Approach*, Belmont, Duxbury Press, 1994.

Castells, M. : *The Rise of the Network Society*. Blackwell, 1996.

Cathy Solheim: *Military Economics: Issues, Policies, and Solutions*, Washington, D.C., Island Press, 1995.

Dixit, Prabla: *Defence Economics: A Struggle for Power*, New Delhi, Orient Longman, 1981.

Dunne, J. P. and Brauer, J.: *Arms Trade and Economic Development: Theory, Policy*, Routledge, London, 2004.

Galtung, Johan: *Pax Pacifica: Terrorism, the Pacific Hemisphere, Globalisation and Peace Studies*. London: Pluto Press, 2005.

Gupta, Asha: *Military Rule and Democratization : Changing Perspectives*, Deep & Deep, Delhi, 2003.

Heimanson, Rudolph: *Dictionary of Economics*, N.Y.: Oceana Publications, 1967.

John M. Seidl: *Politics American Style: Race, Environment and Central Cities*, New York, Prentice-Hall, 1972.

Jones, W.H.: *Government and Politics of India Military*, London, Hutchinson, 1971.

Lovering, J.: *Labour and the Defence Industry: An Alliance for Globalisation*. Capital and Class, Delhi, 1998.

Mary, W.: *Military Space Force: the Cultural Dimensions of Authority*, Cambridge, Belknap Press, 1985.

Prabla, Dixit: *Communalism: A Struggle for Power*, New Delhi, Orient Longman, 1981.

Radhakrishna: *Handbook of Military and Defence Services*, Sumit Enterprises, Delhi, 2009.

Rudolph, Heimanson: *Dictionary of Military*, N.Y.: Oceana Publications, 1967.

Simon, D. : *Public Administration and Policy of Indian Military*, New York, Knopf, 1950.

Sutton, J., *Technology and Market Structure*, MIT Press, 1998.

Wade, J. L.: *Society and Environment: The Coming Collision*, Boston, Allyn and Bacon, 1972.

Index

□□□